Dear Sun

Janine Burke was born in Melbourne in 1952. While studying art history at the University of Melbourne she began writing art criticism and curating exhibitions. The pioneering exhibition *Australian Women Artists, 1840–1940* in 1975 initiated her first book. Between 1977 and 1982, Janine completed an MA on Joy Hester at La Trobe University and lectured in art history at the Victorian College of the Arts, before resigning to write fiction full time. She has contributed to many art journals and newspapers and is the author of ten books of fiction and art history. Her novels include *Lullaby*, *Company of Images* and *Second Sight*, which won the 1987 Victorian Premier's Award for Fiction.

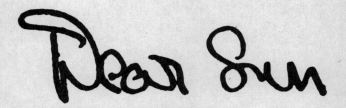

Dear Sun

The Letters of Joy Hester and Sunday Reed

Edited by
Janine Burke

MINERVA

Published 1997 by Minerva
a part of Reed Books Australia
35 Cotham Road, Kew, Victoria, 3101
a division of Reed International Books Australia Pty Limited

First published by William Heinemann Australia 1995

Design by Andrew Burgess
Typeset in Goudy and Frutiger by J&M Typesetting
Printed and bound in Australia by Australian Print Group, Maryborough, Vic.

National Library of Australia
    cataloguing-in-publication data:

Hester, Joy, 1920–1960.
    Dear sun: the letters of Joy Hester and Sunday Reed.

ISBN 1 86330 610 2

1. Hester, Joy, 1920–1960 – Correspondence. 2. Reed, Sunday, 1905–1981 – Correspondence.
3. Artists – Australia – Correspondence. 4. Women artists Australia – Correspondence. I. Burke,
Janine, 1952– . II. Reed, Sunday, 1905–1981. III. Title.

741.092

Every effort has been made to trace and acknowledge copyright material, but should any infringe-
ment have occurred, the publishers extend their apologies and welcome any relevant correspondence. The author and publishers would like to acknowledge permission to reproduce extracts
from the following: 'The Moving Image' from Judith Wright's The Moving Image (1942),
HarperCollins Publishers; Talk: the Australian listener's national monthly magazine, Australian
Broadcasting Corporation; and 'Little Gidding' from The Four Quartets, and 'Preludes IV' by T.S.
Eliot, courtesy of Faber & Faber Ltd.

To Ramona, who knows what friendship is.

Contents

Acknowledgements

I would like to thank Joy's family for their help and involvement. Peregrine and Fern Smith allowed me to quote their mother's letters, as well as lending photographs. Albert Tucker kindly responded to all my questions and lent several of his evocative photographs. Pamela McIntosh shared her memories of Sweeney Reed, her former husband, with me.

Barrett Reid generously gave his time and support, despite passages of ill health. He was a friendly critic of the manuscript, offering valuable suggestions. I am grateful for his permission, on behalf of the Reed Estate, to quote Sunday Reed's letters and also for access to Joy Hester's letters, and others, held in the State Library of Victoria. Jean Langley shared letters, photographs, memories and hospitality with me. Thanks to Nadine Amadio for some long talks and some good advice. Suzanne Heywood, my friend of many years, told me wise stories about families.

I would also like to thank Ruth Bergner, Wendy Bradley, Jane Clark, Alannah Coleman, Peter Cowan, Russell Deeble, Lauraine Diggins, Michael Dugan, Katrina Fraser, Claire Jager, Philip Jones, Michael Keon, Les Kossatz, Shelton Lea, Pauline McCarthy, Jacqueline Mitelman, Mirka Mora, Lady Nolan and John Yule. Special thanks to Richard Haese.

There are others who have given information and advice who wish not to be named and I thank them, too.

Thanks to Jock Murphy and the helpful staff of the Australian Manuscripts Collection, State Library of Victoria, to David Black, Deakin University Library, Burwood Campus and to the Queenscliff Historical Society. Thanks also to Gay Shepherd and Prue Weber of St Catherine's Girls School, and to Ian McDonald of the Copyright Council. And thanks to Louise Stirling for her editorial skills, her lively encouragement and sound counsel.

Maudie Palmer, the former director, and Rachel Young at the Museum of Modern Art at Heide have assisted this project in a variety of ways.

Finally, I am grateful to the Literature Board, Australia Council, for a fellowship which enabled me to work fulltime on the later stages of this manuscript.

A Note about the Letters

There are 92 extant letters from Joy Hester to Sunday Reed, and 38 extant letters of Sunday's to Joy. Of Hester's letters to Sunday, 90 are held in the Reed Collection in Australian Manuscripts at the State Library of Victoria, one is in the collection of Fern Smith and one is in the collection of Peregrine Smith. Sunday's letters are in the collection of Fern Smith, with one in the collection of Peregrine Smith and four in the collection of Albert Tucker. I originally read Joy's letters at Heide where Sunday kept them in manila folders tied up with a blue ribbon. Gray Smith gave me Sunday's letters to read and photocopy in 1981.

Copyright of letters involves dual ownership. For example, regarding the letters of Joy Hester, the paper on which the letter is written is owned by the Reed Estate while the words on the paper are owned by Joy's heirs. Joy Hester's will cannot be located. Letters other than those mentioned above are acknowledged within the text.

Joy's bold handwriting made the transcription of her letters relatively easy, unless she used pencil. Pencil blurs and fades with the years. Sunday's handwriting is nearly indecipherable, so I was grateful that, apart from a short note to Joy in 1945, she typed every letter she wrote. Dating Joy's early letters was difficult: she rarely dated letters until 1948, when Sunday was in Europe. Joy's early letters from Sydney were missives of urgency and dates were superfluous to her. Where a letter is undated, my dating of it is put in brackets. Neither did Joy include her address when she first moved to Sydney, for fear of being discovered.

Neither Reed nor Hester bothered much with punctuation, paragraphs or capital letters, though Hester was by far the worst offender. She used the dash as her chief form of punctuation. Her rendering of poetry is, however, perfect, down to the last comma.

I have used paragraphs and punctuation when otherwise it would prove a strain for the reader. Hester's imaginative spelling is largely intact though where it proved overly confusing (for example, in the case of Heide, which Joy spelled differently in nearly every letter) it has been changed. Ellipses indicate my editing.

An Introduction . . .

> 'Love's intention and the reverse of
> love's intention slowly mark my
> life . . . and on the banks of these dark rivers we become – become what
> we are to each other and become what we are to ourselves.'
> Sunday Reed.[1]

The letters between Joy Hester and Sunday Reed draw a picture of the life of their times. Both were married to men regarded as leaders in the art world. John Reed and Albert Tucker championed modernism through publishing and painting. Neither man shirked confrontation or dispute, both were strong-minded and confident.

Joy and Sunday occupied their positions in the traditional role of wives and helpers and, less traditionally, as women with distinctive voices. Their voices are heard in their letters, dating from 1944 until Joy's death in 1960. And, while it is Joy's voice that dominates, Sunday is both audience and inspiration. Joy's references to Sunday's tastes, queries and needs, her health and well-being, along with a pervasive sense of the beauty of the Heide garden, create a complex role for Sunday as confidante, muse and mother figure.

[1]   Sunday Reed to Gray Smith, undated, Smith Collection.

The letters cover flows and breaks in creativity, struggles with illness and poverty, losses and gains in love. The poetry of T S Eliot, Ezra Pound and Judith Wright is discussed, together with the exchange of Christmas presents, the planting of flowers, critiques of paintings and painters, the Australian landscape as a metaphor for cultural identity, the occult, the care of children, of gardens, of cherished pets. In a personal manner, debates in *Angry Penguins* and *Ern Malley's Journal* are addressed. Friends and loved ones cross the pages of the letters: Albert Tucker, Sidney Nolan, Max Harris, Danila Vassilieff, Barrett Reid, Sam Atyeo, John Perceval and the Boyds. The letters chart the friendship between a young artist and an older woman, their desires and battles for love and understanding.

The letters can be read as a narrative, telling the story of a friendship and covering a time of cultural change. While they illuminate larger issues, it is the personal elements of affection, loyalty and practical necessity that are the subject matter. Sunday was a conservator, treasuring the letters, drawings and poems Joy sent her. Joy was less fastidious, and this is why the bulk of the letters are Joy's. Sunday was not a regular letter writer: it was John who managed that side of life, who responded to the letters of need, the communications to do with art and business, pleasures and worries, humour and anger, the incessant written flow of friendship with artists that shaped the Reeds' lives. Yet Sunday wrote to Joy, and not often to anyone else.

This is a friendship imaged in words, a conversation between two women, an intimacy that we, as readers, were never meant to share. Joy is unashamedly garrulous. It indicates a personal style as much as her tremendous need of Sunday, a need to tell, to explain, to be heard. From the start Joy expected a great deal of Sunday.

◆

Joy had grown up in the Melbourne bayside suburb of Elwood. Dawson Avenue was a solidly middle-class street nudging affluent Brighton. Her father's long career as a city manager for the London Bank ended ignominiously in 1930 when his alcoholism led to the sack. Robert Hester died from a heart attack two years later. Louise, her mother, was a cold, domineering character with whom Joy continually clashed – physically at least once. Joy described Louise as 'a dragon', more like 'a businesswoman than a mother'. Her older brother Neville seemed the favoured one, taking on an irritatingly paternalistic role after Robert's death. From 1935 Louise, who had trained as a teacher, ran an estate agency in Elsternwick in partnership with Neville.

Strikingly attractive, Joy was irreverent, exuberant, earthy and outspoken. She began to run away from home in her early teens, defying Louise and taking refuge with friends and more accommodating members of her family, such as her cousin Marie Bracher. Joy learned the survival skill of trading a bright, engaging self for safety and a sympathetic ear. She developed a resilience, a tough pragmatism about dealing with crises. From her combative relationship with Louise, Joy grew to take subterfuge for granted, conflict as inevitable and flight as a final resort. It was the behaviour of someone who, however gamely she presented her outward, buoyant, larrikin self, was intensely secretive, watchful and anxious.

Joy was a rebellious teenager, to the growing alarm of the Bracher family, who feared she might influence Marie. But Joy was popular and friendly, too, a hedonist who revelled in summers spent sunbaking on Elwood beach with local teenagers. Louise was mean with money so Joy made do with the cheapest, from clothes to fun. Her school years at St Michael's Church of England Girls Grammar in Redan Street, St Kilda were marked by high-jinks, detentions and playing truant. Yet it was at St Michael's where her aunt, Rhoda Hester, taught drawing and encouraged Joy to draw. Joy would later insist she was expelled, though there is no evidence for it. Joy never could pass up the opportunity for a good yarn, the more dramatic the better. She was also sexually adventurous and one early affair led to an abortion. She dealt with the abortion with astonishing equanimity, turning it into a joke to be shared with Marie. Yet abortions in the 1930s were dangerous, illegal and expensive. The waiting room, Joy vowed, was full of women all pregnant to the same wealthy young man Joy was pregnant to. She told Marie she doused her clothes with dry-cleaning fluid on the way home to disguise the odour of chloroform from her mother.

Louise forbade her daughter to attend art school but after a year at Brighton Technical School, George Bracher, Joy's uncle, persuaded Louise that Joy's talent demanded she enrol at the Gallery School. Unwillingly, Louise agreed.

In 1938, Joy met Albert Tucker around the studios of inner Melbourne. By then, in the second year of her course, Joy had grown disenchanted with rendering with minute accuracy the dusty casts of hands and busts of Homer, under the long tin roof of the Gallery School. Tucker, taken with her, invited her to his studio to sit for a portrait. The studio was in Motherwell's Gateway, around the corner from his loft at 26 Little Collins Street. It was part of a web of inner city streets and lanes that had become the centre of Melbourne's intellectual life where studios, cafes and bookshops drew artists, university students and writers.

Tucker's *Portrait of Joy Hester* (1938, Albert Tucker) shows a young woman redolent with sensual promise. Tucker intensified Joy's features, exaggerating her eyes, making them glamorous and exotic and gave her full, ripe lips. Her expression is pensive, dreamy, voluptuous. He is clearly enchanted. It is an image of passion: the sitting marked the start of their love affair. They began living together – though intermittently. Louise Hester, furious that her daughter had taken up with 'one of these mad artists', harassed and pursued Joy.

Louise accosted Joy's landladies; she tried to inveigle one of them to sue Joy for the rent she owed. She visited Bert's mother and insulted her. When all else failed, Louise sent the police after Joy. On the run, Joy stayed with friends, in a series of East Melbourne boarding houses and, whenever she could, with Bert. Money was tight and Joy embraced a frugal way of life. The Little Collins Street loft had no toilet, bathroom or running water. Yosl Bergner, even worse off than Joy and Bert, would call by to share a meagre breakfast.

Joy was an accomplished draughtswoman, winning the Gallery School's Drawing Head from Life prize in 1938. But she found the curriculum tedious; its goal was craft not art. Though she attended the Gallery School irregularly, she was promoted to the Painting and Life School after only three terms in the Drawing Class. Most students stayed in the Drawing Class for three years. Gifted and restless, she went to the life drawing classes held at the Victorian Artists Society in East Melbourne. Joy was in the same boat as many of her contemporaries. The Gallery School was dull. George Bell's studio school in Bourke Street was progressive but expensive, and Bell himself autocratic. The alternatives, Max Meldrum's school where pseudo-scientific theories about tonal painting were preached or the academic practice of the Melbourne Institute of Technology, were equally uninspiring.

Bert set an example. Proudly self-taught, he could not afford the Bell school fees, or even those of the Gallery School, and worked as a commercial artist to make ends meet. Six years older than Joy, Bert educated himself by reading voraciously in the domed Reading Room of the State Library. He attended, and took, life drawing classes at the Victorian Artists Society. Bert was a methodical and deliberate craftsman as well as an impressively original painter. An exacting man, he both practised and provided the discipline Joy felt she lacked. Bert was Joy's father figure. Robert Hester existed only in sporadic, disquieting memories. 'I am made of my mother's hysteria/and my father's weakness', Joy wrote in her poem 'Observation' (1942).

Finally, Joy had no choice about leaving art school. Louise's financial support ended when she left home. To support herself, Joy took various jobs. She was a 'hello' girl at a cab company[2] and a portrait model at the Melbourne Institute of Technology. Like Tucker, she tried her hand at commercial art and attended the Fox Art Academy where she drew movie advertisements from photographs of film stars. But it took only a short stint of designing display and Christmas cards to discourage her.

The art world Bert introduced Joy to was a lively, contentious place, rife with factions and disputes. In 1938, Joy attended the first meeting of the George Bell-led Contemporary Art Society and exhibited in its first annual exhibition (and Hester's first group show) at the National Gallery of Victoria, in the same year. The resolute Bell had begun the CAS as a reaction to Robert Menzies' conservative Australian Academy of Art. If the battle between the moderns and the conservatives was being fought between supporters of the CAS and the Academy, the CAS itself acted as a forum for subtler, though equally trenchant, differences. The political and artistic allegiances that emerged were entwined and fiercely held. The group around CAS lay vice-president John Reed and Tucker, with whom Joy aligned herself, was left-wing, vocal and organised. Bell and his supporters soon found themselves increasingly isolated and out of step.

Not long after Joy and Bert met, he began to figure prominently in the art world, both as an artist and a spokesman. He was elected to the CAS Council at its first meeting. Basil Burdett had singled Tucker out as 'a very young painter of unusual promise.'[3] Bert was fiercely articulate with a sophisticated and coherent sense of himself as an artist; he was also a dominant character. Joy loved Bert, and was in awe of him as a painter.

Despite a truncated art education, Joy's style, even as a young artist, was mature and distinctive. Her life drawings from the the late 1930s handled expressive distortions of form and space easily, rendering homage to Henry Moore. Heavily modelled, then outlined in brush and ink, the male and female nudes are among Joy's first works that contain a plastic power

---

2   Before cabs were radio connected, drivers would wait at the rank for the 'hello girl' to ring through with details of their fare.

3   Basil Burdett, 'Modern Art in Melbourne', *Art in Australia*, November 1938, p. 20.

independent of the small area they cover. Pneumatic and monumental, the nudes have fluid, almost sculptural volumes and a curious asexuality. Joy was learning to compress form within tight perimeters, to present volume without scale and to abbreviate shape at the same time.

The Russian artist Danila Vassilieff also made an impact. Joy had introduced herself to Vassilieff at his 1937 Riddell's Gallery exhibition and he became a friend. Setting up his easel in the lanes of Fitzroy, Vassilieff brought alive the vitality and poverty of Depression Melbourne with rapid brushstrokes. He was an early mentor for Hester, regarding conventional art education as numbing and irrelevant. In the early 1940s Joy drew street scenes, too, often peopled with women. Their melancholy expressions, coupled with a tender and implicit bond, indicate Joy's true interests – the intimate and private aspects of relationships, disturbed states of mind, and the human face.

Her gift was drawing and, from her student days, Joy chose to draw rather than to paint, marking her expression through a sure, rapid manner of execution. Tucker recalled, 'she would be on the floor with a bottle of Quink and a lot of paper and [she would] just produce all these drawings, quick, quick, quick, twenty or thirty or forty in two or three days.'[4]

Drawing was an unusual choice, marking Joy out from her contemporaries, but one apposite for her skills and temperament. Her materials were the cheapest and most accessible; they facilitated speed. She also wrote poetry, creating an evocative and sensuous world in words.[5] In this sense, too, Hester marked out fresh territory for herself. She would be the only artist in her circle to consolidate her literary interests into a body of work.

In 1939 the *Herald* Exhibition of French and British Painting was shown at the Melbourne Town Hall. It was the most important international show to come to Melbourne, giving local artists the chance to see paintings by Van Gogh, Gauguin, Cezanne and Picasso. It was there that Bert introduced Joy to Sunday Reed. Sunday was fifteen years older than Joy, a lean, handsome, stylish woman, fair-haired with brilliant blue eyes. The two struck up a friendship that would last for the rest of Joy's life. Sunday recalled that first meeting when she and Joy sat together at the crowded exhibition. Joy challenged Sunday, demanding to know whether she believed in the 'equality of the classes.' Sunday's reply, that she believed in love, seemed 'satisfactory' to Joy.

4   Janine Burke, *Joy Hester*, Greenhouse Publications, Melbourne, 1983, p. 73.

5   Ibid, pp. 46–7, 62, 102, 143–6.

'From then on, we knew each other.'[6] It is a rather different memory to John's who recalled Hester as a 'little peroxide blonde hoyden mixed up with a lot of half-baked communist ideas.'[7]

After this meeting, Joy and Bert were soon regular visitors to the Reeds' home, Heide, catching the train out on the weekend for 'arvo tea', held on the front lawn, weather permitting. As the friendship deepened, Sunday invited Joy to stay at Heide while Bert was in the army during 1942. By then, Joy and Bert had married. Joy, desperate to keep Bert out of the army, thought marriage might be one solution to stave off his military service. Under the assumed name of Madge Evelyn, against Louise's wishes and slightly under age, Joy and Bert married at the All Saints Church, Greensborough, on 1 January 1941. Louise took her revenge: she had the minister, who had unwittingly married the underage Hester, removed.

Heide was a gathering place for painters, writers and poets. The Reeds fostered an atmosphere of support, of debate and discussion where passionate friendships and loyalties were fostered.

Sunday was a Baillieu, Melbourne's most prominent establishment family. The Baillieu family fortunes had begun in Queenscliff, on Victoria's Bellarine Peninsula. To escape the attentions of a drunken master, James Baillieu had abandoned his ship, which was anchored in quarantine inside Port Phillip Heads, and swum to shore at Queenscliff. It was 1853. The same year he married Emma Pow, a newly arrived immigrant, and they had 14 children. Sunday's father, Arthur, was their third son. In 1881, James built a grand hotel, Baillieu House (now the Ozone Hotel). He was a mayor and a councillor of Queenscliff, involving himself in its growth as a fashionable seaside resort.

Real estate and mining were chief among the interests of the family company, Mutual Trust, with its fortunes built up by the prodigious enterprise of Sunday's uncle, W L Baillieu. Melbourne's 'biggest landboomer' until the boom collapsed in 1892, he would become a member of the Victorian Legislative Council and a founder of the Melbourne *Herald*.[8] Collins House, built by W L in the heart of Melbourne's financial district in 1910, housed some fifty Baillieu companies, and it signified not only the family's wealth but its very public face in Melbourne life. Arthur, not as driven as his older

---

6   Sunday Reed, interview, 5 June 1978.

7   John Reed, Introduction, *Joy Hester Retrospective*, Tolarno Galleries, Melbourne, 1977.

8   Bede Nairn and Geoffrey Serle, eds, *Australian Dictionary of Biography*, 1891–1939, vol. 7, Melbourne University Press, 1979, pp. 138–45.

brother, was a partner in the estate agency Munro & Baillieu, another venture of W L's.

Sunday had grown up in an atmosphere of plenty, living at Balholmen, the family home in Struan Street, Toorak, and staying at Merthon, their holiday home at Sorrento on the Mornington Peninsula. Balholmen, a big, gracious home in Melbourne's most exclusive suburb and Merthon, with its long, winding drive ending in a sumptuous view of Port Phillip Bay, represent a childhood of immense privilege and security. Sunday grew up experiencing, and expecting, the best. She was the only daughter among three brothers, Jack, Darren and younger brother Everard. Jack, nicknamed 'King', was her favourite brother and his early death was a great sadness to her. As a young woman, Sunday had a close relationship with her father. Her upbringing might have been patrician but there were limitations. Sunday reflected,

'I always think the men in our family regard their women in much the same light as a nicely arranged bowl of flowers or a good meal! . . . the prejudice is so strong and I quite understand that I'm never expected to say anything worth listening to and it would cause great annoyance if I did so that I now feel I never want to!'[9]

It was at home, however, that her interest in art was generated. At Balholmen the arts were valued. Arthur Streeton was a family friend and frequent visitor, while Arthur Baillieu collected paintings. Ethel, Sunday's mother, painted watercolours, played the piano and was a keen reader, especially of Katharine Mansfield. She was an elegant woman, yet the kind of life her mother lived – cosseted, cooked for, waited on – Sunday would reject.

Between 1920 and 1922, Sunday attended St Catherine's Girls School in Williams Road, Windsor. Earlier, she had been educated at home. Sport was emphasised – calisthenics and hockey as well as dancing – but languages and music, both important to Sunday, were also on the curriculum. However, it was not a happy experience. Sunday, shy and sensitive, found the regimentation anathema. She didn't fit in. Rather like Joy, Sunday cast doubts over her school years. In fact, Sunday complained so much about school that friends thought she had attended only briefly, if at all. As a teenager, she travelled to Europe with her family. Ethel read and spoke French, a skill Sunday was taught and maintained for the rest of her life. As a young woman, she enjoyed sport and showed a keen interest in food and gardening. Yet it was a lonely girlhood and Sunday had few friends.

[9]   Sunday Reed to John Reed (early 1930s), Reed Collection.

Sunday, however, was no shrinking violet. She learned to drive when few women did and disdained 'bluies' (parking tickets), parking where and when she chose. She had a strong sense of personal style, wearing trousers in the 1930s when it was considered daring, and cut a dash at whatever social gathering she attended. She learned that high society might have been her birthright but its rules, distinctions and hierarchies were definitely not for her.

There was a new image for women in the 1920s – the 'New Woman', 'flapper' or 'career girl' were images imported from America. Though sexual freedoms were more preached than practised, there suddenly seemed to be, for younger women, alternatives to marriage and motherhood. Independent, fashionably dressed and well travelled, the modern woman appeared in rather more control of her destiny than her Edwardian mother. In stolid Australian society, such images were often merely that – appealing but insubstantial. But they did exist and through the popular culture of film and women's magazines such as *The Home* they were pervasive and admired. Sunday seemed to embody some of these possibilities.

In October 1926 Sunday's engagement to Leonard Quinn was announced. It was a disastrous marriage and the family was against it from the start. Quinn, whose family hailed from Boston, Massachusetts, was supposed to be a businessman with interests in journalism but he turned out to be a bit of a phoney. He was probably after Sunday's money. There were ugly rumours circulating about Quinn. Basil Burdett remembered him for passing bad cheques in Barcelona. Married at Sorrento's St Mary's Star of the Sea in December – Quinn was a Catholic – they honeymooned in Paris, then lived for a time in the Cotswolds. Sunday contracted gonorrhoea from Quinn. The subsequent infection led to a hysterectomy. The marriage foundered and Sunday rented rooms in London where she stayed, miserable and alone, until she was rescued by her father. Sunday's inability to have children was a source of grief and longing.

Introduced to John Reed over a tennis match in 1930, Sunday was smitten. 'You'd better marry me', she advised him some time later. And marry they did, in fine style at St Paul's Cathedral in 1932. John's highly proper and religious family had reservations. After all, Sunday was a divorcee. But theirs was to be, like Leonard and Virginia Woolf's, a marriage of true minds and, like the Woolfs, one of sometimes differing satisfactions. John was a Cambridge-educated lawyer whose Tasmanian family were graziers.[10] A

---

[10] See Barrett Reid, 'Making it New in Australia: Some Notes on Sunday and John Reed', *Angry Penguins and Realist Painting in Melbourne in the 1940s*, Hayward Gallery, London, 1988, p. 30.

dark-haired, good-looking man, with a long jaw and mild, deeply lidded eyes, John was quietly spoken and self-assured. Wry humour combined with a sharply perceptive intelligence; he was a staunchly loyal friend, implacable when he believed he was right, and Sunday's champion always.

When they married, John was a partner in the law firm of Blake & Riggall after which he practised as a solicitor from Collins House. John's friends included the cartoonists Will Dyson and Jim Bancks, the creator of 'Ginger Meggs'. Another was designer and cartoonist Fred Ward. The Reeds' involvement with modernism would come soon after their marriage, especially through their friendship with the brilliant young painter Sam Atyeo. Atyeo was introduced to them by Cynthia, John's younger sister.

John's and Sunday's was a relationship of loving-kindness, of almost fraternal protectiveness. In their early letters to one another, disruptive erotic longings are displaced by shared sentiments of emotional security symbolised by physical comforts. The importance of nurturing the other was to be not only the mainstay of their marriage but the dynamic behind so many of their friendships. From the first, John assumed the role of Sunday's caretaker, cheering her flagging spirits, and attending to her sensitivities and her often uneven health. He applied a salve to Sunday's anxieties, a role he would play for the rest of his life and one that she came to utterly depend upon.

In 1934 John and Sunday moved from their apartment at 27 Marne Street, South Yarra to a modest weatherboard house, originally a dairy farm, set in fifteen acres of bush and river flats at Heidelberg near the Yarra River, soon known as Heide.[11] Their life together was begun with gusto. They remodelled the house, adding a modern bathroom and kitchen, along with extensive bookshelves. They also began an ambitious gardening program. Birches, willows, lindens, poplars, walnuts, golden ash, oaks, alders and larches were among the first trees planted. A vegetable garden was started and masses of flowers were planted, too. At Heide John and Sunday could welcome friends such as Atyeo and painter Moya Dyring who would be

[11]   In 1980 John and Sunday sold 11 acres of their 15 acre property which included Heide II (a larger house built on nearby land) to the Victorian State Government for development as an art gallery and public park. The Reeds kept the net amount (about $500,000) of $1.82 million as part of their endowment of the park and gallery. Renamed the Museum of Modern Art at Heide in 1991, it now houses over 500 works from the Reeds' collection. The original Heide building still stands. It was occupied by Sweeney Reed and his family until 1978, then by John and Sunday until their deaths, upon which it was bequeathed to Barrett Reid and Philip Jones.

enticed to help in the garden. Dyring was in her element. Atyeo just wanted to nod off![12] John and Sunday were generous, enlightened hosts and by the late 1930s Heide became a focus for many involved in Melbourne's radical cultural life.

The well-stocked Heide library, and its larder, were twin delights for the visitor. Art books, volumes of poetry, new novels, classics, books about birds and gardens, and the latest journals were all available for the Reeds' mostly impecunious guests. Paintings were everywhere at Heide, hanging on walls, and propped against desks and bookshelves. The garden, as provider for the table and as an exquisite environment, was Sunday's lifelong commitment, a balance of work and pleasure. She employed a number of gardeners over the years to help her tend it. Impressed by potter Neil Douglas' garden at Bayswater, she invited him to stay at Heide and, for a small wage, to help landscape the garden. Sunday's idea for a garden was for 'a heaven on earth all around you.'[13] 'At lunch time we pored over rare garden books, old English cottage lore, garden poetry, herb lore, finding the names of plants that had been found in strange places.'[14]

There were strict routines about gardening, visitors, cats, dogs, food and chores and nothing was allowed to interrupt it. Home *was* life to Sunday and she was miserable away from Heide, even for short periods. Heide was not only central to Sunday, it was a beloved destination for her friends. Joy revelled in the beauties of the garden, the good meals, the gatherings with Arthur Boyd, Sidney Nolan, John Perceval, Mary Boyd and Danila Vassilieff and the arguments about art, music and writing that raged late into the night: it was an environment in which she could feel productive and inspired.

'Sitting on the sofa in front of the fire in the big, soft atmosphere of the [Heide living] room . . . Joy would sit, before dinner or after dinner conjuring magical visions with pen and brush or brush and wash . . . Right out of her imagination, very hot, came these strange drawings of people which were most hauntingly beautiful and evocative, almost ghost-like.'[15]

---

[12] 'Sam wanted to go to sleep when he got out to Heide but Moya made him dig, but I don't think he bust himself over it. He was particularly offended that he should have to dig a bed for marrows! Poor Moya could hardly drag herself away from the veg garden.' John Reed to Sunday Reed, (early 1930s), Reed Papers.

[13] Neil Douglas, interview, 22 September 1980.

[14] Abbie Heathcote, *A Far Cry, Neil Douglas spinning yarns with Abbie Heathcote*, Karella Publishing, n.d., p. 72.

[15] Burke, *Joy Hester*, op. cit. p. 71.

'And yet all the time', John recalled,' [Joy] would be fully participating in the talk going on around her, laughing (sometimes crying) always responding fully to whatever was happening.'[16]

Sunday did not seek a public role for her taste, so she has been seen as a background figure to the cultural movements of the 1940s. She would not hold office in the CAS, as John did, or lecture, or write, or publicly defend the artists she nurtured. Her deafness precluded that as much as her temperament. Unsuited to the hurly burly of public life, its negotiations, politicking and lobbying, the role Sunday defined for herself was to create a very particular kind of home.

Friends were made so welcome they often did not want to leave Heide, or, when they did, felt inextricably bound to the place. That was certainly true of those closest to Sunday, such as Joy and Sidney Nolan. Nolan had arrived at Heide in 1938 a cocky, gifted young painter, unashamedly seeking patronage. It marked the beginning of Nolan's relationship with the Reeds: his love affair with Sunday and his strong, complex friendship with John. The freedoms practised at Heide were not only intellectual and artistic, but moral and sexual. Both John and Sunday distanced themselves from a rigid and conservative upbringing. Both experienced the risk and pain of living outside social conventions, and both were protected by the privileges of their class from suffering the consequences. They belonged to an elite that believed in social responsibility, noblesse oblige. For Sunday and John, their friends became their life.

The move from South Yarra to Heide had made clear the rift with the Melbourne society into which Sunday had been born. For, if Sunday was criticised by her artist friends for her wealth and upper-class background, equally that same class had difficulty accepting her after she threw in her lot with the artists. She was pulled between two social groups, without fitting comfortably into either, and she knew it. It was also a time, as Joy's question about class indicates, when radical politics were part and parcel of artistic definition. Most of Sunday's circle were left-wing, some were members of the Communist Party. In the war years, Joy was an idealistic supporter of communism. Sunday, privileged and generous, was keenly aware of what she had and what her friends did not.

Sunday confided to friends that she didn't deserve her wealth. Unlike her brothers, who were drawn into the family business and felt part of the

---

[16]   Burke, *Joy Hester*, op. cit., p. 71.

Baillieu empire, Sunday was only 'trained' for marriage. She believed her inheritance was unwarranted and unearned. It was the impulse behind her philanthropy.

The support of left-wing artists and causes strained relations with Sunday's family, especially with her father. The regular Thursday night meals with Arthur at his Anderson Street, South Yarra flat, often ended in arguments. Or there would be explosive phone calls. Once Sunday was in town when an expensive black car drew past her. She glanced inside. 'What a horrible group of men', she thought. She looked closer. They were her uncles. Sunday and John relinquished their old lives when they set up house in the bush outside Melbourne but they gained a new one, and they did not renege.

Sunday had briefly studied painting at George Bell's Bourke Street studio school in 1933. Sam Atyeo was impressed by her work. 'You've got quality in your work', he told her.[17] Dismissive of Bell's school – 'good for grey people to learn to paint' – Atyeo went on, 'There is something . . . you have . . . these bloody grey people will never be able to realise.' If the art George Bell admired was 'disciplined, objective and mindful of European classicism' then it's unlikely Sunday would have found it to her taste.[18] The approach to art, and its appreciation, that she developed was not for the crafted object but for the primacy of the artist's intention and vision. Sunday and John thought tuition a waste of time, even an impediment to creative expression, and they argued about it with Joy who, in 1942, was still uncertain about its advantages.

There may have been other reasons for Sunday's dislike of art school. Many women attended Bell's school (Maie Casey was a student there in 1933) and when Bell resigned from the CAS in 1940, he took most of the women members with him. Their loyalty to him and his teachings turned them away from the CAS's radical politics fomented by John Reed, Albert Tucker and Noel Counihan. Yet Bell was no supporter of women artists, despite the many talented women he instructed. He believed they were not serious about art, and saved his finer efforts for the men. It was an attitude Sunday could not have failed to notice. Sunday did not continue to paint and never referred to herself as an artist, yet it shows her curiosity and indicates how aware she was of the aesthetics, as well as the practicalities, of art. Perhaps it also made her realise just how much support a woman artist like Joy needed.

---

[17]   Sam Atyeo to Sunday Reed, (mid 1930s), Reed Collection.
[18]   James Mollison in Felicity St John Moore, *Classical Modernism: the George Bell School*, Foreword, National Gallery of Victoria, Melbourne, 1992, n.p.

The only sketches of Sunday's that remain are the stick figures scrawled on her letters to Joy.

Sunday was a sharer. She cooked, cleaned, ironed John's shirts, milked the cows and ran the house – although everyone who stayed was meant to lend a hand. She was not entirely on her own. There was Jimmy, the odd-job man and, occasionally, domestic help. Nolan was a bit of a slouch about house-work although he got involved in the garden; Neil Douglas pitched in while Barrett Reid offered to clean the milk separators, a job nobody wanted. Joy made breakfast – a time when Sunday was notoriously touchy – and on sunny days it was held in the garden at seven-thirty.

Sunday's emphasis was on simplicity, quality and naturalness. Food was a celebration. For her, diet was immensely important, the difference between well-being and ill-health. Edward Dyason, Sam Atyeo's patron, introduced Sunday and John to the Hay system. American Dr William Hay had devised a diet where carbohydrates and protein were never combined in the same meal, and which emphasised whole grains, unrefined sugars and fresh, home-grown vegetables. Sunday gave up rich French cooking: she and John became healthier and the vegetable garden became even more important in their lives. Mirka Mora, newly arrived from Paris in 1951, was impressed by Sunday's skill and style as cook, housekeeper and host. Sunday 'took as much pride in keeping her kauri draining board scrubbed as the rarest flower in the garden. The bleached linen sheets and pillows . . . were like white camellias.'[19]

While Sunday's background gave her the freedom to pursue whatever she chose, to indulge her interests and merely dabble in the arts, she was not a dilettante. Her intellectual curiosity and powerful personality expressed them-selves through the environment she created, through intimate relationships with artists, and through the financial support she supplied to the artists she believed in. Sunday's was an acute, refined, subtle sensibility. Albert Tucker would call Sunday 'the eye' of the group, 'the real force that drew us together.'

Sunday fully participated in the publication of *Angry Penguins* and *Ern Malley's Journal* and in the ideas behind the formation of the Contemporary Art Society and the Museum of Modern Art of Australia. She may not have attended CAS Council meetings but she would thoroughly question John afterwards, acquainting herself with every detail, and offering criticism and

[19] Heathcote, op. cit., p. 70.

advice. No decisions were made without her. Her translations of Rimbaud introduced the poet to her circle, having a particularly fecund impact on Nolan's work.

Together with John, Max Harris and Nolan, Sunday was an active director of Reed & Harris, the company which published *Angry Penguins*. Sunday's opinion shaped direction. In all these ventures, Sunday came up with ideas and backed them with money. Together with suggesting articles, poems and exhibitions, and soundly criticising the fruits of their labours, Sunday also did the hackwork of reading proofs and hanging shows. At Museum of Modern Art openings she served the drinks. 'I wash up five hundred glasses in two pink and blue plastic buckets.'[20] Her visual sense was crucial in layout and design. Sunday and John were a team but Sunday was the inspirational force.

Sunday wanted to be as closely involved with the ideas and the production of a work of art as possible. She was not averse to suggesting to Sidney Nolan, or any other artist for that matter, the direction his work should explore. Sunday's was a frank and challenging voice, her insights both apposite and original. It was after seeing Streeton's *Yarra Valley at Heidelberg* (c. 1888, National Gallery of Victoria) at Heide that Nolan began to rethink his attitude towards the landscape. 'Sunday discussed the possibility of using all this modern experience, and the abstract painting experience, in the service of a revival of Australian landscape.'[21] 'We did discuss it and I did start to change course as a result.'[22] Ned Kelly's exploits not only offered Nolan possibilities for landscape painting and for developing the bushranger's mythic potential for Australian culture – ideas thrashed out with Sunday and John – but a private narrative based on his deep, and often troubled, involvement with the Reeds. The *Kelly* series traced 'emotional and complicated events in my own life. It's an inner history of my own life.'[23] When Nolan painted on the long refectory table in the Heide dining room, Sunday was there beside him, part of the process. Sometimes Nolan would work on the *Kelly* series with one arm draped around Sunday's waist.

---

[20] 'Lately I have been managing the domestic and housekeeping side of things for John which means I spend a lot more time in the Museum. It is hard work.' Sunday Reed to Jean Langley, 16 July 1960, Langley Collection.

[21] *Sidney Nolan,* interview with Peter Ross, ABC TV, 1992. *Yarra Valley at Heidelberg* was the first painting the Reeds had bought together in the 1930s.

[22] Richard Haese, *Sidney Nolan: The City and the Plain*, National Gallery of Victoria, 1983, p. 12.

[23] Noel Barber, *Conversations with Artists*, Collins, London, 1964, p. 90.

Nolan and Sunday enjoyed a great, creative partnership for nearly a decade. If she forsook her ambitions as an artist in the 1930s, then she realised them vicariously through her role as muse for Nolan in the crucial passages of his work: the 1942 Wimmera paintings and the 1946 *Kelly* series. She was not only his adviser and sounding board, while he was in the army in 1942 she prepared his materials and supplied him with books – Rilke, Auden, Spender, Baudelaire, Proust and Joyce. Theirs was a congress of shared vision, a potent union of passion and spirit that helped to inspire some of Nolan's best landscape paintings.

Sunday was as ready with praise as she was with criticism. Yet her criticism was leavened with respect and, in many cases, it earned her devotion. The beam of Sunday's approval bestowed radiance on its recipients. Two of her most admired artists, Hester and Nolan, made art publicly – Nolan on the dining room table and Joy on the floor by the fire in the library. 'I miss your work', she told Joy, 'I miss watching you work.' This was the kind of relationship with art Sunday sought and enjoyed. It was an unconventional and wholehearted patronage that was undeterred by prevailing canons of taste. Sunday may have been glad to see the fortunes of John Perceval or Arthur Boyd gradually rise but she stuck by artists such as Hester and Vassilieff, who were not as lucky, keenly following their progress and acquainting herself with their work in every detail.

Her commitment to Australian culture was uninfected by the subservience to English culture that was such a feature of Australian society in those years. She loved Australia and did not want to live anywhere else. Her interest in French culture did not lead her to make Paris her home, as did so many American and English intellectuals of her generation, and her trip there in 1948 is recorded in her letters as a catalogue of woes and discomforts.

Sunday recognised that the Australian landscape needed to be re-invented by modernism and given the same significance that Tom Roberts and Arthur Streeton accorded it. She was knowledgeable about the bush and wildflowers, and John had imparted his knowledge of native birds to her, yet Sunday was no sojourner to the back of beyond, no traveller roughing it in remote regions. Heide was her creation and her reality. She developed her taste within its walls. With John, she gathered around her like-minded artists who may have felt isolated and dissatisfied in Australia but who were, equally, concerned to change the culture, not merely escape it. This project – to participate in and radically alter Australian culture – was Heide's great dynamic, fuelled by the intense friendships of those associated with it.

If Sunday's involvement in publishing and running galleries was practical, intellectual and financial, it was also heartfelt. For Sunday, the life of the feelings was meshed with any enterprise, artistic or otherwise. If her struggling friends needed Sunday, she was equally dependent on being fed by their ambitions. Sunday wanted her friends to be as complete a part of her life as possible. A private person who valued intimacy, Sunday was also hospitable, keen for new contacts and acquaintances, and open to current ideas. Such qualities made Heide a busy place.

It was in contrast to the Boyds' home, Open Country, at Murrumbeena, where the casual, bohemian atmosphere was generated by the spirit of the Boyd family as much as by their less affluent circumstances. Friends drifted in and participated in whatever was going on – from a sit-down dinner to a discussion about literature or art. An invitation to Heide was deemed a privilege by some and Sunday was seen as remote, imperious and intimidating by those hearts and minds with whom she did not click.

Though much has been made of the philosophical differences between the Heide and Open Country groups, from the letters it is evident there were regular comings and goings between the two households in the 1940s, and a sharing, between the women, of domestic concerns. At Open Country, Yvonne Lennie and Mary Boyd were young artists who did not continue with their careers while Doris, matriarch of the Boyd clan, was a painter and potter.

The mood at Heide was governed by Sunday. She was sensitive, intuitive and easily hurt. For her there was no limit to the need to know and understand those she loved. For Sunday 'any time was relationship time.'[24] Heide was, as Max Harris has written, exacting and demanding in terms of the testing of sensibility.[25] And Heide, in this instance, can be taken to mean Sunday. Around her, there existed a huge emotional climate. Sunday was a mistress of atmospheres. Her capacity for friendship meant she insisted on playing a major role in the lives of those she loved, whether they liked it or not. This could lead to demands, restrictions and a desire for control. 'When will I be able to leave my loves alone I wonder?' Sunday mused. 'Go quietly into the earth and be as dead as a doornail.'[26]

She had an uncanny ability to know precisely what her friends needed, nurturing those close to her with inspired acts of largesse but she imposed

---

[24] Barrett Reid, interview, 19 August 1994.
[25] Max Harris, *Angry Penguins*, op. cit., p. 23.
[26] Sunday Reed to Joy Hester, (1950), Smith Collection.

values and had high expectations. Sunday could be 'worse than God.'[27] Her craving for reassurance required a constant, attentive solicitude from her friends: gifts of poems and drawings, of hair ribbons and favourite cuttings were the tithes of love. Sunday wanted to be needed. Conflict was an inevitable element, and one that Sunday was not afraid of. Arguments eddied and swirled in the Heide air. Friendships could veer from a happy balance to the brink of disaster in moments. If she was quick to forgive, she also expected forgiveness. Barrett Reid recalled, 'Sunday didn't give Joy enough space. She didn't give any of us enough space.'

She was a woman of energy and organisation whose nervous temperament often left her strained and tired. She could be peevish and impossible to please, stretching the patience of those near her, especially John, to breaking point. Sunday was capable of broad gestures of benevolence and small acts of petulance. Single-minded, stubborn and swiftly discerning in matters of taste, she was also lavish with encouragement when it was due. Her devotion to contemporary culture meant she was impatient with those less engaged, alert, impassioned. Art, for Sunday, was a life of dedication, not a career or a hobby. For it, everything and anything could be sacrificed. Once she was convinced of an artist's worth, that artist's personal behaviour, no matter how irregular or unsociable, was of little account.

She was plagued by minor illnesses which, coupled with a soft, quavering voice, gave the impression that she was delicate, ethereal. A hearing problem bedevilled Sunday and led to vexations, confusions and the hearing aids she detested. Sure of her own domain, she could also be timid. On one occasion, Neville, Joy's brother, arrived at Heide. Sunday found him overbearing and a bit mad. Alone in the house, she offered to make tea. She walked down the hall and through the garden and all the way to Heidelberg station where she caught the train to town.

◆

Joy had grown as an artist under Sunday's eyes. In the 1940s, she was the only woman member of the so-called *Angry Penguins*, which included her husband, along with Sidney Nolan, John Perceval, Arthur Boyd and Danila Vassilieff. It is this association which has placed her securely in Australian art history, though it has taken years for her value to be assessed. *Angry Penguins* 'was not a literary quarterly at all but a common cultural workshop', stated

---

[27] Nadine Amadio, interview, 26 March 1995.

Max Harris.[28] It certainly functioned that way for Hester. The talented and ambitious men associated with *Angry Penguins* were her friends and peers. It was a period where rowdy arguments about the function of art and vitriolic exchanges about the moral imperatives of painting, and the role of the artist, divided the art world. Melbourne art politics in the war years were not for the faint-hearted. Ailsa O'Connor, married to social realist Vic O'Connor, commented ironically on the 'other' art politics of the time,

'In the Contemporary Art Society a clear division showed up between those artists grouped around John Reed, and ourselves (communist-social realist artists). Joy Hester and Yvonne Lennie were their slightly invisible women members (as I was within the left group).'[29]

Joy was the only woman of her group exhibiting regularly alongside the men. Between 1939 and 1946, she showed a dozen works in six consecutive CAS shows. Joy was also the only woman to have her work reproduced in *Angry Penguins* – a stark pen drawing *The time-lag / a middle-class dressing-room* (1943, Private Collection). But how was a smart, bold and attractive young woman artist viewed? In a startling note on contributors in the same issue of *Angry Penguins* Hester is described as, 'Joy Hester. Peroxide blonde in the early 20s; former pupil at the Melbourne Gallery; natural and prolific draughtsman; exhibits with CAS; writes poetry; married to painter A L Tucker.'[30]

John Reed has prefaced his professional information about Joy with a description of her hair – her appearance, in effect, her sexuality. George Bell had taken Tucker aside to warn him about Joy: she was 'wild' and not a suitable companion for him. John might have been a friend but he had reservations about her, and elsewhere described her as 'a hoyden'. Bell certainly did not approve. To many others she was simply 'Bert's girlfriend'. When I began my research on Hester in 1977, this was how several men, including Noel Counihan, first recalled her. Yet another young artist, Alannah Coleman, was impressed by Joy. 'She was wonderful, free speaking. She used language I dared not use.'[31]

Sunday was a role model for Joy – an influential and respected woman, the creator of the Heide ambience. The few older women artists from whom

[28] Jane Clark, *Sidney Nolan: Landscapes and Legends*, Cambridge University Press, Melbourne, 1987, p. 58.

[29] Ailsa O'Connor, *Unfinished Work, Articles and Notes on Women and the Politics of Art*, Greenhouse Publications, Melbourne, 1982, p. 35.

[30] *Angry Penguins*, no. 5, 1943, n.p.

[31] Alannah Coleman, interview, 8 February 1995.

Joy could have sought advice and guidance were in the discredited Bell group. Yet, for all the contradictions in her role, Joy was the woman artist at the centre of her circle. Noel Counihan may have ticked her off for being a political backslider and she may not have attended as many CAS meetings as she should, but politically, artistically, Joy belonged. She helped to define the visual culture of the 1940s.

Joy was uniquely placed to benefit from a diverse number of influences. In the early 1940s, social realism had a pervasive rather than a distinctive effect on her work while surrealism, the other major current, surfaces in one or two drawings. Her art responded to a variety of influences as she began to sort out a personal language: Picasso, Diego Rivera, George Grosz and German Expressionism as well as Tucker, Vassilieff and Bergner appear as useful references at this time.

In 1945, Joy's work developed the psychological and formal power that marked her maturity. The head and eyes become the focus in drawings that no longer hint at disturbed states of mind but abrasively portray them. Suddenly Joy could exploit the dramatic qualities of brush and ink to their full potential.

Discovering she was pregnant in May 1944, Joy tried to have an abortion. An infection precluded that and, with grim resignation, Joy announced to her friend Pauline McCarthy that she would have to have the baby. If motherhood marked the end of her freedom, it also brought with it fear and guilt. No one knew that she had been having an affair. The man, a drummer in local jazz bands, was one of Joy's secret lovers. Harry, a taxi driver at a company where Joy worked in 1942, was another. A watercolour of *Harry* (1942, University Art Museum, University of Queensland) shows a pink, naked, hairy, distorted body, with a sensual, leering face; violence oozes from *Harry*. Joy confided to writer Michael Keon, another Heide guest, that Harry whipped her.

After a time, Joy seemed to accept the pregnancy and happily settled into planning the birth but when Sweeney was born, in February 1945, her dissatisfactions resurfaced. She declared to Bert she 'wasn't cut out' to be a mother. The time she had spent drawing and writing was now spent tending her son. Depressed and housebound as Sweeney grew, Joy took her frustrations out on her husband.

The other trigger for Joy, and the place where she was able to locate these new emotions, was in the newsreel footage of the concentration camps. Liberated by the Allies in 1945, first Auschwitz by the Russians in January, then Bergen-Belsen by the British in April, footage of the camps was soon screening worldwide.

Joy drew on the films directly, and she appears to be the only Australian artist to have done so. She saw them in cinemas in Little Collins Street, taking Sweeney, only a few months old. In one drawing, sourced from footage from Ravensbruck, the cadaverous bodies of a mother and child hang from a gallows. In another, an emaciated form is propped against a wire fence. One skeletal figure lies dead: an image of personal suffering, it is titled *Birth of Sweeney* (c.1945, Private Collection). Joy's angry, wounded relationship with her mother is pictured, too. The withered torso of *A Human Being* (1945, National Gallery of Australia) has rolling, double eyes that create an expression of icy malevolence. It is an image of a person stripped to the bone, sexless, ghastly, yet malignantly powerful. This 'victim' is none other than a portrait of Louise.

But it is in *A Frightened Woman* (1945, Private Collection) that Joy concentrates and achieves what was essential to her art and what would subsequently direct it: the eye as carrier of meaning. Significantly, it is one of the few works from this period she signed, dated and titled. Crazed pinwheel eyes register the depths of violence and injury that a human being can experience, a point where what is human is itself on the verge of shattering and dissolving. But, for all her starkness, *A Frightened Woman* directly engages the viewer, communicating with her anguished eyes that there is no escape from our condition, no recourse, spiritual or otherwise. At the extreme point of emotion where, from pressures within or without, personality verges on disintegration and reason slips away, the saving grace, and the last resort, is an available and palpable humanity, a sane, cool knowledge in the heat of terror, that human beings are defined by such limits, by such extreme points. They chart the nature of humanity, transforming and substantiating it.

Hallucinatory masks of terror, passion and love delivered in black and white would now become the subject of Joy's work. Key series such as *From an Incredible Night Dream* (c.1946), *Gethsemane* (c.1946) and *Faces* (1947–48) indicate the intensity of emotion Joy saw shaping her life and relationships. The exaggerated, staring eye not only came to symbolise feeling but was the stylistic and compositional focus of her drawings. Bliss, suffering and revelation are all suggested by the upward gazing eye. In the *Love* series (1949) Joy drew lovers, their eyes merged – sight unified in the sexual embrace. She limned the trembling edge of feeling, a place of extremes, of conflict, change and loneliness. What is most human about her work is also its most abstract quality, the essence of expression, feeling at its most concentrated.

Hester's art indicates darker, more troubled aspects of her personality. She might have been dubbed 'Sunshine' by her friends because 'I am always giggling and laughing',[32] but her drawings reveal a nervous, introspective self – her creative self – which was matched by her anguished poetry and related writings of the early 1940s.[33] In 1949, Joy would admit to Sunday, 'I wished to die for many years.' The sadness and violence of her home life, her father's death, guilt and fear from the early abortion may have all contributed to her feelings of despair – though her art is not one of despair. It signposts the abyss but is not trapped within it. Nonetheless, Hester's was a tragic vision.

By early 1947, Joy had completed two new series of drawings. They were *From an Incredible Night Dream* and *Gethsemane*. Joy had read an English translation of Jean Cocteau's *Opium* (1930) that Bert had bought. The tale of Cocteau's withdrawal from the drug was, according to its author, like describing 'a wound in slow motion.' The title *From an Incredible Night Dream* was inspired by one of Cocteau's tortured drawings, though his drawings were no more the product of hallucination than Joy's. It is unlikely that she had access to opium or any other drug. Joy's drawings are a visual approximation to Rimbaud's 'long, immense and reasoned deranging of all the senses.' Bodies are realised with a minimum of brush strokes, eyes roll, mouths gape, heads are thrown back in ecstasy or terror. The Night Dreamers are witnesses of a nightmare journey of the senses.

Gethsemane was Sunday's doll. Faceless, long-haired and stuffed with lavender from the Heide garden, it sat on her bed like a surrealist personage where it was duly greeted by visitors. For Sunday, it was an emblem of grieving, of her infertility. Gethsemane was the garden where Christ waited to be arrested and taken to his execution. It was a site of lonely vigil and suffering, a place of betrayal, where Christ's sacrifice is fully apprehended by him and where, in Christ's fear, what is divine is made human.

If in *Gethsemane I* (c. 1946, Museum of Modern Art at Heide) Joy renders in rapid strokes the doll's blank face, then by *Gethsemane V* (c. 1946, Museum of Modern Art at Heide) she is no longer satisfied with such abstractions: the doll has been endowed with intense, upward gazing eyes and a beatific smile. *Gethsemane V* is a portrait of Sweeney. Sunday's doll, the locus of suffering love, is symbolised by Joy's son. If Gethsemane represented the child Sunday could not have, then in Joy's drawing loss has been

[32]   Joy Hester to Albert Tucker, (1942), Tucker Collection.
[33]   Burke, *Joy Hester*, op. cit., pp. 47, 63.

transformed – Sweeney's face has replaced the doll's, just as Sweeney himself would replace Sunday's longing by becoming her adopted son.

Hester had completed her best drawings so far. A new confidence added to the restlessness she already felt about her marriage and motherhood.

◆

In April 1947, Joy's life changed dramatically. She left Melbourne for Sydney, abandoning her marriage and her two-year-old son. Her companion was Gray Smith, with whom she would spend the rest of her life. She would hear from a specialist in Sydney what she had already been told in Melbourne: that her illness, Hodgkin's disease, a cancer of the lymph glands, was terminal. Smith, who had also left his family, suffered from grand mal epilepsy and was often ill.

Joy met Gray in late March while Bert was in Japan. Joy had wanted to accompany Bert on the trip and was disappointed when it proved untenable. She stayed on alone, looking after Sweeney at their flat in Martin Street, Elwood. Introduced by Pauline and Jack McCarthy at their Kismet Bookshop in Johnston Street, Fitzroy, the attraction between Joy and Gray was instantaneous. They spent the weekend together in the McCarthy's spare room.

Like Bert, Gray was a man of strong personality but, where Bert was cerebral, organised and ambitious, Gray was subject to mercurial moods and a debilitating illness. Epilesy was a social stigma then; more than an affliction it was regarded as a disgrace, even as evidence of insanity. Gray's life was dominated by it. His condition made many of the normal social duties, exchanges and pleasures difficult, and encouraged a private rather than a public life. The outside world could be a threatening place and the prospect of a fit, frightening and humiliating.

Gray's sense of himself as an artist was nascent in 1947. Older brothers Max and Martin had been friends of Nolan's. Gray had hung around the St Kilda baths with them, an interested listener to their conversations about painting. Gray had studied under Max Meldrum and had shown in the 1946 CAS Annual Exhibition. He was a compact, nuggety, roughly handsome man, balding, with intense blue eyes. With his heat, spontaneity and bawdy humour, Gray mirrored aspects of Joy. 'He is the man of me', she wrote to Sunday, 'and I am the woman of him.'

At first, Joy had not planned to leave Bert. Bert was unaware of Joy's affairs, even of the depth of her friendship with Sunday. Though he received a stipend from the Reeds, Bert refused to be drawn closely into the Heide circle, finding it too rarified for his taste. Nor did the Reeds feel at ease with him. Sunday respected Bert as an artist but she was a little afraid of him. Bert made no bones about his trenchantly held views and delivered them forcefully. The role Bert played in Joy's life would now be severed while her connections with Heide strengthened.

There was a further element in the situation. Joy had been sick for some time. A lump had formed on her neck. When Sunday asked Joy about it Joy was dismissive: she had been to a hospital where she was told the lump was 'nothing'. Joy had a hacking cough and had lost weight. Sunday insisted Joy see her own doctor, who in turn recommended Doctor Littlejohn, a specialist.

Shortly after Bert arrived back in Melbourne, John arranged a meeting where he told Bert the diagnosis which Joy did not, as yet, know: she had Hodgkin's disease and had been given two years to live. After they returned to their Elwood flat, the strain proved too much for Joy. She burst out with the news of her affair, said she had to leave to think things through. She ran from the flat, leaving Sweeney there. Later she went to Heide where she, too, was told the results of her tests. She told Pauline McCarthy the news kept 'pouring into my head'. Bert stayed on at the flat with Sweeney. A few days later, he took Sweeney out to Heide.

Joy and Gray left for Sydney in such a rush, Joy did not even have a change of clothes. When they arrived in Sydney, Joy and Gray had no money and nowhere to live, staying first in Coogee, then Mosman. They got by on postal notes from the Reeds and Elsie Smith, Gray's mother. For several months, the red light district of King's Cross was home. They could find work only sporadically.

The early letters to Sunday cover a time of fear, sickness and insecurity, of art being made under difficult conditions. Joy's eye for absurd detail and appreciation of a sensual world of natural, physical beauty lightened the troubled moment. Joy tried to amuse and entertain Sunday, even when the going got tough, rather like the story Joy told about her abortion. It was an element of their friendship, and a balance Joy was keen to maintain – both for Sunday and herself. As she finished one letter to Sunday, 'You do not have to answer my letters, I just like talking to you.'

Joy was involved in a battle for her health. Within a month of arriving in Sydney an operation to remove a gland from her neck was followed by the ray treatment she loathed. At the same time she was writing poetry and producing the *Faces* and *Sleep* series. Sunday supplied her with brushes and instructions on how to mix Chinese ink. Nolan sent paper. Joy had never enjoyed the solitude and contemplation of a studio or the luxury of expensive materials. She was used to working fast with whatever came to hand, putting down everything she had to say with speed, clarity and economy: it served her well now.

The *Faces* are not just a document of her own fears and insights though Joy admitted 'they're frightening things to hang on the wall . . . my "eyes" really seem to be running away with my drawings and somehow when I put brush to paper I start with an eye, do the eye and the rest is dictated by that.' The face *was* Joy's vehicle of expression: streetscapes appear as background to drawings from the early 1940s but the landscape and the mythic or bibli- cal themes that captivated Nolan or Boyd held no interest for her, nor, for that matter, did pictorial narrative of any kind. The *Night Dream* and *Gethsemane* series prefigure the *Faces* in form and content.

All attention is now concentrated on the eye. The drawings themselves were approximately life-size, making the eyes the immediate focus point. In *Faces* Joy's observations of people surface in a more innovative way than in portraits such as *Harry* or *Michael Keon* (1942, Museum of Modern Art at Heide). Emotional intensity, already explored in *Night Dream*, reaches a higher level of substance and articulation.

A time of crisis can be one of illumination where circumstances are seen from a fresh perspective and new strengths are realised within the individual. Self-knowledge can be the gift of such passages, where what has been repressed or denied flows out, awakening resolution and change. Joy's art flourished: she began the work of her maturity, the drawings exhibited in her first solo show. Her love for Gray was a healing resource, a balm to the pres- sure and a passionately fulfilling union. Despite her problems, Joy's identity as an artist remained intact because she continued to address and maintain it. If there was a test of her commitment to drawing she met it in 1947, and triumphed.

A symptom of Hodgkin's disease was night sweats, where Joy would wake in fright, shaking and drenched in perspiration. Some *Faces* have the quality of a nightmare emerging from a shadowy background, yet their resolution as images, as coherent and moving works of art firmly grounded in human experience means the *Faces* are more than either a therapeutic exercise or a diary of sensations of distress. Art is an act of self-criticism on the part of the artist, a rigorous and willed performance where whatever is weakest in the artist's creative vocabulary is banished and whatever is strongest is pushed to the limit. Good art's first challenge is always to its creator.

Face II (1947–48, Janine Burke) is a portrait of Gray. His face entranced her. She wrote to Sunday, 'I would like to tell you about Gray's face but I don't think I can except to say it is like and he himself is like every drawing I have ever done . . . It is a quite wondrous face and changes so swiftly and so subtly.'

Gray's abstracted face emerges from a dark wash, Joy's companion on her perilous journey. Apart from an ear, no other features clutter the direct inquiry of the gaze. *Face II* is a calm and soothing, though not a transcendent, image. Joy may have been fascinated by the supernatural, by ghosts, poltergeists and things that go bump in the night, but she did not try to visually equate them in her drawings. *Face II* is not an angelic messenger but a visitation, both gutsy and real. 'The heads I do are the heads that pass me in the street', she told Sunday.

The *Sleep* series also uses Gray as inspiration; the form of her sleeping lover becomes a motif for rest, but with the deeper resonance that haunts Joy's drawings, the body in *Sleep I* (1948, Museum of Modern Art at Heide) takes on a deathly pallor and stillness, the anonymity of a corpse in a morgue.

Apart from outings with Alannah Coleman, Joy and Gray were lonely in Sydney, though Joy made light of it. She knew she had lost friends by leaving Sweeney. Connections with Guy Boyd and his pottery business did not work out, nor did the various ill-conceived money-making schemes Gray and Joy dreamed up and attacked with wild enthusiasm. The letters to Sunday were a reminder of what she had left in Melbourne, and what she still loved – Heide and, in a more complicated way, her son.

Nolan was a good friend to Joy and Gray in Sydney after he arrived late in 1947. He had been travelling in Queensland with the precocious young Brisbane poet Barrett Reid. Nolan had left Melbourne in July, unravelling the tight web of his relationship with Sunday and John. For eight years, Sunday had been his lover, and John, his friend and business partner. With Joy, Gray and Alannah Coleman, Nolan celebrated New Year's Eve on Bondi beach. Nolan helped Gray with stoking the furnace at their Point Piper flat and he was sympathetic towards Joy's worries over Gray's health – and her own. Nolan felt a deepening of his friendship with Joy. She seemed to have become wise, confident and balanced in her dealings with the world.[34]

---

[34] Sidney Nolan to John Reed, 14 January 1948, Reed Collection.

Nolan felt the changes in Joy had to do with 'the way you have dealt with your knowledge of defeat, energies and hope which has now made you into something like a real woman.'[35]

But, after their tense and trying year in Sydney, Joy and Gray were making new plans. A shack in the bush was their goal, a place to make art, live quietly and keep well. After all, it seemed the miracle had happened: Joy believed she had conquered Hodgkin's disease. She was in remission. It was time to come home.

When they returned to Melbourne early in 1948, Joy and Gray stayed at Heide. On 25 March Nolan married Cynthia Reed. Nolan and Cynthia's was a whirlwind, ten-week romance. To compound matters, Cynthia and Sunday did not get on. Perhaps they were too alike: both were formidably intelligent and attractive women.

Cynthia was part of Melbourne's modernism in the early 1930s, educating a clientele that included H V and Mary Alice Evatt in the clean lines of European style.[36] Cynthia had run Modern Furnishings, an interior design shop at 367 Little Collins Street. At her invitation Atyeo showed one of his controversial, modernist paintings at Fred Ward's Collins Street design shop, the same painting that Bernard Hall had refused to hang in the 1932 National Gallery of Victoria Travelling Scholarship exhibition. Reportedly, it stopped the traffic. Alert to Atyeo's talent, Cynthia offered him a show, and design work, as he struggled to make a living. In the early 1940s Cynthia and Atyeo were lovers.

Cynthia's was a varied and unusual life marked by phases that included both writing and psychiatric nursing. Her first novel *Lucky Alphonse* (1944) was published by Reed & Harris. A vivid, edgy, forthright woman, Cynthia was physically frail with a powerful spirit. She abhorred her childhood at Mount Pleasant, the Reed family home outside Launceston, and memories of it plagued her life. Cynthia was rather awed by Sunday, regarding her as a genius and an egoist. Sunday's personality could be overwhelming. There was rivalry, too. Cynthia had an intense relationship with her older brother. According to Cynthia, John was crazy about her. The two women, Cynthia, dark, and Sunday, fair, shared lean good looks and an elegant mien. Could these similarities, Cynthia speculated, have prompted John's attraction to Sunday?[37]

[35] Sidney Nolan to Joy Hester, (1948), Smith Collection.
[36] Jennifer Phipps, *Atyeo*, Heide Park and Art Gallery, 1982, p. 13.
[37] Cynthia Reed to Sunday Reed, (early 1930s), Reed Collection.

The day after their marriage, Nolan and Cynthia went to Heide to make the peace. A terrific row ensued involving both Sunday and John. Neither wanted Nolan to leave. Joy and Gray ended up being a part of it. When Nolan did go, his break with Sunday was complete, though neither Sunday – nor John – ever stopped hoping for a reconciliation. More than two decades later, Sunday wrote to Jean Langley, 'There is just Nolan. You must believe me that I would give you tickets, money, everything, tomorrow if you could bring Nolan to Heide for even five minutes. Every day I think it will be today. He will come today.'[38]

John had lost his sister and his friend. Nolan's powerful feelings for his lover and her husband manifested as dismissal – after a few months of an increasingly tense correspondence, he refused all contact. John wrote, 'For you your life is through with us . . . Sun's letter to you . . . will have made it quite clear that it is not so for us. We ask then that you will accept this as our reality.'[39]

But the feelings ran too deep for Nolan to keep them private. The third party in a ménage à trois becomes the inner commentator and observer of the marriage, a symbol of the marriage's problems. Sometimes the lover can provide the fillip to marital boredom, strengthening bonds through tension. In Nolan's case, he was a witness both to Sunday's sexual dissatisfactions with John and John's helpless inability to remedy the situation. At the same time, Nolan was dependent on the Reeds for money and for the kind of intellectual stimulation only they could offer. He pressed Sunday to leave John. She wouldn't. The three were ensnared in an intimacy of claustrophobic fervour. They were circumstances which were not conducive to frailties of the heart.

The destructive rage of the poems in *Paradise Garden* (1971) indicate the level of frustration Nolan suffered loving Sunday and just how much he wanted revenge. Dignified and circumspect though he may have presented himself in his letters to John, it masked his true sentiments. In *Paradise Garden*, self-loathing and betrayal form harsh rhythms in an erotics of jealousy and despair. Nolan positions himself as the victim, manipulated and corrupted by the Reeds. He is an artist-child, robbed of his paintings and his innocence. Sunday is cast as a monstrous muse, frigid yet rapacious, a vessel of vile desires. In his efforts to lay bare his carnal compact with the Reeds, the point at which he seems to have suffered the most hurt, Nolan displays a savaged pride. Though *Paradise Garden* was, Sunday reflected, 'an evil

38   Sunday Reed to Jean Langley, (c.1972), Langley Collection.
39   John Reed to Sidney Nolan, 12 May 1948, Reed Collection.

book' that would 'slowly poison me in my lifetime as well as my death', she could not bring herself to hate Nolan.[40] 'A great river of love and tenderness pours over this consuming darkness.' For Cynthia, her marriage to Nolan was mostly a happy one, yet she did not find her own peace. Cynthia committed suicide in 1976.

In 1948 Sunday was distraught over the break-up with Nolan and, for the first months, often stayed in bed. Joy looked after the house, Sweeney too. Sweeney's response to his mother's return after nearly a year's absence must have been a mixture of relief and confusion. After all, she was back – but not to stay. Sweeney was Sunday's little boy now. Joy made that clear. She was 'Mumma Joy', a distinct and separate being.

Sunday developed a close relationship with Gray and he would spend hours sitting on her bed, comforting her. Sunday would always be mindful of Gray's 'love and strength' which 'meant so much at a time when there [was] practically nothing else . . . which mattered at all.'[41] For Gray, his encounter with Heide – and Sunday – was profound. He wanted to live there and twice put this proposal to John, who delicately rebuffed him.[42] For many, the enchantments of Heide were inextricably mixed with Sunday herself, and the style of life they felt she could offer them.

In August 1948, Sunday and John sailed to Paris with Sweeney. It was an emotional voyage. The Reeds wanted to sort out Sweeney's adoption with Bert who was, by then, living in Paris. With them they took Nolan's *Ned Kelly* series which they hoped to give a European showing. They had been shown in Melbourne in April to a dismal response.[43] After much trouble, including a wait of three months to get the paintings out of customs, the Reeds managed to arrange a show of the twenty-seven *Kellys*. Through their connection with H V Evatt and Peter Bellew, they were exhibited at Maison de l'Unesco in Paris in December 1949.[44] By this time the Reeds had returned to Melbourne. Jean

[40] Sunday Reed to Jean Langley, (c.1971), Langley Collection.
[41] Sunday Reed to Gray Smith, undated, Smith Collection.
[42] Gray Smith to John Reed, (1949), Reed Collection.
[43] The *Kelly* paintings of Sidney Nolan 1946–47, Velasquez Gallery, Tye's Furniture Store, Bourke Street, Melbourne, April 1948.
[44] H V Evatt (1894–1965) was an old friend of the Reeds. A defender of modern art and a former High Court Judge, Evatt was President of the UN General Assembly in 1948–49. Peter Bellew (1912–86), also an old friend of John and Sunday's, was founder of the Contemporary Art Society, Sydney, in 1939, art critic for the *Sydney Morning Herald*, 1939–42, and editor of *Art in Australia*, 1939–42. From 1947 he was head of the arts division of the headquarters staff at UNESCO, Paris.

Cassou, curator-in-chief of the Musée national d'art moderne, wrote the catalogue introduction. But organising the exhibition was a disappointing experience. Sunday wrote to Gray, 'I suppose if names mean anything then the Kellys have already arrived and we were glad that at least Cassou and others have seen the paintings and apparently been moved by them.'[45]

Finally, the Reeds wanted a break and to revisit some favourite places such as the Ile de Porquerolle, off Hyères in the south of France. They bought a car and toured through France, Italy and England, leaving Sweeney for a time with a French family in Tours.

For Joy and Gray a new life began in rural Hurstbridge. They had never lived in the country and badly wanted to make a go of it. Garford, familiarly known as Gar, in Haley's Gully Road, Hurstbridge, was on less than a hectare and it had no electricity or sewerage. Though Joy might have made disparaging comments about Gray's aunt, Susan McKay, when they stayed with her in Sydney in 1947, it was she who bought Gar for them. It was tiny: there were two big rooms and a smaller one that was used as a bedroom. Sometimes Joy used the back verandah as a studio. A small apple and pear orchard was attached to the property and John came up with his rotary hoe and hoed the rocky soil. Gray built a dam. Joy planted a flower and vegetable garden, with help from Heide. She also produced more of the Faces, continuing her practice of drawing on her knee by the fire, cross-legged on the floor or at the kitchen table. She discussed her poems with Gray and read them aloud.

For Joy it was a time of happiness and health, despite the hardships of country life and poverty. 'I am changing,' she wrote to Sunday, 'becoming much more quiet and composed.' Yet there was sadness, too. Louise Hester died in 1948 and there was, at last, something of a reconciliation between mother and daughter. Louise admitted to Joy that had she been faced with Joy's dilemma regarding her marriage at the same age she would have acted similarly. As Gray observed, it had a 'rather severe effect on Joy' who began 'wondering if maybe she had been hard on [Louise] in the past – this coming from the softness her ma had shown in the latter stages of her life.'[46] In her will, Louise left the house at Dawson Avenue to Sweeney when he came of age. She had cut Joy out of her will when Joy went away with Gray. Typically, Joy did not complain. She received the interest the estate drew, and two hundred pounds. At the last, Louise may have been forgiving – but not enough to leave Joy the house.

45 Sunday Reed to Gray Smith, 30 June 1949, Smith Collection.
46 Gray Smith to John Reed, (November 1948), Reed Collection.

Though Joy felt settled at Gar, for Gray it was a 'place of waiting . . . We would like to share your life', he told the Reeds, 'Joy for her reasons and I for mine.'[47] If Joy sought greater closeness with her son her letters do not reveal it. Joy and Gray stuck it out at Gar for another couple of years before moving to Avonsleigh in the Dandenongs in 1952.[48]

Cherry's Lane, Avonsleigh, was a larger property of fifteen acres and they tried to make a living by growing potatoes, keeping chickens, planting oats and selling wood but after a year they realised their crops would not give them sufficient income. 'It's going to be a hard fight to keep this place', Gray noted. There were mad schemes to supply chickens to the local delicatessen at Belgrave or to pick blackberries, but these were doomed. Avonsleigh was further from the city, too, a trek by bus and train to town, but they had an inside toilet and plenty of water.

It was a semi-reclusive life, and meant that, more than ever, Joy was cut off from the Melbourne art world. Her central role had ended when she left Tucker. Indeed, their break-up signalled the cultural disapora of Melbourne's post-war years. Whatever ambitions Joy may have had as a young artist, illness created a fresh agenda that required constant adjustment. Yet her ambition remained. After she left Bert, and despite the difficulties, Joy went on to produce a significant body of drawings and poetry. She did not devote herself to family and marriage as her sole occupation. But there were risks involved in being an artist for women of Joy's generation. Perhaps that is why there are so few of them.

Creative forces are unconscious and untrammelled and the need to express them can be destructive to the established pattern of a life, and certainly to the conventional expectations of a woman's role. Creativity is like a hunger, and it needs to be fed time, ideas, energy, books, art, landscapes, journeys, changes of all kinds. Joy did not leave her husband and her son to develop as an artist, at least not consciously. Nonetheless, she made a distinct choice at a certain point. In 1944 Sunday had a sense of Joy as an impressively talented young artist who needed to discipline herself to realise her gifts. No one except Sunday was prepared to tell her so because she was the one who took Joy seriously. In her first (extant) letter to Joy, Sunday wrote, 'In spite of what Bert used to call my feminist attitude, which in its fullest sense is true of me I think, you only prove the rule by being obviously the exception

---

[47] Gray Smith to John Reed, (1952), Reed Collection.

[48] Like Garford, Cherry's Lane, Avonsleigh was bought for Gray and Joy by Susan McKay.

– more than ever perhaps because of the touching and simple fact that you still do nothing about it. I wish you would.'

Was 'the rule' that there are no great women artists and did Joy prove it by being the exception?

Art, for Joy, was an integrated part of her life and this pragmatism served her well in her straitened circumstances. If her imperatives had been a studio, canvas, oil paints, a model and days of silence it is unlikely that she would have continued at all. Working on the floor, at the kitchen table, on her knee was how she made art for most of her life – in bursts, intently, spontaneously. At the same time, it meant that her work was not taken seriously. It seemed too casual, too quick, too raw. Drawing was seen as preliminary to the act of painting. For Joy, it was the finished work.

At Avonsleigh, Charles Blackman would be a neighbour for one memorable summer in 1954, while other visitors included Georges and Mirka Mora. With friends like the Reeds, the Moras, Charles Blackman and Barrett Reid, Joy's connections with the Contemporary Art Society could be maintained, albeit tenuously. She continued to exhibit in CAS exhibitions and Georges Mora, president of the CAS in 1957, was keen to have Joy on the CAS Council. Yet these were Joy's friends, powerful individuals in the local scene who recognised her talent as an artist. Joy had to maintain a balance as a professional artist with Gray, also an artist but not a very gifted one. If Joy attracted little success, Gray attracted less and this must have provoked tensions, especially in a man of such a febrile disposition.

When Gray and Joy could not meet the repayments on Avonsleigh, they lost it and rented a house at Upwey, also in the Dandenongs, before Sunday bought them a house at Clydesdale Street, Box Hill, in 1956. For the first time, Joy would have a separate room as a studio where she worked at night. She would produce *The Lovers* series and other late, large works. With a sense of her own history as an artist forming, she began to sign and date her work.

The Lovers picture sites of passion between men and women. A woman's head is thrown back in ecstasy – or does she cry for help? A man's grasp on his lover is tight as a stranglehold. A woman gazes up at the looming form of her lover with a troubling mixture of need and fear. His embrace is tentative, uncomfortable, threatening to the woman. Yet voluptuous sexual abandon, the moment of orgasm, is celebrated, too. Joy is the only Australian woman artist, until the late 1960s, to celebrate the pleasures of the flesh and the contradictions of love. Her view of the relations between men and women is bleak and unflinching. Love is a battle that must be fought as a primary way of realising the self. Within it, Joy suggests, there can be tenderness and fulfilment but violence that borders on madness and annihilation can also be part of it. Women are constrained, watched and shadowed by men. They are radiant but vulnerable, sexually potent but powerless once in the embrace. Desire involves rapture but also dissolution. Keeping distance, maintaining autonomy is pictured as important but nearly impossible in these drawings. Love is the enactment of a tragedy.

What do *The Lovers* depict of Hester's emotional life? Gray was a reckless man who was also capable of great gentleness and sensitivity. They had physical fights, big rows. Sometimes Gray drank, which only worsened his condition. On more than one occasion, he attempted suicide. Their life together was bounded by sickness, support and survival. Her protective love for him is evident from the letters and he inspired many drawings, but Gray must have also been at times a tough, intractable companion. *The Lovers* could also refer to the past, to restraints Joy felt in her marriage to Bert.

◆

The reason for the move back to town was that, after a remission of nine years, the symptoms of Hodgkin's disease had re-emerged. Joy had been warned that pregnancy would precipitate her symptoms but she went ahead with her two pregnancies. In Sydney in December 1947 Joy had an abortion under her doctor's advice. She was told they were twin boys. A son, Peregrine, was born in 1951 and a daughter, Fern, in 1954. The letters from Sunday are unflagging in their belief that, together, they can beat the disease. Gray was bitter about the final move, believing Joy was healthier and happier in the country, and that the Reeds had taken the decision out of their hands.

There was a feverish radiance to Joy in these years, a hunger for sensation. Joy had always relished the big, dramatic moments as much as the minutiae of daily life. Yarn-spinning was a favourite pastime. She took a hectic delight in the ordinary, rendering it an entertainment, fantastic, hilarious or rare. The recognition that time was running out for Joy emphasised the narrative of her own life, where mortality was defined like the perimeter of a page. 'Somehow one never really runs away, or I never have,' she wrote to Barrett Reid, 'and I find that the faster I go the more catches up with me . . . all the while time stands, to me, still – straight up and down like a great white sheet.'[49]

[49] Quoted in Barrett Reid, 'Joy Hester, Draughtsman of Identity', *Art and Australia*, June 1966, p. 45.

In her studio at Clydesdale Street, Joy began to draw on her experience of the bush – revealingly, after she had moved back to the suburbs. She probed neither its 'romance' nor its anecdotal aspects, both of which she appreciated: she isolated the figure, usually a child, in an empty space where it clutched an animal, a chicken, a lizard, a small bird. The Child was a popular image in the 1950s, especially in Melbourne painting. Charles Blackman, Arthur Boyd, John Perceval, Laurence Hope and Robert Dickerson had all depicted big-eyed, innocent waifs at the mercy of circumstance, emissaries of a gentler, more poetic world. *Girl with Turkey* (1957, Private Collection) and *Girl with Hen* (1956, National Gallery of Australia) show the Child protecting that which cannot be saved, an animal about to be slaughtered. They are images of loss and betrayal, richly toned in golds and browns, large, confident, controlled; Joy's final statements as an artist.

Though Hester went on making drawings and poems until the last months of her life, she felt defeated about her status as an artist. Gray recalled Joy 'cried all night' because 'she didn't have enough time to find another track. The track she was following wasn't reaching anybody.' At the time of her death in December 1960, her audience was a small group of artists and friends. Her solo exhibitions in 1950, 1956 and 1957 received uneven reviews and no sales. On its closure, she had presented the entire 1950 exhibition of drawings and poems to Sunday. 'They're all yours, Sun. Take them home.' It was only in 1963 at Hester's Commemorative Exhibition, organised by John at the Museum of Modern Art, that her drawings received their first critical praise.

◆

Though Joy sent her drawings and poems to Sunday, she rarely mentioned her work. In the period of the letters, Joy produced hundreds of drawings and many poems. Her first one-woman exhibition at the Melbourne Bookclub Gallery in 1950 was the fruition of three years' work. She showed the *Faces, Love* and *Sleep* series together with her own handwritten poems, tacked on the wall beside *Love* and *Sleep*. Privileging the poems in this way indicated their importance to her, a dual creativity. Yet Joy refers to the 'little show' to Sunday only in passing, although it must have been an exciting and nervewracking experience, her solo professional debut.

While the act of producing drawings and poetry was crucial, Joy's comments on it were not. It may have been the result of a natural modesty, a temperament that was uncomfortable articulating the creative process. Joy's production was swift and intuitive, uncluttered by preparation. But this absence may indicate a 'feminine' reticence learned among her more confident male peers, a language of self-presentation she did not believe she could command, even when addressing the exclusively female audience of her patron and trusted friend. This silence forms a curious and persistent lacuna through the letters. Joy may have been a remarkable tall tale-teller and a great gossip, a magpie of incident and anecdote, but she was also capable of editing and repressing what she did not wish Sunday to know.

Joy was keen to compliment Sunday on her new role as parent, without ever offering the advice which, as Sweeney's mother, must have been on the tip of her tongue. Joy created a distance between herself and her son which was specific and final. If she had anxieties about his welfare, she would not divulge them. The absences Joy created in her letters could be as poignant as their brimming fullness.

At first, Joy did not tell Sunday, or anyone else, that she doubted whether Sweeney was Bert's child. The truth of it can never be known. Joy confided in Gray but all through Sweeney's adoption process, and in the ensuing letters with Sunday, she kept it to herself. Perhaps she did not want to jeopardise the adoption. Perhaps she was ashamed. Most likely she also wanted to protect Bert from any further humiliation, until he had begun a new life. By late 1948, a new relationship had begun for him in Paris with an American woman, Mary. Later, when he returned to Australia, Bert would marry again. His connection with Joy remained, however, profound, anguished and very much alive.

Joy did not confront the other man, the drummer, who had his own family. He never knew. Much later, Sunday came to accept it. Whatever Joy told her about the circumstances of Sweeney's conception must have convinced Sunday. No doubt she felt shocked and more than a little betrayed. After all, Sunday had negotiated an adoption process with Bert that had caused distress to all concerned. But her friendship with Joy endured.

All of this may go part way towards explaining Joy's attitude towards Sweeney. She did not want her son back, despite the improvement in her health and her return to Melbourne. Joy rarely negotiated situations. She made a decision, stuck to it and didn't complain about the consequences. Yet the affair she had, and its aftermath, must have been a source of shame and anger. Sweeney seems to have been the unfortunate inheritor of that.

Gray's circumstances – he had left behind a young daughter – meant that he may not have wanted Sweeney with them, either. But, at the same time, Joy felt she had made the right choice for her son to be adopted by her best friend, who was wealthy, responsible and caring, and who had formed a strong relationship with him.

Joy tried to keep other secrets, too. Shortly after Nolan arrived in Sydney, he began visiting Cynthia. Nolan had left Melbourne in July to travel to Queensland after asking Sunday, not for the first time, to divorce John and marry him. Nolan reflected, 'in threesomes, there has to be a crack-up . . . one or the other has to go.'[50] Sunday refused. After eight turbulent years as Nolan's mistress, she must have realised the demands that would be placed on her, once she was his wife. Twelve years older than Nolan, Sunday had given her lover a sentimental education, intricate and painful, not only for themselves but for those close to them. Great art had been made but the human cost was high. In 1941, Nolan had left his wife Elizabeth Paterson and baby daughter Amelda for Sunday. It was a slow, agonising break-up. Sunday, alternately jealous and concerned for Nolan's family, suggested they live at Heide – an unacceptable solution. Nolan dithered but finally made his choice: his future lay with the Reeds. Yet when it came to deciding her future with this questing young man, Sunday's answer was unequivocal. Nolan wanted to travel the world and make a name for himself. Sunday wanted to stay at home. She needed succour, constancy, peace. Nolan was not the man to supply these needs.

The role of an artist's wife has been, traditionally, one of subservience, feeding aspirations and energies other than her own and basking, when success came, in the reflected glory. Sunday was the centre of the Heide circle, attracting and controlling a small galaxy of friendships and projects. She had a husband who worshipped her. She dwelt in a fixed, resplendent environment. In Nolan's new world there would be no such certainties. Sunday might have conducted her personal affairs with a bohemian flourish but she came from a cautious class. She would not discard her security for vagabond pleasures, no matter how much she yearned for Nolan. Apart from her commitment to John, which, despite the complexities, was unswerving, Sunday had the added complication of Sweeney. Taking on a two year old at forty-two, after being childless, must have been quite an undertaking. It is easy enough to see Nolan, wounded by Sunday's rejection,

---

50   Peter Ross interview, op. cit.

together with being broke and needing support, making Cynthia the target of his affections. He was a shrewd and personable man, used to charming women and impressing men.

But Nolan had recognised that, for some time, as far as the Reeds went, 'We have all gone full circle.'[51] Things had to change. 'There will not be an involvement in the old sense.'[52] Cynthia was wary, too. Her previous relationships had been hurtful, destructive. Despite its compromised beginning, theirs was a marriage of adventure and, for Nolan, of great success. Cynthia, devoted to him, was companion to his travels, the elegant designer of their life together, the fierce, uncompromising manager. Yet Cynthia always remained afraid of Sunday's hold over Nolan.

Cynthia, once observing the ménage at Heide in 1940, and concerned about the effects the emotional temperature was having on Nolan, had advised him to get out in no uncertain terms. In Sydney in 1948, Joy must have realised – if Nolan did not tell her himself – that a relationship had started with Cynthia. Yet Joy refers to Cynthia in an oblique, critical manner that gives nothing away. Sunday, expecting Nolan to return to her, would have been frantic with jealousy if she had guessed. Which she finally did. Gray recalled, 'We made the big mistake of telling Sun what was going on. We'd been asked to. We were very silly.'[53]

Sunday, for her part, prized, and demanded, honesty. She was keen to clarify the unexplained phrase, the blurred explanation, or any attempt to smooth over the difficult or hesitant moment. Joy may seem open, yet despite her spontaneity, she was quick to turn from confrontation. Given the intensity of Sunday's friendship, it was a form of self-protection. Joy fends Sunday off. Sunday deliberated over how true or valid an interaction had been, she questioned and examined. Her insistence on seeking resolutions created discomfort both for herself and Joy.

Anxiety surfaces, too. Joy had given Sunday her child, given a baby to a woman who could not have one, though Sweeney arrived in circumstances that neither Sunday nor John were prepared for. They might have been overwhelmed by their new roles, and by the expectations that both Bert and Joy had of them, but from a mixture of love, need and responsibility, Sunday and John kept Sweeney. By July 1947, Bert was planning to leave the country.

---

51 Sidney Nolan to John Reed, 31 October 1947, Reed Collection.
52 Ibid.
53 Gray Smith, interview, 22 March 1982.

John wrote to Bert, expressing his surprise.[54] Devastated by the break-up with Joy, Bert did not feel he could take care of Sweeney. Suddenly, Sunday and John were not merely minding Sweeney while his parents sorted out their lives: they were his parents. Though Joy and Sunday had discussed the possibility of Sunday taking Sweeney, probably during the first, unhappy months of her pregnancy, the reality was rather different.

It is evident that in the winter of 1947, Sunday was not only alarmed by Sweeney's 'sudden placing into my care' but astonished that Joy had left Bert so peremptorily. To Sunday, such an act was inconceivable. She tried to get a response from Joy about Sweeney and Bert, to make her face up to her actions and resolve the situation. Joy agreed she had a left 'a trail of dirt' behind her but, as far as she was concerned, her previous life was just that. 'I thought I had made it clear that when I met Gray someone shut the door on the rest of my life . . . It's over.' Of course, it was not that simple. Within a year Sunday would want to seal the situation with adoption.

Joy wanted Sweeney to be cared for by Sunday. Joy was also reliant on Sunday for money, and would be for the rest of her life. She did not want to alienate Sunday, ever. They had struck a complicated bargain. Joy felt the pressure, especially where the touchy business of money was concerned. She wrote to Elsie Smith, 'We have been officially invited to Heide to dinner on Thursday evening . . . Gray thought he'd better collect the dough this week. So it'll be the personal appearance tour.'[55]

In Sydney, during Nolan's visits, there were bitter conversations between he, Joy and Gray, about their dependence on the Reeds. The Reeds were rather less wealthy than their desperately hard-up friends realised. Sunday and John gave artists and their families small, regular contributions, stretching over decades. And, once the Reeds had become the bank, many were disinclined to allow them to stop. It made for envy, resentment and no small degree of manipulation – and Joy was no exception. Sunday gave gifts of money and love and she expected loyalty, reassurance and the production of art in return. The transactions were rarely smooth, making for disappointments and misunderstandings on both sides. But the bond between Sunday and Joy, formed in the years before Sweeney was born, endured. Sweeney became an inextricable element, both in the problems Sunday and Joy encountered in their friendship, and in its growth and continuity.

[54]   John Reed to Albert Tucker, (June/July 1947), Tucker Collection.
[55]   Joy Hester to Elsie Smith, undated, Peregrine Smith Collection.

Their personalities – Joy, warm, outgoing, earthy, vital, and Sunday, intuitive, sentimental, sensitive and reflective – were, in many ways, complementary. Though Joy could sever herself from her past – from Bert, from Sweeney – Sunday brooded, and was prone to self-criticism and fits of weeping self-recrimination. Sunday did not let go. They shared an emotional intensity, a hot, passionate response to life, and articulating that response was essential to both. To observers they could seem as close as two sisters. Sometimes, it could be an exclusive friendship where Joy, frankly jealous, made it clear others were not welcome in the zone of their intimacy. There were other differences, too, apart from temperament.

Joy had a strong belief in the supernatural. She had psychic experiences with poltergeists and ghosts which made reality an even more heightened experience for her. She believed in divining the future through reading a crystal ball. In the last year of her life, when she saw a straight black line appear in the ball she knew she was going to die. After her first encounter with cancer, her belief in God was strengthened, though she did not formalise her faith by attending church. The poltergeists who visited her were reckless messengers from a disordered universe where violence and injustice were meted out with gay abandon. Joy could be punched on the nose by a 'polly', or a ghost would ride up to Gar and ask directions. 'Ghosts have trivial minds', Joy sniffed. Sunday was a firm non-believer. Her beliefs were fixed on the human realm, on human choice and responsibility.

Sunday respected details. Nothing was too minor or intimate for her opinion. Ringing close friends on a daily basis was maintained with the same determined rigorousness as the housework. Heide was kept spotless through Sunday's efforts. Nothing was allowed to get shabby. Sunday's appearance was individual, stylish and casual, and she dressed with flair into old age. Joy was a beautiful woman who thought fashion was trifling and was happy in hand-me-downs. In her youth she might have dressed with a 'secretarial smartness' and peroxided her hair but poverty and country living made her less fastidious. Joy was slapdash. She tended to be casual about housework and cooking, and her succession of rather unfortunate pets. Neither Joy nor Sunday could bear to be alone. If Joy was by herself at Heide, she would lock herself in with all the lights on. On bush walks, Sunday would become agitated if John was out of her sight even briefly.

Sunday, unafraid of speaking her feelings, eloquently expressed love, and there is a sensuous quality to her love for Joy. Hester is much more reserved, wondering if it sounds 'mushy' to tell Sunday she has 'a deep love' for her. If one of Sunday's roles was that of mother, then Joy can be read as the wayward, demanding daughter. Indeed, the torrent of Joy's letters are at times exhausting in their need for affection and affirmation. Despite the sensuousness of her love for Joy, Sunday and Joy did not take their friendship further. Sunday had a coyly disapproving attitude towards homosexuality. 'Boys and girls were made for each other', she would say. It could make close friends who were homosexual feel uncomfortable.

While Sunday and Joy exercised a suprising degree of sexual licence in their lives, their husbands did not, and were faithful. Sunday lived openly with Nolan at Heide, and managed, not without stress for all concerned, a household that included her husband and her lover. Before Nolan, Sunday had had affairs with Sam Atyeo and Peter Bellew. Sunday was a very sexual woman, flirtatious, seductive and possessive. If John found her affairs distressing, he did not have the power to forbid them. Emotional control in the marriage was negotiated by Sunday.

While Joy was living at Heide in 1942 she drew a picture of the situation and her own powerful, ambivalent feelings towards Sunday.

'Not a day goes by,' she wrote to Bert, 'that, in the same day, I alternately love her, hate her and despise her but also always admire her . . . Something I feel that is eternal and good. So very good. And good again. This is Sun.'[56] Joy was appalled by 'the way Sun treats John. The utter selfishness of some of her actions is unbelievable. John bites back and looks as if he could kill her at times. She is terribly spoilt . . . It is the same with Nolan except not quite as bad as he is a newer toy . . . Sun has a power over everyone which she uses very subtley [sic] to its fullest extent. She has the power of Nolan over John. He daren't make a false move if he wants to keep her. She has the power of "giving" over Nolan. Also he is in love with her and cannot see lots of things.'

It reminded Joy of Cathy and Heathcliff in *Wuthering Heights*. 'Loving nature as those two in the book did, loving the moors and trees and living, in actual fact, the meanest, [most] spiteful lives they could live, they both gave each other spite but they also gave love. This is what Sun does. She gives a lot of love and I have the greatest admiration for the sensitivity she possesses which is on a high level, higher than I have ever met before.' Joy even wished she had 'that selfishness so cunningly disguised that I could get my own way whenever I wanted it.' Yet she admitted, 'to me it is unhealthy, one loses one's laughter. I get sad. I could cry to be away from it all', while recognising

[56]   Joy Hester to Albert Tucker, (September/October 1942), Tucker Collection.

that 'tonight [Sunday] will do something that will be so charmingly thought-ful and sweet that I will forget her cunning.'

Joy ended her letter, 'I am very fond of John. I love Sun, too, in a different way. I am not sure that I, in the final analysis, would stick by her as she is now with all her little ways. I would, for ultimately she does and says things which transcend for me those little differences. Even though at time she hurts me, perhaps I hurt her unknowingly.'

In the 1950s, Sunday had a deep, but platonic relationship with Charles Blackman. After Nolan there were no more affairs. Perhaps she loved Nolan too much for him to be replaced in her affections. Sunday's needs were in the foreground, and John did not compete. His needs were satisfied by his marriage. Not strongly sexual, he did not seek solace in other loves, either men or women. John was a man of astonishing restraint, secure in himself, the manager of Sunday's relationship with Nolan. John would discreetly leave the house if Nolan arrived unexpectedly to see Sunday. He would chide Nolan if he did not write to Sunday often enough and encouraged Sunday to put up with rough digs in Dimboola when she went to visit her lover, stationed there in 1942. But if John had the generosity to allow Sunday her affairs, nor did Sunday have conventional expectations of him.

After Reed & Harris collapsed in 1946, John did not have a job again until the 1950s. Reed & Harris had been a bright hope but it had lost the Reeds thousands of pounds. Never an ambitious lawyer, John did not return to the law: he and Sunday lived from their incomes. Sunday did not expect John to be the provider, but rather to pursue his own interests. From 1946 for the next ten years, John was at Heide working alongside Sunday in the garden, and rearing Sweeney. In 1953, the Contemporary Art Society was revived with John as president. In 1956, the CAS gallery would become a permanent exhi-bition space, the Gallery of Contemporary Art, with John as director. Then, in 1958, with his and Sunday's collection as its foundation, and backed by local business people, the Gallery of Contemporary Art became the ambitiously titled Museum of Modern Art of Australia. John was its director until 1965.[57]

Sunday and John remained together, and lovingly so. In their seventies, John and Sunday were alive to each other; emotionally and intellectually, there was no distance between them. In the meantime, John had endured a great deal. He remained a champion of Nolan's work and, personally, he was

[57] See Janine Burke, 'The Museum of Modern Art of Australia', *Art and Australia*, September 1977, p. 70.

very fond of Nolan. Together with Sunday, he was saddened that Nolan left – yet there must have been relief. In 1964, John wrote to Nolan, 'I have a certain tough resilience that once served you well.'[58]

Such matters were not discussed in Joy's and Sunday's letters. After all, their letters were shared: John would read Joy's and Gray, Sunday's. Joy writes about Nolan with a determinedly cheerful objectivity. She casts him as a family friend, rather than as Sunday's cherished love.

If Hester made radical decisions about her life, she was certainly not free from guilt. In regard to Bert, Joy regretted the hurt she had caused. She did not criticise him, even when it would serve to justify her own actions. A similar discretion overcame mentioning Gray's violent outbursts in the letters. These could precipitate a fit or they could be caused by alcohol or his inflammatory temper. Nolan, as well as the Moras and Barrett Reid, were involved in some dangerous scenes with Gray. So, for that matter, was John. Gray once chased John around the trees on Heide's front lawn with a gun. Joy seemed the only one capable of calming Gray. Though, if she had the devil in her, she might just as likely egg him on.

◆

My own connection with the Reeds began in 1974 when I was researching my BA on Australian painting in the 1960s. I went to Heide to interview John about the Museum of Modern Art. Later, Sweeney became a friend. In 1977, he was a student at the Victorian College of the Arts where I taught art history. Before that, he had run galleries in Carlton and Fitzroy.

In 1976 I had seen an exhibition of Hester's, organised by Sweeney, at Tolarno Galleries, Melbourne, and decided to make her the subject of my MA, later published as a book. Sweeney was helpful in the early stages of my research. He contacted Albert Tucker and discussed my project with him, then, knowing how distressed Sunday remained at Joy's death, offered to accompany me to Heide for that interview.

John, Sweeney and I sat at the marble table in the Heide II living room, and waited for Sunday. It was an austere, pale room, full of winter light. John told me that Sunday didn't want to be interviewed about Joy, didn't like the formality, and perhaps wouldn't come down. Meanwhile John, the good host, made coffee and brought out a plate of biscuits. We had decided to

[58]   John Reed to Sidney Nolan, 13 October 1964, Reed Collection.

begin without her when Sunday appeared at the top of the nervewracking stairs. The stairs ran at right angles to a hallway that ended abruptly, over-looking the living room. Without the comfort of a stair rail, I felt I was about to walk into thin air, and it made me concerned for the two elderly people who lived there. Heide II was dramatic and elegantly proportioned but not homely, more like an art gallery, which it has become.[59]

Sunday, silver-haired, dressed in white, descended slowly. I felt a knot of tension. How was this going to go? To break the ice, Sweeney began making conversation. Sunday didn't meet my eyes. I switched on the tape recorder. Sunday's hearing problem meant she would talk over – or under – John, Sweeney, or me, counterpointing questions and comments in a frail, clear, insistent voice. Now that she had decided to be part of the interview, Sunday was keen to help, asking exactly what I needed to know, warning me not to let her ramble, and seeking John's corroboration when dates and facts eluded her. Sunday's recollections were, however, sharper than his. Her manner was diffident and courteous – she seemed shy – but she was confi-dent about her views, and put them succinctly. Yet there were undercurrents, even a sense of contest. Sunday remained guarded. I had not won her trust. I was not sure whether she approved of me, or my research on Joy. After all, Joy was her treasured friend, and she held Joy's memory closely. I had the feeling that my tape recorder and my questions were unsettling a previously established balance for Sunday between herself and Joy, a dialogue she did not wish interrupted. Sunday seemed tuned to inner realities of time and place that intersected with the room we were in. Hers was a compelling, disquieting presence, the focus of the interview, of its mood and flow. Sunday could, in a flash, exert emotional pressures that were subtle, forceful and very much under her control. And so, I felt, were we. I pushed on with my questions. After nearly an hour, the memories overwhelmed Sunday, and she wept. It would be a scene repeated time and again with Joy's family and friends. I felt guilty. 'This is awful', I said to Sweeney, driving back to town. 'I leave people in tears.'

Becoming involved in my research was a personally difficult undertaking for Sweeney. He told me several times that when Joy was dying, and he was

---

[59] In 1966, John and Sunday commissioned architect David McGlashan to design and build a new home for them, 'a romantic building, ageless with a sense of mystery . . . a gallery to be lived in.' Constructed from Mount Gambier limestone, terrazzo tiles and treated pine, Heide II was judged building of the year in 1968 by the Royal Australian Institute of Architects.

fifteen, he refused to go to see her in hospital. He recounted the occasions spent with her as a child as fractious and irritating. It sounded as if it was so for both of them. Yet he admired her work and similarities arise in their poetry, particularly in their use of metaphor. Though Sweeney did have the opportunity to renew and re-establish a relationship with Bert, this did not occur with Joy. The doubts cast on Sweeney's paternity were ones he shared. He was not the first who told me about the jazz drummer, believed to be his father. He had known the story for many years. When this man died, Sunday brought his obituary to Sweeney, then living at Heide I, and explained that his father was dead. 'What do you think of that?' Sweeney demanded of me, outraged. It was months after the event. 'What do you think?' Sunday may have believed she was acting in Sweeney's best interests but he was angered by the way she had handled the situation.

Sweeney wanted to talk about Joy and to hear what I was discovering. In retrospect, I realise that he spoke more to me about Joy than he did to others. Perhaps because I was the outsider I could be entrusted with secrets.

Sweeney had led a troubled life. At sixteen he had a daughter to a local Heidelberg girl. John and Sunday ended the marriage by packing Sweeney off to London. Prior to that, he attended Preshil, a progressive school, before becoming a boarder at John's old school, Geelong Grammar. His adolescence was wild and he was briefly placed in Turana, a youth correctional institution. In 1969 he married Pamela Westh and they had two sons, Mishka and Danila. Between the late 1960s and mid 1970s, Strines in Carlton and Sweeney Reed Galleries in Fitzroy (where he was briefly in partnership with Julian Stirling) were lively indicators of current art.

For years Sweeney had been involved with concrete poetry, starting Still Earth, a small publishing house. He had an ambition to work in non-commercial galleries and strived to be, though he was not, financially independent of John and Sunday. At art school, Sweeney made pale, exquisite prints incorporating his own short, lyrical poems. These tender and sentimental works, where hearts like delicate tattoos veiled in watercolour mists were laced by words of love and yearning, are aesthetic objects in themselves. Yet it was an uneasy situation for him, trying to make a fresh start as an artist in his early thirties, though Sweeney was committed to it. The combined reputations of Joy Hester and Albert Tucker cast a long shadow over his creative aspirations.

Among his lecturers were artists he had exhibited and Sweeney, older than his peers, and sporting an immaculate appearance, cut a somewhat lonely figure among the scruffy hippies and casual exchanges of the student scene.

He was precise, cluey, intense, and fancied himself as a bit of a wheeler-dealer. Equally, he was generous, humble and kind. He measured his words, and it added to a tightly leashed quality, as if beneath the controlled surface, stronger and less comfortable emotions strained. Sweeney seemed intent on proving he could manage, he could cope, he could tough it out. Despite his streetwise bravado, he struck me as someone who didn't know how to protect himself.

Sweeney had grown up, indulged and adored by Sunday, into a kind of living museum. High expectations were placed upon him. His relations with Sunday, though strong, were often, from Sweeney's side, discomfiting and contradictory. Though Heide meant everything to him, Sweeney was burdened by his past in a way that made him feel helpless to effect change. Towards the end of his life his unresolved anger towards Joy increased. It was some time after his marriage broke up that Sweeney committed suicide in March 1979. It was not the first attempt.

◆

I had considered that the letters between Joy and Sunday would make an interesting book when I was researching Hester's life. Transcribing and editing them became something of an emotional voyage for me. I could not help feeling sad and angry at the way Sweeney was treated. There is always a lingering guilt among the friends of someone who has committed suicide, the sense that we should have done, known, understood more. Freud remarked that every suicide is an act of murder. Though it might be hard to imagine abandoning one's children in order to kill one's self, Sweeney's inner distress may have been exacerbated by just that – his children, and the recognition of how much he loved them. It must have made him wonder how Joy could have left him. This painful awareness of rejection made Sweeney's own sense of loss acute and intolerable. Most tragically of all, Sweeney repeated the pattern.

Writing about the recent past, while many of those involved are still alive, requires that discretion and diplomacy is balanced with fact and evidence. Mostly I am a writer of fiction, and fiction has no such responsibilities. It is, largely, an act of imagination, independent of factual strings and tugs, free of the weight of veracity. Interviewing the Heide protagonists a second time around while researching the background to the letters made me feel at times that I was part of a large and complicated family – with all the inherent allegiances, squabbles, sympathies, intrigues, confidences and betrayals. For those associated with Heide the past is very real indeed. What happened fifty years ago is as tangible as if it happened yesterday. Some want to control the representation of that past. All feel proprietorially involved, and none agree with one another.

Sunday, in particular, evokes powerful emotions. She has been the subject of an intense, critical scrutiny by some former friends and an immense, passionate loyalty on the part of others. Sunday attracted, and enjoyed, the raging egos of creative people. Rivalries and disputes that existed then remain now, placing her at the centre of conflicting opinion. Despite the generosity Sunday lavished on her friends, she lost many of them. The price of a certain kind of patronage is high. Nolan, for example, was vigilant in his campaign to denigrate the Reeds. They did not fight back and avoided the glare of public debate. Nolan may have tried to contact Patrick White to heal their famous feud when White was dying, but the breach remained with John and Sunday.

In 1977 the contact with Nolan for which Sunday had longed for thirty years eventuated. Mary Boyd was Nolan's companion on his trip to Australia. They would marry the following year. After Mary's visit to Heide, she persuaded Nolan to ring Sunday. Bitterly disappointed with the conversation, where Nolan lightly parried her remarks, Sunday burned his love letters. However, many of Nolan's letters to Sunday, vibrant accounts of landscape, art and poetry, written while he was based in the Wimmera in 1942, remain.

After a long battle with cancer, John died on 6 December 1981. The following week, I went out to Heide to return a drawing belonging to Sunday, together with several original poems that she had loaned for the retrospective of Hester's I had curated at the National Gallery of Victoria.

We had afternoon tea in the library where Joy, sitting on the floor near the fireplace, had produced many of her early drawings. Sunday was abstracted and strangely calm. Though her old friend Barrett Reid, ill himself with Hodgkin's disease, was at her side, she seemed utterly alone and the house, empty. The unease that had marked our previous meetings, my unsureness about her support for my research and my hesitancy in her presence, were gone. Whatever resistance we had met, and recognised, in one another dissolved that afternoon.

To my surprise, knowing how ill John was, they had attended the opening, both dressed in white, a dapper, handsome couple, holding hands. I was nervous about Sunday's response to the show. When she and John arrived, I noticed they didn't bother socialising; they went straight to the works. Her congratulations, quick, firm and warm, were the turning point between us.

I took her hand as we said goodbye at the front door. On each side of the door were glass panels, etched with the roses Joy had designed. Sunday said she had been happy to see so much of Joy's work together. The exhibition would lead to greater interest in Joy's drawings and poems: Sunday knew it. On 14 December Sunday died in her sleep.

Chapter 1

**1944
46**

Heide, Sunday night
(1944)

Dear Joy

Just a quick note to tell you that the
other day when I was wandering about the shed between the sparrows'
nests and mice and all else, I found a small painting of yours crumpled
up on the floor which I like a great deal; a disturbing head with an arm
around its neck and another smaller head at the side. Do you remember?
It is mouldy and a bit torn but I hope I can keep it and I am enclosing a
cheque. I miss your work. I miss watching you work. You must believe
this please. Always I find your response so organic, so completely
natural, that almost everything you paint is at once both vital and very
real for me and I was happy after so long a separation to discover something that I had not seen before. In spite of what Bert used to call my
feminist attitude, which in its fullest sense is true of me I think, you only
prove the rule by being obviously the exception – more than ever
perhaps because of the touching and simple fact you still do nothing
about it. I wish you would. With love to all three of you. Goodnight.

S

28 Dawson Avenue, Elwood
(1944)

Dear Sun

I really don't know what to say
except that for the whole day I ran round feeling a bit light in the head
after receiving your letter. I would have felt a bit light just to know that
you should write about the old painting but then to receive the cheque
on top of it all! It was delicious! There is one sentence at the bottom of
your letter that I think I know what you mean but one day I will get you
to decipher it for me.

I have not touched a pencil or pen for at least three months now (but
I must say that your letter spurs me on). Now don't laugh – but the
reason being that I have recently discovered for the first time that there
is an occolt or is it spelt occoult? and my mind has been sort of groping

round the outskirts of these subjects for some time now. It has sort of upset the order of my previous mind and left me in a bit of chaos consequently no painting – (or is this just another rationalization? – for not painting I mean) but I feel sure that if I have *ever* (which I doubt) had anything to say I could not have said it fully had I not come to these thoughts for I feel that my whole life has been waiting to stumble on these things and particularly my painting has been geared up to it but has never really put its finger on the spot so to speak – for my work (to me at any rate) has always been groping for an expression of the psyshological [sic] and pshyic [sic] aspect of a moment or not even a moment but a split flash that half a moment can give.

This may all sound double dutch, I can't really express myself clearly and spelling worries me – I hope it doesn't sound as though I am about to attend seances or something. It is a mode of interpretation of life that I have always had basically, but I have just never been aware of its existence. I really have not got anything very clear at the moment in my own mind but thanks to your letter it has spurred me out of my lethargy and makes me want to do something about it. This all sounds very self-centred.

I must stop but there is one thing I would like to say that you must probably know anyway and I cannot say it very easily but that is how Bert and I feel for both you and John, especially now when all this rumpus is on over *Angry Penguins*.[1] I have thought such a lot about it and for you during it all wondering how it will turn out.

My mother is pretty bad with her feet. Gangreen [sic] broke out in them and she has been having sulpha drugs and they seem to have cleared up that part of it but she has to keep off her feet until Xmas at least and so after much apprehension on our part Bert and I have come down to the sleep-out here and things seem pretty smooth in the relations at the moment. She is a bit too ill and old to fight much now and as we did not seem to be able to get the house we were promised in Brunswick it seemed a solution temporarily except that there is nowhere for Bert to paint. So we are going to try and get a dump somewhere in

---

[1] Joy is referring to the Ern Malley hoax perpetrated by Sydney poets James McAuley and Harold Stewart. The Ern Malley poems were published in the art and literary journal *Angry Penguins* in 1944 in a special autumn edition (actually early June). Exposed as a fraud shortly afterwards, the poems did much, at the time, to discredit *Angry Penguins*. See also Michael Heyward, *The Ern Malley Affair*, UQP, Brisbane, 1993.

the city if we can for about 5/– a week or something but as per usual they don't seem to exist. We would keep it just to paint in, and go on living here as long as relations were not too strained then I think things would work out. Thank you for the £5 5/ – I will put it in the bank for junior.

Thank God I never read a letter over once I have written it. That is one torture I spare myself.

Love to you and Heide and the ducks and dogs.

Joy

PS   I would like to borrow your Ezra Pound cantos if I may – I have been reading and rereading his poems and cannot understand the lack of interest there seems to be in his work. To me they are (the poems) the most vital and significant work and I really believe him to rank with the first six poets. His translations from the Chinese are superb. If they are not strictly accurate who cares? Their value as poetry is the only thing which should concern the reader but everybody I mention the name Pound to so far draws themselves up to their full height and sneers audibly and sighs beneath the sneer, poor thing! as though I have some disease or other. To me he is the Picasso of poetry. Have you read any of his work before the cantos? It is extremely hard to get. I am trying very hard to get a book of his poems that has a very good introduction in it by T S Eliot. If you have that I would like to borrow it also – I suppose you have read his work. I would like to hear your opinion and feelings about him. Very much.

In 1945 Joy and Bert moved from rooms in Powlett Street, East Melbourne, to live at 47 Robe Street, St Kilda.

St Kilda during the war years was one of the hottest spots in town. Soldiers on leave and visitors flocked there. On the weekends, the foreshore was thronged with amusement seekers. The Palais de Dance, Luna Park and St Moritz ice-skating rink provided entertainment, as did the coffee lounges and cabarets where jazz and swing bands played. After dark the streets and parks became scenes of clandestine trysts. Prostitutes did business on Fitzroy Street, just as they do today. Once a fashionable seaside resort, St Kilda had become sleazy. Tucker's *Images of Modern Evil* series (1943–46) was inspired by the sexual licence and conspicuous carnality of the war years.

Joy had quit her job as a waitress at the Hotel Australia in Collins Street midway through 1944 when she found out she was pregnant. Joy had had two or three abortions by the time she was twenty-four. She sought to terminate this pregnancy, too. An infection precluded that.

Their flat in Robe Street was part of a ninteenth-century, two-storey terrace divided into a boarding house. It comprised a big double-fronted room with a wrought iron balcony. The landing housed a large kitchen where Bert painted several works from his *Images of Modern Evil* series. It was the most spacious and comfortable place Joy and Bert had lived in.

On 4 February 1945 Joy gave birth to Sweeney. He was named after Sweeney Agonistes, a character of T S Eliot's.

(1945)

TO MY DARLING SUN AND JOHN

My whole being in flight – I sit motionless in bed but my blood is 'en route' – I am in rapport with the birth that I am about to experience – the villa has already, to me, become the mansion, awaiting only my residence to consume the flowering – in all ways – in so many directions

In the weeks I have been with you both at Heide surrounded by LOVE, and your living, and your dedications – plus the mysterious X, I know I have been revived from the cold soil of my leaking heart. I would never have believed it possible for such a thing to happen to a human being twice! All your love pouring to me has made me not quite steady, not quite here – just as though I have partaken of a very rare wine, but the difference is I haven't. You both have done this for me – cast miracle[s] everywhere making wonderful transparencies of my darknesses.

What can I say to you? Just that I wish you to know this.

XXXX

Joy

Heide
(February 1945)

Dear Joy
We are all so happy about you and
Sweeney and want to see you both. Perhaps we will be allowed in by
Thursday.

Bless Sweeney for me and give him the enclosed birthday present.

Love to you and is there anything you want? Please let me know if
there is.

S

In the following letter, Joy refers to the dispute that erupted between Tucker
and Reed & Harris. Tucker contributed reviews and essays to *Angry Penguins*
and was closely involved in all aspects of the journal. However, at the end of
1945, Tucker wrote to the Reed & Harris partners protesting that he had
been 'shut out of what he felt was an increasingly closed group'. He
demanded 'full and equal partnership on the grounds of his contribution to
Angry Penguins.'[1] John Reed was shocked by Tucker's 'final and absolute'
demand for partnership, perceiving the relationship as one fostered by
personal commitment and a sense of artistic community rather than as a
professional contract. For a time it led to a breach between Tucker and John.
Sunday and John were a united front on most issues, this one included.

47 Robe Street, St Kilda
(March 1946)

Dear Sun
John mentioned that you were very
surprised at my endorsing Bert's statement – and I feel I would like to
clarify things a little from my side – now that things have settled down
a little.

I have been thinking a lot lately of how many worlds there are
contained in very small spaces and how every person is really one world

[1]   Richard Haese, *Rebels and Precursors*, Penguin, Ringwood, 1981, p.124.

to himself, uncontacted by any one or any thing. But just occasionally, when one little suggestion or the meeting of a memory or perhaps a smell of a flower touches off some deep stirring in one unconsciously, even to the person it belongs – one feels – 'Ah, here is contact' – but when this contact occurs the person thinks in his enthusiasm of the situation that it is complete identification – as I say, it can occur from such a small thing as a remembered odour of a flower or a house.

But I am convinced that what actually happens is a small part of one's ego rises to the surface [for] a moment, smiles, then recedes into its own protected world. Between husband and wife, between parents, or friends this ego really gets daring and pokes its head out further, so the other can see the 'color of its eyes' so to speak.

Your world, my world, Bert's world are all private and hidden from each other and sometimes from ourselves. But we have contacted! Somewhere! Who can say where and on what level. I can't. It would be so much easier if I could then I could state in *exact* words precisely where things start and finish with us all.

But there is also our other sort of world . . . our social being, conditioned by all sorts of winds that blow. Well, somewhere in this outer world we have got into a muddle and the gulf of contact has become wider and wider – I cannot say my definite reasons for feeling Bert's statement was right – but I can say I was not influenced by Bert to endorse it. I just did. It was a sudden angle I got on the whole thing but it is too late now to put it down here. All I want to say is that if we can by some means measure the length and breadth of our inner contacts we will be able to work together in an oblique way that is *its own* force beyond our control. I know from my side and yours that this force is for good even though we cannot contact it in our outer world of the moment.

I feel it's just like the business with the atom – it has shown us, and opened, publicly any way, forces of energy working unseen – but working in definite cycles and directions, contacting here and there. Those contacts are the things that make for a completion of our personalities. After all that seems to be all we are here for.

I do not feel I have [made] myself very clear but perhaps you can sort out what I mean.

Love to you
Joy

Heide
Saturday night (March 1946)

Dear Joy

Thank you for your letter which I felt was so much an expression of your reality and I am sensitive to it although my response is not the same. It would seem to me that I spring from many various sources, private and otherwise, but what probably goes out in the world, as far as one knows oneself, is for better or worse, one whole piece. I suppose then, I mean that in this way human activity finds resolution: changed by the mysterious and personal as well as the social worlds, and at its deepest to the point of love or hate, it coheres and must not split to justify survival. Isn't to do this to betray the heart (and the head) at any given moment – involvement in struggle becomes reality and not the cause itself – which perhaps at one level is the only kind of communism we all know so well.

Does this sound too heavy, too saturated? If it does then I would rather be a dragon fly. But surely somewhere here there must be a striving towards totality that is common to us all and the measure, that you speak of, to work by – which for myself anyway is always a healing point. I wanted to write more to you but I am not well and I feel there is nothing I can say except that John and I are very sad. We are sorry for whatever mistakes we have made. In fact we hope it is a real way of learning to be better, learning to be more than we are, not to cause hurt. I hope that all is well with Bert and with you and if Bert was painting that would be the best possible news.

S

Chapter 2

April
July
1947

Late in March, while Tucker was in Japan, Joy met Gray Smith. Introduced by friends Jack and Pauline McCarthy at their Kismet Bookshop in Johnston Street, Fitzroy, Joy and Gray spent the next days there together.

Joy had been ill for some time. A lump had formed on her neck and she had a hacking cough. Sunday recommended her own doctor who in turn recommended a specialist, Doctor Littlejohn. Early in April, when Bert returned from Japan, John summoned Bert to his office in the city to tell Bert what Joy did not, as yet, know: she had Hodgkin's disease, a cancer of the lymph glands, and had been given two years to live. Returning home to their flat at Martin Street, Elwood, Joy burst out with the news of her affair with Gray. She ran from the flat, leaving Sweeney there. Soon after, Joy went to Heide where John and Sunday told her the news of her condition.

Joy met with Gray and, over the next few days, they planned what to do. Joy would not return to Bert and Sweeney. Gray would leave his wife, Yvonne, and young daughter. Borrowing some money for the fare, Joy and Gray caught the train for Sydney. They found rooms in Coogee, then Mosman, before moving to 61 Bayswater Road, King's Cross.

Joy had to seek medical attention immediately. On Dr Littlejohn's advice she saw Doctor McCallum, then Doctor Lovell. By 12 May, she was in the Royal Prince Alfred Hospital where she had an operation to remove a gland from her neck. By 14 May, she was given a 'final diagnosis' by Doctor Lovell.

Coogee
Sunday, 13 April 1947

Dear Sun

I would have liked to have seen you before I left but somehow things caught up with me and all I knew was that I had to get out and I'm sorry to admit that it sort of became an obsession, the words 'get out' – this is not how one should work – but it seems to me how I have worked ever since I was a little girl in long green grass at school – I would have liked to have seen you, Sun, but I blocked out on everything just about – except those two words. I'm glad I did – I feel a sort of return of 'Edme'¹, [of] the calm somewhere deep

¹ Edme was a character in Julien Green's gothic novel *Midnight*, Harper & Bros, New York, 1945, a favourite book of Joy's and Sunday's.

inside that I have not felt for a long long time – it is impossible to do as Bert would have liked me to do – that is explain myself – these things cannot be explained even to oneself for to explain is to destroy it or injure it somewhere – we all try to preserve that thing for it is [as] precious to us as our bodies which we so frantically try to preserve – or try to.

When death is near or illness we have to save something for ourselves – Nolan knows that, in painting – I think Max [Harris] once called it our holy ghost, our very personal one – I'm sorry for Bert that I gave him such a shock but if it comes – to break it slowly or to try to plan these things does not work and in the end does more harm to both parties. We are in Sydney and in being together we are both finding out how far away Edme had gone from both of us – these things, once they slip [away] are not easy to regain, and one thing we both know is that it is not easy. Love, in the sense that Bert and I knew, does not exist in either of us and I doubt if it ever will. Had I continued with Bert I think ultimately the results would have hurt him far more than doing it this way.

It is not easy in the practical sense either, Sun, as we have no money and I would appreciate it [if] you could lend me something, about £5, which I would pay back to you for we hope to be able to make a fair bit soon if we can get a cheap place to live but accommodation is very hard to get and very expensive and until Gray gets some sort of income it would tide us over. We are in Coogee at the moment but have met a very nice woman who thinks she'll be able to give us a little place for us to paint but she won't know until she sees her husband tonight. So if you can send the money send it to Mrs J Tucker c/- GPO Sydney. I am going to the doctor as soon as I can find out from [Dr] Littlejohn the name of a good one here. I have written to him to find out – and then if the doctor he recommends is in a public hospital I shall see him there – if not I shall see him and ask him about treatment in Public Hospitals and if he thinks they will be able to do it.

Also, could you please send me a couple of Chinese brushes, thick ones, as they are not obtainable here and I think I left mine at Heide. Send c/- GPO as our address is as yet uncertain – I will send you any geraniums I see here that I think you have not got. We do not intend to stay in Sydney and as soon as my neck is fixed and we have enough money we will go north.

Gray is a good boy, Sun, and I know it will work out well. I know we've both hurt people through this but there are times when it cannot be avoided which ever way it's done. As far as Swene is concerned it is better that it happens now than later – I hope you can feel for me, Sun, as in fact I know you do for you are all that I have that I want of the past. You are the only thing that has kept me steady somewhere inside. I hope you don't think this sounds 'mushy' but I have a very deep love for you. Write to me as soon as you can – and I hope John can be not so sad as when I last saw him after the books had gone.[2] I only wished I could have been able to offer him some solacing but I could think of none.

Good night Sun

GPO Sydney
(April 1947)

Dear Sun
Needless to say I was very pleased to get the £5 and Carl Plate cashed the cheque for me.[1] We are both working over here but have not been working long enough to get any wages. And I was going mad for something to read – I bought two little postcard prints and some ink and paper and brush and Gray bought about ¹/₂ dozen little tubes of watercolor and we both feel very good about it because after all the upheaval and having to leave our books and being in an awful 'autumn toning' room and not even having any money for a little bit of paint can be depressing but we have been looking long and hard at the wonderful ocean and I am quite drugged with cliffs and sea and at night the whole town we live in is covered with what looks like fog for about ¹/₂ a mile inland but it's spray from the ocean and with the houses silhouetted against the street lamps and the mist [it] looks like some remote Cornish village.

[2] Hester is probably referring to the collapse of Reed & Harris. Late in 1946, the firm began to wind down. Max Harris resigned from the partnership and returned to Adelaide. In early 1947 future projects were cancelled, though it would not be until the end of the year that John Reed would finally close the business.

[1] Carl Plate (1909–77) was a painter who ran Notanda Gallery in Sydney where Joy probably cashed the cheque.

I am writing from [the] GPO and come to town one day a week so if you write me, post letters to [the] GPO where I can collect them. Littlejohn sent me a letter about who to see in Sydney and I will get in touch with him Monday.

This afternoon am going to CAS [Contemporary Art Society] Sydney branch exhibition and I am on the look out for geraniums.

Love to you and John

Fragment
Mosman
(April 1947)

... Can't send drawings yet. They are too bad to send yet.

We went to Sydney CAS show. There is not *one* even half good painting in [the] show. All at Donald Friend level and not *one* with even a touch of anything worthwhile. There were Dobells there and I did not recognize them – [they're] just the same as the others – and not a soul in there looking at them and it was as big as our annual [CAS] show. I came out in an awful mood after seeing all those – so many bad pictures.

Have no books to read. Can't afford them. Wrote to Bert and asked him to send a couple but I won't get them so if you have any spare ones I'd be glad. I left the little Judith Wright at Elwood unfortunately.[1] You said in your letter something about Nolan sending the paper and you said at the end of the line c/- GPO. The funny part was you started the line from the wrong part of the letter and it read something like this 'I see this in hundreds of your drawings c/- of the GPO'. I could not get the words 'c/- of the GPO' out of my mind in connection with my drawings, as the heads I do are the heads that pass me in the streets. Anonymous most of them, impersonal in some way but on the other hand, looked at individually, they seem personal ...

[1] Judith Wright, *The Moving Image*, Angus & Robertson, Sydney, 1942.

Mosman
Tuesday, 29 April 1947

Dear Sun

Thanks for the very sweet telegram – that sounds awful but it was a nice telegram – but I didn't have my gland out – I went to [Dr] McCallum as you know and he sent me to the surgeon who asked me about which hospital and I said a cheap one and he suggested the intermediate section of [Royal] Prince Alfred which is akin to our Alfred in Melb.

He asked me about finance and I said I had none but he [will] send a/c to Melb – so far OK – so he booked me in [to] the hospital for 10.30 am and I rang [the] hospital and they said be there [at] 10.30. Got there and they asked for fees in advance which I did not have and said John was posting money to hospital and would be OK. Well, the bastards wouldn't let me in, said it was all in advance and it turned out to [be] (for the hospital) 30/- so I said I'd ring Gray and he'd bring it in that afternoon and they still wouldn't do it as I had no guarantee for the anaesthetic doctor and the surgeon and the operating room etc. – I got mad and did my block and called them all the B's I could think of and went home.

It mucked us up a lot – for the place we are working and living (at a hotel I think I told you about) wants only the two of us or neither and said, when I told them about going into hospital and not being able to work, they told us to go and Gray was gone when I got back, gone to look for a room or something – anything, anyway after a hell of a lot of persuasion they are letting us stay till Thursday when I go into hospital.

The money I rang John about should be there by then – accommodation is quite a fantastic problem here – one cannot even get a room in a pub for a night! – but after all we have done, that is worn the soles of our shoes walking in the heat from one end of Sydney to the other, we have managed to get a nice little 2 rooms and back yard and linen [place] for £2 a week – and we got it quite by accident. We have both been working together in this pub and I told John, I think, over the phone about the doctor saying I would not be able to work for a fair while while I was having treatment. This of course is quite fantastic and I will have to go and have a talk with him about it. Anyway he says I have to rest after the gland is out for a week – Gray as you know cannot work in a full time job and he can work if we both are together as I can watch him and look after him if he gets sick.

It has not been easy, what with not knowing where we'd sleep for each night of the first week we were here and walking our feet off each day and paying about 14/- each for a bed for the night and [I] felt quite good in the job, having a lovely big room and our board provided and looking at the rolling ocean all day and [I] thought I'd just be able to go to hospital and come back to work in a couple of days – God, things seem to get complicated sometimes – and the mad thing is we go into town and set out to do or go somewhere and both get lost – I can't for the life of me remember how the streets go. Anyway, we have a roof over our heads now and if Gray can get a part time job somewhere. We have not met any people we know over here at all only Alannah[1] and have only seen her once.

I'm sorry you've had trouble with Swene, Sun. I seem to have or we both have left a trail of dirt behind us and caused a lot of trouble to a lot of people but even had we known of the trouble we'd have ourselves and of what we've caused others we'd have still done it – Gray is having trouble with his wife who has come over here in the hope of getting alimony I think – but so far we've been able to steer clear of her. It seems the blessed world works on the 'eye for an eye' principle as she does not need money as she is being looked after by Gray's aunt. My mother is sending me maudlin terrible, upsetting sort of letters. She, I suppose naively thinks I [will] read them and come rushing home – no, Sun, it's no illusion, Gray and I have found something and we intend to keep it – it's a mutual thing.

[1] Alannah Coleman (b.1920) began her training at the Gallery School in Melbourne when she was 13. It was there that she and Joy became friends, both joining the CAS at its first meeting in 1938. Alannah was also a good friend of John's and Sunday's, sharing Sunday's passion for cats. Coleman managed the 1946 CAS exhibition in Sydney, and moved there early in 1947. She exhibited paintings, produced murals and was a photographic model. A beautiful, charming and sociable woman, Coleman found her metier in promoting Australian art, when she moved to London and founded the Australian Artists Association in 1951 and the Alannah Coleman Gallery in 1959. She showed the work of Boyd, Tucker, Nolan, Blackman and Whiteley. In 1963, Coleman was Commissioner General of the Paris Biennale. In 1971 she managed Bonython Gallery, Sydney, before returning to London where she continued to promote Australian art, cf Wendy Bradley, 'Alannah Coleman', MA thesis, Deakin University, Burwood Campus. Also, Alannah Coleman, interview with the editor, 8 February 1995.

You have been or you are the only thing that is 'good' and wholesome to me Sun, you are the thing I have in my mind everytime I draw a drawing for it is you who have [sic] fashioned my drawing – although you may not know it. This may be a dubious sort of compliment but I find it hard to tell you how much you actually mean to me for I have never had a mother and my father died too soon and without being affected or anything I love you, Sun – and I hope some day to be able to be worthy of what you have done for me by just being 'you'. When I say worthy I don't mean in the conventional sense – for if you love some-one, one desires always to sort of be able to be as good as the one, one loves so the other person will be able to know and there is only one way I can do that and I will do it one day, Sun – don't think this is as maudlin as it sounds – for it is really simple and un-neurotic deep down but I cannot say these things as simply and innocently as I mean them.

An awful thing [is] occurring in a big building here right on the street. A man hung himself and people saw it and the police came and put him down – the worst thing were [sic] in the comments of the crowd who got excited and merry although it was suppressed and only showed in the glints in their eyes, their craving for something sensational – the man himself did a pure simple act – but God what distortion happens after!

Goodnight Sun, love to you all

Mosman
(April/May 1947)

Dear Sun

Got your letter from Lonsdale.[1] It must have crossed with one I sent down there to you. I s'pose you'll not get the one I sent you and it was my first cheerful letter to you, realizing how selfish I'd been moaning about myself in all my letters and you and John being exhausted and going to Lonsdale ... But your letter, apart

[1] Sunday and John stayed regularly at Jack and Molly Bellew's house at Point Lonsdale on Victoria's Bellarine Peninsula. They also rented their own beach house at Point Lonsdale. In 1946 Jack Bellew had edited the short-lived broadsheet *Tomorrow*, the last publication of Reed & Harris.

from it being cold down there cheered me because you sounded happy – Swene sounds the perfect 'rogue'.

I missed McCallum at hospital and thought he'd more or less handed me over to [Dr] *Lovell*, to whom I took an instant liking and he has an excellent name here – at the hospitals etc. where he lectures. He's a lovely man with honest light brown eyes, about 38–40 yrs and young looking – I didn't take to McCallum so well – but on [a] subsequent meeting I understand his particular Scotch personalitie [sic] and I like him and he's looking after me well and is, as you say, 'fatherly'. All I have to do now is see him in about 3 wks for observation but I feel better and brighter than I have felt since I've been here and am very cheerful.

Weather is bloody awful rain, rain for 3 or 4 days. Traffic has no rules here and they blatantly disobey the copper on point duty and the cop nonchalantly takes no notice. [They have] these signs in the middle of the streets which make me laugh every time [sketch of sign reading 'Pedestrian refuge'] and I spend my life running from gutter to 'refuge' and 'refuge' to gutter. It's a nightmare!

. . . In Melbourne one thinks one is lucky if one knows where black market commodities are to be got. Over here one is damned lucky to know where to get things at normal price – cigarettes and tobacco are only sold at normal prices on Saturdays if you're in a mile long queue at 9 am – so the smoke screen is not so thick. No geraniums, not even common red ones, in fact there is a dearth of green[n]ess. No art shows worth reporting. Have made no friends here as yet. The US fleet has gone, the streets look quite respectable. Lovely places down near the Bridge. Houses over 105 years old and all into solid rock and little stairs in the streets and looking like Capri or the 'casba' [sic] in Algiers.

I am not 'prego' sigh of relief! or I don't think so – !!! The two poems enclosed were written about 2 or 3 weeks ago.[2] How are the cows? If they are in good milk and no one is using an odd butter coupon out that way you could float one over here – as BM butter is 4/- a pound. Love to John and hope he feels and looks not sad and tell him not to the 'hog the cream' and scrub all the floors.

Love to all and you and Swene
Me

---

[2] Missing.

61 Bayswater Road, King's Cross
2 May 1947

Dear Sun
I received your letter and read and
reread it – it was a lovely letter.

I am still not in hospital, not till Monday next now. [Dr] Lovell had
to attend a doctors' conference or something so it is put off now till
Monday – if you write me or John sends hospital money better send it to
GPO as God knows when I'll be there in hospital, though it is certain
almost for Monday now. John said something about the money Bert and
I were getting – I had considered that finished or I understood it to be
when Bert came [back] from Japan and I don't know why he said he will
tell me about that later on. If he does intend to continue any part of it,
I'd appreciate it now while I cannot work as we are pretty broke but if
that is not what he meant when he mentioned it forgive me for
mentioning it.

Sydney is a funny place. It is Americanized compared to Melb. and it
makes me think I'd loathe to live in New York. The traffic here is
fantastic, I get quite panic[k]ed every time I try to cross a street – there
seem to be no rules at all except the survival of the fittest – the cafes all
serve breakfasts, even the suburban ones. Most of the bread sold is 'cut'
and wrapped in cellophane or rather sliced bread. Of course I'm forgetting you've been here on your way home from Brisbane – but I feel as
though I am in a foreign country ... I am enjoying having our own
couple of rooms instead of the lousy food we got at the pub where we
worked, I don't think one could have got worse. The quality of Sydney
food in [the] shops is much poorer than Melb. and dearer.

Gray has been pretty well over here with the exception of a few para-
lyzing migraines – though he tells me they are not bad [compared] to
what he has had.

I feel a bit tired – the strain of having nowhere to live and not having
my gland out etc. but really apart from that I feel good and am loving
being over here.

Royal Prince Alfred Hospital, Sydney
Wednesday
(c. 12 May 1947)

Dear Sun
I have been thinking of you. Last
night Gray brought in a book of Spender's poetry, or rather it was an
early anthology of those boys, Auden etc. with a lot of Spender in it —
seems quite odd to read them now — thinking of the time when we read
Spender when a new poem of his came out, and how excited we were —
Gray bought this book for 1/- at a funny little secondhand bookshop
over here where I saw some books Nolan would like and when I'm out
of this confounded place I'll go and have a look [at] what there [is] for
him. It's quite a quaint old shop.

Had my gland taken out on Monday and they'll take the stitches out
Friday. I had another sort of anaesthetic not ether, no lovely dreams. I
was disapppointed. It just put me out and no sensations at all. Not even
aware I was going to sleep. They are keeping me here for a week while
they start me on the therapy ray treatment. They did not remove the
lump in my throat, [they] only took one gland from there. It hurt for a
couple of days and made me feel sick but I had a terrible time today. I
was taken into the 'ray' room which looks something like an H G Wells
picture. A huge wall that looks like a Nazi wireless wall and big things
in the air like this [sketch] and this [sketch] quite terrifying and they lie
you on a bed in this square padded room lie you staring at all this appa-
ratus in the air and a large sheet of black glass above you and a thing
sticking onto your gland and weights over your head to stop movement
and cover your head practically all of it with rubber and the stifling
'cramped in' feeling and then they leave you in this room alone. Shut a
huge iron door behind you and 'turn it on' — terrific buzzing and burring
etc. lights and numbers jump up and down on the dial and you are
supposed to stay there 11 minutes. Well, you know what I'm like — I
panic[k]ed. My heart beat like a thrashing machine my throat seemed to
nearly choke and I yelled my head off — at last after 4 minutes [of]
yelling they came and saved me (from myself) and I was booing and
beside myself and feeling very ashamed and I'll have to have 11 minutes
of this a day ad infinitum or at least until something happens.

I'll be alright tomorrow I hope. I'll have to be. Because of the scene I only had 4 minutes today – God I have not been so frightened since I was a little girl alone in the dark. It was not exactly fear but a sort of panic caused by [the] thought of all the power of unknown things harnessed in that room – the final diagnosis has not come through yet of what is wrong with me ... and they can only reduce the glands by ray and they have to do that first – apparently Littlejohn had mentioned Hodgkin's Disease to them as both McCallum and Lovell said they agreed as far as they could with Littlejohn that it was that but still they may find it's all due to tonsils or something equally silly. After all this I hope they do – it is the most perfect weather over here and would you believe it, it's too hot even in the hospital and hospitals are cold even in summer.

I feel very lonely in here with things happening to me and seeing Gray for only ½ hr each day and the long hospital nights with people groaning etc. (including me at times for my neck is sore still). So much has happened since we've been here that I've forgotten Melbourne things. Except for one or two personalities everything else seems never to have existed – the mind is curious. Things can happen to it and we have little or no control over those things. The mind flips this way and that and the only thing we can control, and it's remote control, is what happens to the things we think ...

Write and tell me what has happened to the firm [Reed & Harris] and how you all are – What will John do?

I find it very hard to write a letter since I have been here. I find I have forgotten what I said in the last letter and forgive me if I say the same thing each time. In fact life seems to have been very disjointed and I have been overconscious of physical things owing to this blasted treatment. I had just started to write you when I was whisked off for another 'ray' treatment. I am not frightened now and I am going home for the weekend and I come in again on Monday and Tuesday and then get discharged and have to come back each day for ray treatment. It'll cost 1/- a day in fares and God knows how long in time. I s'pose knowing how hospitals muck you around it'll be the best part of half a day.

... I have not done any more drawings as I have been in this death chamber where life stands still – even though I suppose some of the greatest human dramas are enacted in hospitals they seem devoid of all emotion and sterile in every way.

Thank Nolan very much for the paper which I received OK and was very glad to get it. You cannot buy any over here. Gray has been doing paintings on it as there is no board of any sort here either.

It is very funny, our lives together because I get exhausted very easily and have to lie down and I cannot walk far at all these days before I have to rest. The business before I left Melbourne has left me exhausted somewhere and then all this doctor business etc. so when I feel good-oh Gray gets sick and vice versa but I think it is rather funny for us both to be together and somehow out of it all we want it that way. When Gray gets a migraine I usually draw or write and when I feel exhausted, he feels good and paints. It really works quite well as the kitchen is the only room light enough to work in and we couldn't both do things at the same time in that tiny little room.

At night when we open our back door there is a blaze of neon signs [which] smacks [us] in the face and silhouetting the only tree in the district and it's in our backyard. [Sketch of Hester and Smith's home with backyard and tree.] Our poor little leafless tree. That's just about the shape of the tree. Can't tell what sort it is until it gets leaves. In this little yard one feels as though one is in the centre of a huge metropolis like New York and [it] never fails to give me a shock.

I'll post you these poems written in hospital between pans and thermometers and nurses mucking around so forgive them.[1]

Love to you all and Heide must be looking wonderful if it's nice autumn weather.

Did I tell you David Boyd has gone to Tahiti to go into partnership with a Tahitian (not native) potter or something?[2]

---

[1] Though Joy does not name them and though she would rework and refine poems over months, and sometimes years, it is probable that 'Untitled' and 'Anaesthetic' are two of the poems she sent in earlier draft form to Sunday. Both are unpublished. Photocopy collection the editor.

[2] David Boyd (b.1924) is the younger brother of Arthur. Although he continued to have pottery exhibitions with his wife, Hermia Lloyd-Jones (b.1931), David Boyd would turn to painting in the 1950s. In 1947, Boyd travelled to New Caledonia with the writer Hugh Atkinson.

Untitled

There is one small room I cannot forget – where no life was – where rivers went on timelessly, endlessly, and the seepage above my head made the green for me to look on – where murmurings are, voices, then the damp, being alone and waiting anxiously for a time unknown in that square room.

Anaesthetic

Through the green well
ascended, came out clean
on level ground. light bulbs
above the head, and surgeons
snipping scissors
their reflection
more real than flowers
beside the bed
FLOWERS that hold all summer
suspended in this room.
girls' blue eyes, efficient
averting time
taking from life
those precious moments.
RIVOTED ceiling meaning
more than eyes more
than lovers call
witnessing more intimately
my own secrets . . .
green and white receding
visible now the well
through which I entered.

61 Bayswater Road, King's Cross
Wednesday, 14 May 1947

Dear Sun
Received the books and they are good and I will promise not to lose them and take care of them. Today I received your letter after I came home from the doctors'. I came out of hospital yesterday and am under X ray treatment for a period of 11 minutes each day for an indefinite period then I have 6 weeks off it and then one finds out if it is having any effect in that period then I go on to more and so on. I have quite definitely got Hodgkin's disease and am a blue duck apparently unless they find a new miracle overnight on how to cure it. The ray can clear up the disease for a while. It comes back. The doctor spoke pretty plainly to me as I asked him to. I do not intend to come back to Bert and Swene. I am sorry for Bert and quite decided and Gray has not tried to influence my decision but I was disappointed by your letter although I was asking too much but I thought I had made it clear that when I met Gray someone shut the door on the rest of my life before that and it was not conscious just an unconscious thing that happened to my mind and it was as quick and final as someone shutting a door. It's over.

I deeply love Gray and I am staying with him – I have been very sick with the ray treatment – it has made all my other glands swell and made me feel pretty awful – but Lovell says that'll pass. Gray has poisoned his foot and we seem to be very hard up. I did not go to Glou[ce]ster House but to the Public Hospital and spent the £5 you sent us to live on. My treatment is free and the only expense I can see for you is Lovell's bill although I have only to visit him now and then so it should not be much. I am sorry I mentioned ... the money you and John gave Bert and I and I would not have thought about it had John not mentioned it in his letter.

Goodnight Sun

61 Bayswater Road, King's Cross
20 May 1947

Dear Sun

I have read your letter thru very quickly once and I have about 20 minutes before I go to the hospital for treatment to write this letter, I cannot wait until I come back to write, it must be done now. Forget you received my last letter if you can. I am sorry. It is only today that I feel at all normal since I wrote. It was a terrible day and I was afraid and have been until today – I came out of hospital, we had no money, about 2/- I think. I went to Lovell and he had prepared to tell me what he had to and I could see this and [I] let him tell me and did not ask him any of the things I had gone there with the intention of asking. Gray could hardly walk on his poisoned foot and I received a letter suggesting Bert might be coming over here and your letter all too suddenly one on top of the other and was at my lowest ebb and had failed that Friday to go to my treatment and on Monday yesterday went to treatment and got on the bed and they put all the blasted rubber over my face and I broke down hopped off the bed and went away without the treatment and crying. The man who works the machine was rude to me and I felt lousy but fortunately Gray has a job now and I have taken a pull at myself and feel like facing the world once more. The last week I have really been off key – it's this blasted treatment.

It makes me so weak and sick headaches sore throat glands sore and the most terrifying of all a feeling of will I get the next breath or not – it all comes at once. Sometimes I come out in an awful sweat. This is not physiological after what Lovell said as I had the reaction in hospital and it lasts for the rest of the blessed day on and off. Naturally I have been introspective and self-absorbed and morose. I am over it now and will not get that way again.

God! I know what I have asked of you in the mental and physical sense (as far as Swene is concerned) and I have told you what I think and that stands always but I have sorted myself out. It is hard to do when you feel exhausted, as you know by your own experience. Forgive me Sun. I will not send the cheque back as I would like to, it will tide us over till 'pay day'. To add to my depression that silly bitch Rosemary seems to have mislaid my case and I am still, except for my overcoat, in the one costume and undies which I wash each night.[1] It is rather funny really and I feel like laughing at myself for taking myself so seriously.

Anyway I went to David Jones [Gallery] and saw the Royal Society of Artists' exhibition which is worse than awful. They have some nice little [William] Gould bird prints there and the National Gallery here is full of beautiful facsimiles of modern masters badly framed and badly hung. It is a shoddy town and makes one realise how dreadful it must be to be poor in London or New York. The Yankie [sic] fleet is here, 11 boat loads of them and the town stinks.

I'm glad I'm living with Gray. He has the most rare sense of humour and makes me laugh a lot and made me wild last week by joking when I felt lousy but it is the thing that has taken my moroseness away. I am taking care of the books, dear Sun, and loved *Thunder on the Left*.[2] There are a couple of passages in it which are rare insights into kids looking at adults. I will post you a drawing tonight, it is the best so far but it doesn't last when it is hung up – I think it must be superficial. When you are not so tired write and tell me of the Boyd/Yule show if you see it.[3] Love to you and John and forgive me please. You do not have to answer my letters. I just like talking to you inadequately as one does in letters.

Love to you all

61 Bayswater Road, King's Cross
Sunday (mid? June 1947)

Dear Sun
... Sydney to me yesterday was anywhere but Australia. There is a part at the foot of the bridge where houses jut up like stark reminders of other cities and other times. Very old and all built one above the other with stone stairs cut in the rock

---

[1] Rosemary Smith was married to Martin, Gray's older brother.
[2] Christopher Morley, *Thunder on the Left*, Cornstalk Publishing, Sydney, 1926.
[3] Doris Boyd–John Yule exhibition, May 1947, Velasquez Gallery, Melbourne. Doris Boyd (1883–1960) painter and potter, was married to Merric Boyd and was the mother of Lucy, Arthur, Guy, David and Mary. John Yule (b.1923) had met Martin Smith and Neil Douglas in 1942 while in the army and through them became friendly with the Boyd family. He worked at Arthur Merric Boyd Pottery at Murrumbeena in 1945 and studied at the Gallery School with David Boyd in 1946.

and green moss and seepige [sic] making the stairs look ancient and worn and gardens old ones, from time past ... Here is the place to lose oneself. Quite frightening too, because it look[s] alien and old and somehow one feels one is not in Australia anymore ... but then one thinks that it *is* Australia and Australians have built this city and these old rock stairs and somehow it does not altogether reassure one.

When the train passed the bridge shook and I was sick with panic and finally had to take [the] bull by the horns and pull myself together for I was only still halfway across the damn thing – I got across, of course, without mishap but my stomach is not made for the march of time. I was crossing the bridge on my way over to see dear Guy Boyd[1] – he is truly a lovely person of the stuff [of which] saints are made – he is the most abstract of the family and he is the most lovable. He is so completely natural in every way and [has] two beautiful shy blue eyes. He was working at his potter's wheel again and he is very close to it and the shapes he fashions there. He does not stop when one arrives. He prefers to work while he's talking which is very nice for the visitor – I don't think I have ever met anyone as simple as he is – or as pure. David [Boyd] is in Numea [sic] and it is very expensive living there he says, £3 for lodgings. I forget whether that's for a day or a week.

It is impossible to buy tube color with the exception of earth colors and they are scarce. Powdered color is worse for they only sell poster colors but one can mix them with oil if one can get it! Linseed oil is the catch. Got about ¹/₂ full by luck the other day but it is not enough to mix up powdered color.

Have seen a couple more of these lousy Sydney exhibitions. Oh my God! Bonnard is the latest fad here and they have all crudely interrupted [sic] his color and style – I have not contacted any of those people. I feel I don't want to. The only person we know is Guy and he is not in any way connected with the 'art' circles.

Have great fun here with seeing Chips Rafferty and Muriel Steinback

[1] Guy Boyd (1923–88) began his professional life as a designer and manufacturer of commercial pottery at his family's pottery works. Later he would become a successful sculptor. In 1946, David helped Guy set up a pottery in Neutral Bay, calling it the Martin Boyd Pottery. It was in a shed behind a house where David boarded with friends. During the day, David threw pots while Guy attended a sculpture course. Sales to Sydney stores were sufficient to make the pottery viable. John Vader, *The Pottery and Ceramics of David and Hermia Boyd*, Matthews/Hutchison, 1977, p. 24.

who live not far from us. Chips is a tall streak and is growing an enormous beard for the Eureka Stockade film.[2] In fact, the amount of beards over here is fantastic! They must all be hopeful of being picked by a 'star-finder' – it is quite humorous for if they don't decide definitely on the cast soon the whole of Sydney's male population will be bearded – Eureka!

I am to see McCallum sometime next week – the lump in my neck has vanished! and a few smaller lumps appeared at the back of my neck. They may go too. I feel excellent and with the exception of a very dry mouth and a bit of congestion in my nose there seems nothing much wrong. The spit glands are affected in some way, causing the dryness – I have noticed that I cannot take shock of any kind. Even the slightest makes me terribly weak all over but this I think is probably nervous.

My blasted mother wrote me to say she was coming over and I've written her and told her I won't see her if she does – just writing about her makes me tremble. Sun, why is it I can never escape the dreadful fear of her and the feeling of insecurity she gives me? I feel her presence like a cunning animal about me and I am frightened of which way it will jump – I feel she can outwit me – but I am not worr[y]ing for if she does come over. She'll have to find me first!

There is one other thing. Do you think John could send me postal notes instead of money orders as money orders take about 2 or 3 days sometimes for the money to come through and like this week I will not be able to collect it until Tuesday as it's a holiday Monday and also the blasted money cashier shuts his place in the [G]PO at 4 pm and that's a bit awkward, too.

My neck is a brown – red as a berry where the ray was put and now looks quite disgusting as it's peeling – just like a burn.

Your book[s] are all intact and [I] will send them over at first opp. to you . . . Did Nolan get the photos? Are they any good to him? Guy Boyd is coming tonight to take us to some friends of his who paint pots. This is our first invite since being in Sydney. Feel quite excited! They live at the romantic name of Lavender Bay – go by ferry in the night.

I think the enclosed poem is the best I've done. Let's know what you think. Maybe [I'm] blinded, I have a sneaking suspicion.[3]

I'm still worried about you, no word. Are you sick Sun dear? How is

---

[2]   *The Eureka Stockade* (1949) directed by Harry Watt.
[3]   Missing.

the violet tunnel?[4] The pointsetia [sic] over here is a tropical dream, huge and bright against the city's dust. The violets have no smell here. Rosebuds are in profusion in the shops – lovely things.

My love to you and John and the two terrible twins Swene and Syd.[5]

Goodnight Sun

61 Bayswater Road, King's Cross
Tuesday (c. June 1947)

Sun

Your sunny letter came smack bang on top of one from mother so I 'saved yours up' and read it second – thank God! What a dirge! All about me being 'decadent' and Gray being a foul beast, and what's more, accusing me of pinching one of her diamente brooches which is worth about 2/6 (I s'pose) – well, enough of that.

Your description at the end of your letter makes me 'smell' Heide again – the daphne and the dear [violet] tunnel in the wind – one can almost forgive people like Rupert Brooke for his 'O to be in England now that April's there' or something[1] – that is how it makes me feel, the smell! There is nowhere except Heide have I had such smells. Rereading that it makes me laugh, sounds funny doesn't it? Was not meant to be – talking of nostalgia – I met Alannah for the 2nd time in Sydney and she was bursting with a letter from Paris from a cafe on a boulevard with the traditional young poet drinking wine – How many does that make? It was Alister.[2] He arrived in England with £10 and is now in Paris and still has

---

4   A long drainage trench at Heide, planted out with violets.
5   Syd here means Sidney Nolan.

---

1   It was Robert Browning who opened his famous poem 'Home-thoughts, from Abroad' with the lines 'O to be in England/Now that April's there'.
2   The poet and critic Alister Kershaw (1921–95) contributed to *Angry Penguins, A Comment* and *Art in Australia* before leaving for Europe in 1947 where he broadcast for the BBC. He moved to France in 1948 to work as secretary to the writer Richard Aldington, before becoming the ABC's Paris correspondent. A flamboyant young man, Kershaw was best known for his satire 'The Denunciad', part of which was published in *Angry Penguins*, September 1943. It mercilessly lampooned members of the local literary and artistic scene. Hester refers here to Kershaw's poem 'Lands in Force', published in the second edition of *Angry Penguins*, which was also the title of a volume of Kershaw's poetry published by Reed & Harris. See also Alister Kershaw, *Hey Days; memories and glimpses of Melbourne's Bohemia 1937–1947*, Angus & Robertson, Sydney, 1991.

his £10! and will have a job back in England (he'll be back there now)
doing the BBC talks on Aussie literature. At present he is dreaming in
the Luxemburg [Gardens] [sic] with Aldington and his (Aldington's)
wife. He is Aldington's house guest. Let's hope the Aldington knocks
some of the Aldington out of Alister and sends him in verse to 'Lands in
Force' to start off from. He's of course busting himself with pride and
sniffing the Parisian air to the full – this is what he dreamed of – must be
lovely for dreams to come true. I don't mean that sarcastically . . .

No, Gray did not get job as posh waiter. He made all arrangements to
take job, interviewed slicker than slick head waiter and we went one
night and crept round to an alley where the kitchen window was and
noted all the wrinkles that a posh waiter must note. Forgot one thing!
The suit! They said he had to have an evening suit of most elaborate
style and flyaway black jacket just as elaborate and pants, evening pants
and black shoes and black socks!! We like stupids had completely over-
looked that. So that was that. It would cost about £7!! even secondhand, so instead he got a job as a part-time 'reader' of the local rag
which comes out once a week – but, not daunted, we have a scheme!
Gray is painting some flower studies, tiny ones and we are going to
frame them ourselves, gold too! and hawk them in the 'arcade' shops for
about £1 each and we'll be millionaires in no time!! . . . But, really, it
should pay, and it only takes ½ [an hour] to paint them and if we sell 20
we will turn it in till we have used up the £20. Ha! Ha! It sounds too
good. I s'pose there'll be a catch somewhere.

McCallum today. Nothing to report till I have my X rays taken and I
have to ring hospital and make an appointment and when McCallum
has a look at the X rays I have to see him again and he'll have some
news for me. You get the X rays done for nix I'm almost sure at the
hospital and if they charge it's only about 2/- at the most – this blasted
pen keeps catching on the paper! I keep forgetting to buy a writing pad.

Swene sounds a bit of a tiger – you are to be admired for your training
him on his pot, but did you hear the sequel? Bert took him to mother's
(the only decent bit in her letter!) and went armed with pot – Swene
peed in pot – went to back door, tipped contents out [the] door, brushed
his hands – went into lav. and pulled chain.

No wonder you feel depressed and want to be born again, with all
that sulpha! I do hope the abscess has gone, Sun. I s'pose you feel like
Van Gogh and want to cut your wretched ear off – I can imagine the

agony you were in and hope it's gone. You must have been hogging a few chocolates on the sly to get an abscess! Ask John what he thinks. I bet he'll agree, no one will believe it just <u>CAME</u>.

We have all round our little yard big flats and when we go out the back door we have to be very careful. Just like crossing a road, look about us, look right, look left, and it's only luck if there are no slop buckets emptied, plum on top of your head. I just missed one today, but my clean washing on [the] line didn't so I started an inter-flat screaming match – 'Why don't yer look what yer doing?' sort of thing and screaming about council laws and hygiene and what – I outscreamed them – won by a head so to speak.

Love to you all and ST too'

61 Bayswater Road, King's Cross
Friday (June 1947)

Dear Sun
Your letter was lovely and cheery – it's rather funny. Gray hangs on letters from his mother and I on letters from Heide, so we have a saying each day – Any letters from Sun? No, any from Mum? No or yes as they come. Gray will sit down to write a letter and usually sits for about 10 minutes in front of a blank piece of paper and then says aloud 'Dear Mum' just as I am about to write 'Dear Sun' and I nearly write 'mum' and he nearly and sometimes does if I say aloud 'Dear Sun'. So between Mum and Sun it's rather funny.

I am writing this in bed and Gray is painting a street scene at night which rather amuses me because he has neons and street lamps. But instead of a series of blues, it's a series of browns and yellows and really quite different but I am not saying anything for if I did it would get wiped out in one foul sweep and it looks as though it's a rather good one so far. I may mention it when finished. No, perhaps not, it would get wiped out for sure.

Did I tell you we both hope to make a few extra bob doing pottery designs for Guy Boyd? We had a shot on ashtrays yesterday and he wants us to do lamp bases. It's fun. He has a good set up and I love the feel of

³   Sweeney Tucker.

the clay, even if it is only painting on it. Unfortunately [we] cannot let our heads go as they have to be 'slick' to sell – crabs and seudo [sic] modern leaves etc ...

The photos of Swene are superb. What a card he looks on the 'trike'. I look at it and say 'surely not', that bloated little so and so but he looks such a tiger I s'pose he must be – when I say bloated, no reflection is meant on Hay or you as he always looked like that – only it gives me a shock every time I realize it.[1]

Nolan going north! It's good news and bad. It's bad as he is tired, I have thought he looked tired for a long time now – it's good, too, because I think once in every Aussie's life they have to do two things – 'go bush' and 'go north'. They usually do, too. Of course I'll see him and I'll go down to Mascot. I'd love to. In fact it's a pity in a way [I] did not know sooner. He could have stayed a night in our kitchen. Still he can if he wants to on the way back.

I have had X ray and am going to see McCallum next Friday so won't know results till then. Even if they mean more treatment, I'll not be depressed as I cannot be an invalid. I have decided that much and I must live my life as it comes and just see I don't get too tired and have early nights and apart from that what can I do? I might live longer if I retired from [the] city and went out in [to] the country and took things easy and that's impossible for I'd go mad even in heaven not being involved in life – such is my fate, or my nature, or my glands! I don't know who to blame.

You ask how I am getting on apart from the stories I tell in letters – I worry sometimes, about one evening a week and I get perhaps a bit depressed but that soon passes as I get no sympathy from my stormy partner and that is good. It smacks me into a proper mood again. I could think of no better partner for the present as he is such a many sided curious, infuriating, lovely and laughing character. I am constantly

---

[1]   Dr William Hay was a popular American nutritionist of the 1930s. The Hay System emphasised natural foods including whole grain cereals, unrefined sugars, nuts and fresh vegetables. His 'chemistry of digestion' was founded on the principle that carbohydrates and protein should never be combined, so meat would be consumed at one meal and bread at another. Sunday, health and diet conscious, also took it to mean that vegetables should be garden grown. Neil Douglas recalled, 'Sam [Atyeo] and I brought [Edward] Dyason into their lives and Sun and John went on Hay ... they became healthier ... and the vegie garden became an even more important part of their lives.' Abbie Heathcote, *A Far Cry, Neil Douglas spinning yarns with Abbie Heathcote*, Karella Publishing, n.d., p. 71. Sunday passed on her interest in Hay to Joy.

amused and on my metal [sic] and this is good, stops [any] introversion –
he is never the same for $^1/_2$ [an] hour and [is] always making jokes, [is]
delightfully vain and really has a shocking inferiority or superiority
complex, I can't make up my mind which – he never says he loves me.
If I ask him it puts him in an awful 'mood' and I roar laughing.

All this is good for me and new to me and it has made me realize that
what I thought love was is just what love isn't. This knowledge has
made me mature in that regard deep down somewhere – something like
having a baby matures one somewhere, somehow in a way one can't
exactly say but it does. We have a lovely time dreaming and romancing
together and making up stories about people and incidents we see here
and there and we are both about as impressionable, so you can imagine
what a madhouse it is. We come down to earth quickly, though sometimes so quickly that we both nearly howl. Then the 'stormy one'
usually says something very funny and we're off again roaring with
laughter and passers-by give us queer glances etc. So you see that is how
I am. There is a laugh or a storm every minute and I am happy in this
way for I think it is most probably the best thing for Hodgkin's and I felt
cheered, too, about your news from [Drs] Shaw and Florence[2] even
though Lovell managed to convince me pretty well that I'm a dead duck
as far as permanent cure goes.

It all seems like a dream now, his little talk to me. I'm sure he stepped
over 'doctors' rules' that day but I begged [the] truth of him at all costs.
He even told me to put my 'affairs' in order so as not to be caught
unawares. Don't tell Littlejohn this as he may tell McCallum and they'll
think Lovell is a bit rich as doctors aren't supposed to tell patients this.
I'm glad he did for I have had the reverse effect and instead of feeling
sorry for myself, unconsciously the 'will to live' has come uppermost and
I know I'll live to 98 and nark everyone – I still remember how I gulp-
ingly asked him if it was a gorey [sic] death and he replied 'no, you just
get progressively weaker.' Well I'm as strong as a horse and putting on
weight and a transformation has occurred inside me since hearing this, a
bodily transformation and I feel stronger every day.

As far as the wolf at the door goes, we are just keeping him at bay
very well really considering how dear things are here … Still if our
scheme to sell the potboilers comes off and the pottery designs pay off

---

[2] Sunday consulted doctors in Melbourne for their opinions about Joy's condition and
      forwarded them to Joy.

we should be on easy street and before long I'll be sending John a cheque – I can hear John saying 'Gosh Sun, do you think she will' – Ha! Ha! might even win Tatts. Pigs might fly too.

What's this I hear from Alannah about John getting a job with CEMA?[3] Is it true? She knew no more than that – Sun, I do hope the sadness is over. It's been very sad and sort of hopeless for you both, hopeless it seems but I know things will turn and when they look blackest – this is a cliche, I know but it's true – since I have been preparing my mind to die I find something has been released and the things I thought important and essential have gone and the unimportant have become a source, a new spring of life and hope. A new spring is around the corner for you and John. We only go on because we know somewhere the new spring is and the problem is only to find it – and this sounds a bit audacious for God knows you and John have looked for new springs and found them and it seems as though you've found them all. I know you're (and who wouldn't be in your place!) tired now to look – but you won't have to look. They'll come and grab you before you know they've got you – yes that's true – banal as it sounds.

A tit bit of news before I close down (you don't have to answer these epistles, you know – this was meant to be a short letter!!)

Some friends were invited to Cynthia Reed's place for arvo [tea] and dinner presumably as they had to arrive at about 3 o'clock.[4] After 2 hrs travel to Pymble, [they] arrived tired and thirsty – no cup of tea but at 6 pm when dinner time was imminent, they got coffee and nuts. At 9.30 pm still no dinner. They got coffee and cakes and 10.30 pm [then] they went home for a meal. This story came from Alannah as she was telling me of an old flame of mine who lives at Pymble who wants us to go out there. Remember Terry?[5] Nolan will anyway – so Cynthia cropped up.

Having talked about myself for the last hour I feel quite good so I hope it doesn't have [a] reverse effect on you.

Love to you all and SSST too

---

[3] The Council for the Encouragement of Music and the Arts, formed during the second world war. The first CEMA art exhibition was held in Sydney in 1946. John did not work for it.

[4] Cynthia Reed (1908–76) was then living at 8 Woniora Avenue, Wahroonga, with her six-year-old daughter Jinx. Her first novel, *Lucky Alphonse* (1944), was published by Reed & Harris, and her second novel *Daddy Sowed a Wind* was published in 1947. Cynthia would also publish four volumes of travel writing between 1962 and 1971. See *Outback and Beyond, The travels of Cynthia and Sidney Nolan*, Angus & Roberston, Sydney, 1994.

[5] Terry Cornioley, fellow student of Joy's at the Gallery School.

61 Bayswater Road, King's Cross
(June 1947)

Dear Sun

I bet it can't be as cold and drear over there as it is here. Has rained for a week solidly! with [the] exception of one day in the midweek and it was so hot we had no coats at all and the place we live in gets no sun as there are tall flats on either side – looking out all the time for a cheaper and cheerier abode. The place we have is a bit of a shambles but it seemed like heaven when we got it.

Called out and saw Guy Boyd. He is really a dear quiet boy and makes lovely pottery. [He] has a huge kiln [which] cost £300 and it's electric so he can regulate it much better than [the] Murrumbeena boys and gets a steady *even* temperature which seems essential. He has wonderful clay (which if you saw it, you could not resist buying a huge bag, it's so white!). It costs £2.10/- a bag as against about 6/- a bag [for] the Murrumbeena stuff but bad luck for Arthur. Even if Guy sent some over he could not bake it as Arthur has to have his kiln at too high a temperature.

Guy's pottery is in lovely superb yellows (looks like cadmium) and marone [sic] and all colors in fact which Arthur cannot get as they are made over here [Sydney] by Dulux and they have a German ex-internee and color specialist working for them and it can only be obtained in small quantities as it's expensive and rare. Guy has to pick it up personally. I'm going to find out how they're going (for Nolan) if I can, if [the] new Dulux colors post war can be obtained for 'outsiders' yet. Apparently you have to be in the know to get it.

David is actually in Numea [sic] and has asked Guy to send him clay so God knows what he's up to over there! Guy's stuff is more 'commercial' in design and decoration – not a patch on John Perceval or Arthur's lovely chook and cock pots but he has the baking, glazing and finishing down to a 'tee' and it's not without its charm. Guy only does this during the night and goes to Syd[ney] Tech[nical] School during the day on the army's rehab. scheme to learn modelling etc. from [Lyndon] Dadswell who is a nice man but BA [bloody awful] sculptor.[1] It is having

---

[1] Lyndon Dadswell (1908–92) was a sculptor and influential teacher. After serving in the second world war, Dadswell was appointed as an official war artist. He returned to teach at Sydney's National Art School in 1945.

(at the moment) a tightening effect on [Guy's] work but that will pass and he's got enough Boyd in him to pull thru or something.

Apart from Guy have not met any Melburnians thank God as I don't particularly care to get the address of where we live back to Melb. My mother has written a couple of her usual sort of letters to GPO saying things like 'women always pay – come back dear' and in the next breath 'where are my such and suchs?' Something worth about 6d that she lent me and 'I want them back Joy and I intend to get them' 'goodnight darling mother loves' sort of rot.

Heard that Max [Harris] had acquired a 93-year-old house with shingled roof and telephone and five acres of orchard and bush – sounds lovely so I s'pose Vonnie[2] will love it too and they'll take their lovely baby out there and live – I don't suppose it is far from Adelaide either.

How are you and John, Sun? You're frozen and hybinating [sic] I s'pose. Swene getting too much for you? I think now he's out of nappies he should be a lot easier – and that I think is miraculous. I'm sure he'd be in naps until 21 if I had him. I would like one day when you have time for you to send me a copy of those lovely little Rimbaud translations you did for AP.[3]

By the way how is everything straightening out for you and John? I hope you feel more cheerful now and things are happier in that regard from now on. It seems such a pity. Really it [Angry Penguins] could have been so good but still it did good and was the best we've had in Aussie so you can always know that it was not a failure in that sense. Looking back it did wonders, really, for the time it was going and Aussie artists and writers ought to be jolly thankful for what it did for them but they're a rum crowd when it comes to the point. People all are I s'pose, not just sections of them, but it seems pretty hard to me that it should have been [allowed to] just let slide by them.

[2] Yvonne Harris, Max Harris's wife.
[3] 'Three Poems by Arthur Rimbaud Translated by Sunday Reed' appeared in *Angry Penguins*, no. 4, 1942, pp. 42–3. 'Poem', 'Dream for Winter' and 'Dreamer' were Sunday's only public contributions to the journal and her only published translations.

(left)
1. Louise Hester, c. 1932.

(below)
2. Sunday and Ethel at Sorrento, c. 1913

(top)
3. National Gallery students, 1938. Joy is seated far left, third row, and Alannah Coleman is seated second from right, second row. Other students include Nornie Gude (next to Joy) and Laurence Pendlebury (top centre). WB MacInnes, head of the Painting and Drawing School, is seated fourth from right, second row.

(above)
4. Sunday and Arthur, c. 1930.

(right)
5. Joy at 16.

6. Albert Tucker and Joy at Heide, 1942, while Tucker was on leave.

(top)
7. Joy, John, Sunday and Sidney Nolan holding Sweeney at Sorrento, 1945.

(above)
8. Heide.

(left)
9. John Sinclair (?) cutting Joy's hair at Heide with
Sunday looking on, c. 1944.

(above)
10. John, Nolan and Sunday in the library at Heide.

(top)
11. Joy and Max Harris in the train to Heide, c. 1944.

(above)
12. Sunday with Joy holding Sweeney in the train to Heide, c. 1945.

Poem

On the fine nights of summer, I will go on the paths
Pricked by the wheat, to tread on the slender grass;
Dreamer, I will feel the freshness on my feet,
And let the wind bathe my bare head.
I will not speak, I will not think,
But love will fill my heart,
And I will go far, far away, bohemian
By nature, – happy as with a woman.

Dream for Winter

In winter we go in a little pink carriage
With blue cushions
We will be happy. A nest of kisses rests
In each soft corner.
You will close your eyes so as not to see
The evening shadows making faces through the window,
Those snarling monstrosities,
Mob of black demons and black wolves.
Then you will feel a scratching on your cheek.
A little kiss, like a mad spider,
Will run on your neck.
And you will say to me, 'Look!'
Leaning your head,
And we will take a long time to find that little beast
– who travels so much.

Dreamer

Away I went fists in my torn pockets.
My coat too became perfection.
Under the stars Muse your faithful friend,
Oh what love I dreamed.

My only trousers had a big hole.
Tom Thumb dreamer, shedding rhymes on my way.
My inn was the Big Bear.
My stars in heaven softly rustled their silk.

And I listened sitting on the side of the road,
Those good September nights where I felt
Dewdrops on my face like strong wine:

Where rhyming in the middle of those faery shadows
like lyres, I held the rubber of my worn out shoes,
A foot against my heart

> 61 Bayswater Road, King's Cross
> Saturday (June 1947)

Dear Sun and John
... We went one night to a new
therter [sic] show here of Geo. Farwell's *Sons of the South*[1] – Never seen
worse!! That Indian dancer is here at the moment and Ruth Bergner is
dancing with him (she is very remarkable I've heard).[2] Believe the
Indian is good but accompanying ballet is made up of huge bell bottom
virgins with enormous legs and they do this sort of Indian hand wiggles
[sketch] with a perpetual grin and then turn round, bottoms to audience
and do it again. Well, I believe it's terrific!! In voile pants or something!!
Funny thing, the papers have announced the cast is set for *Eureka*
[Stockade] and well, wot der yer know there are now only about
three beards left in Sydney and I think they're sailors! The others

---

[1] George Farwell (1911–76) arrived in Australia from England in 1936. He wrote plays,
stories, biographies, travel accounts and documentaries for radio and television. In 1943
he established *Australian New Writing* with Bernard Smith and Katharine Susannah
Prichard.

[2] Sivaram was an Indian dancer brought to Australia in 1947 by Louise Lightfoot. Ruth
Bergner partnered Sivaram during his Australian tour. The company performed at the
Radio Theatre, Sydney, for a month and Melbourne's National Theatre. Ruth Bergner
(b.1927) had emigrated to Melbourne from Warsaw in 1936. Her brother, Yosl Bergner,
arrived the following year.

have all been cast and taken on 'location' or shaved themselves with disillusionment.

... Today ... we walked for miles and felt like Burke and Wills as we pushed through uncharted virgin bush at the Spit – a truly glorious place [which is] only 7d tram fare from [the] city with a wonderful, simple, manly and workmanlike little suspension bridge joining a sort of is[th]mus. Makes the Harbour Bridge look an awful sham show ... We found a little bay like that [sketch] and we had to climb down from the cliffs above. It was like a lovely miniature jungle and huge rocks and wonderful glimpses of this tiny bay at the bottom and we went home dog tired as the sun was setting and the glorious Sydney sky-blanket closing us in all round – all this for 7d. It's a superb place. We asked if there were any shacks to let around – alas alack!

My 'Pollys' [poltergeists] who have not been in touch with me for about 6 mths have decided to visit with a vengeance. Last night I was wide awake at about 3 am cursing our milkman to hell for making such a noise – when suddenly I received a terrific blow on the mouth, so I naturally roared like a bull and gave Gray a bang – he roared like a bull and banged me back saying, 'What the hell are you doing?' Poor cow, I awoke him from a lovely slumber only to find that it was not he who hit me in his dreams as he was on his face and had [his] arms tucked well underneath him. I still have a swollen lip where I was hit – it could have only been a polly but I was wide awake!

Sounds a bit intimate this story of a double bed – but blame the housing shortage! (PS don't tell anyone) ha! ha! Perhaps that's the sort of story one in my 'position' should not repeat but the incident was so queer and my lips so sore I had to tell someone – I don't know whether I told you or not but I did have a polly before I left Melb. [which] I had forgotten and it gave me a blood nose and [I] woke up with a sore and bloody nose but everyone said it must have been the way I slept on it. Perhaps it was, but last night I felt the blow!! – enough of that.

How's Nolan?

I have done a few more drawings – but they seem a little better – I don't know – all I know is they're frightening things to have on the wall. I had to take them down as they nearly sent me nuts – I'm sure a psychologist would not approve of them. My 'eyes' really seem to be running away with my drawings and somehow when I put brush to paper I start with an eye, do the eye and the rest is dictated by that.

I'm shutting up now, this letter looks too long! Love to you all – still no geraniums over here – saw one plain red one in a box in a garden [which looked] as though it was made of gold.

Chapter 3

July
October
1947

61 Bayswater Road, King's Cross
(July 1947)

Dear Sun
I do hope you are all right. I have
been having some dreams about you so write and let me know you're
OK. John was in one dream and he was tangled in a tree down in the
paddock and he couldn't get out and a bull gored him. They were really
nightmares and the ones I dreamt about you were indistinct, no story
and no events just some sort of sadness that made me want to cry but I
don't know what was wrong with you and I dreamt the same feeling two
nights running and it's lasted thru my waking hours.

I have a 2 hr daily job with lovely people named Solomon. A really
delightful family who make me feel I am also a member of [their] family.
A nice boy about 21, a girl 20 (big, Jewish, and on the loud side but
completely lovable) and a delicate one of 16 who has a flare [sic] for
dressmaking. I get 30/- a week and fresh eggs (from their farm) and 'old'
(which are not) clothes they don't want. They have a large flat and I go
there at 10ish in the morning and 'tidy it' as they have all mod. cons
and a cook etc. and there is no work except to (not even make bed[s])
tidy and sweep (with [a] vacuum) the wall to walls – and numerous cups
of tea and cigs (supplied). And 'Dadda' who suffers with heart and gets
up at 11 am comes and makes jokes with me about money and finding
sovereigns that he [has] lost etc. They are very wealthy and are very
simple – and they paid £500 for the key of their flat.

They had to come to Sydney because of the weather and dadda's
heart – and 'mumma' who is young (a lot younger than Mr S, so she says
and looks. He is 70) and pretty feeds me with gossip of family and relations. It is really ideal and I get my lunch too and do hardly any work
and 'mumma' says I'm a 'gem' and she was lucky to find me. McCallum
said if I *had* to work I was to get only a couple of hours and easy and
luckily (I think I was lucky) I got this and it's just round the corner from
where I live. I got it through an ad in [the] local suburban rag. So I
think mumma's a 'gem' and she thinks I am. She thinks she's lucky and
so do I.

I have not posted photos yet that I bought for Nolan and will do so
tomorrow. Apologise for me as what with getting [a] job etc. I just forgot
– love to him also.

Today is hot and dry with a north wind and the harbour looks like a bay and I love it. The only thing to spoil it is the Bridge and I hate it. It looks like [a] Walt Disney and one only should see Walt Disneys in the dark. I never *once* look at the harbour but I see it as it was when the first boats pushed in through the heads. How lovely it must have looked to those sailors, green on either side, as they found all the lovely little bays hidden away . . .

Went to La Perouse the other day, [we were] wandering over the cliffs and there were rats in the rocks. It was a grey ominous day and the Aborigines all look dejected and Botany Bay was grey and still and depressing and it was sad like the Dead Sea at the back of Point Lonsdale and I felt the atmosphere hanging heavily even when [we] got back to the city and people – it's lovely, really remote, and lost in history but one cannot stay there too long or one would vanish mysteriously like Monsuir [sic] Antoine de la Perouse to whom they have a monument and [the inscription] in French . . . [says] something like this,

'On the day of (about 1901) Monsuir Antoine de la Perouse sailed into this bay and was never heard of' and then the French were sent to look for him and sailed away to the shores of France and did not see him again. The iron round the monument is eaten away and cor[r]oded by the sea.

I went into a little house that was open and found some Abos had a pottery kiln and were [making] clay wreaths for cemetries and little clasped hands [sketch of clasped hands] all white and death-like so I came away after that just as the sun was setting on the small white sands of the old bay where people were long ago. It is still uninhabited except for a couple of fishermen and the old Abos.

The evenings across the harbour look like Heide in the mist.

Love to you all and my thoughts are with you, Sun.

Goodnight

In July, Nolan left Melbourne on his trip north. When the plane refuelled at Sydney, Joy and Gray were waiting at Mascot Airport for Nolan. They had less than half an hour before Nolan's flight for Brisbane departed, so they hurried upstairs to an American-style cafe where they had a cup of coffee.

Nolan wrote to John that Joy was delighted with the daphne Sunday had sent from the Heide garden, and held it to her, talking quickly and excitedly, her eyes bright.[1] Nolan thought Joy had lost weight and looked older, yet there seemed a new calmness to her. Though Nolan expressed concern about her health, Joy evaded his questions, insisting the swelling in her neck had subsided. She pulled back her coat to show him, but only for a moment, and he was not convinced.

Eagerly, Joy asked about Heide but when the topic of Sweeney came up, she once again avoided Nolan's questions, closing the possibility of further discussion. Nolan wondered if it were the rushed circumstances that prevented Joy speaking about her son but decided it was Joy herself. Gray, Nolan considered, seemed thinner and quieter. Though Nolan sensed a quiet harmony in their relationship, it did not impress him as anything remarkable. He felt a certain loneliness about them, too, and when he left Gray and Joy, standing at the gates, waving, Nolan felt moved by their deep connections with one another.

> 61 Bayswater Road, King's Cross
> Tuesday (July 1947)

Dear Sun

Well – the plane's gone and I've gone, but here I am only half of me, smelling my lavender bag. I s'pose you and John feel the same way for it was only today, of course (I suppose you did the same) waved frantically until [the] plane vanished into the air, and then the inevitable flatness!

How excitedly we tore down to Mascot – there are no trams there or so we were told, only one bus to Doll's Point a day, so off in a taxi. There was a tram but we'd never have made it – bundle out of taxi – we've got ½ hr. Plop! smack bang into another world of [sketch of wind socket] those things and flat ground and hangars with big shiny steel beetles poised, with their noses heavenward as though they're not really shut up but almost looking as they know it's only an interim [period] and [then] off into their heavens. Big notices with such arousing statements as 'Wing your way with A.N.A.' – another curious little placard about 'Company takes no responsibility for such things as public disturbance,

---

[1] Sidney Nolan to John Reed, 14 July 1947, Brisbane, Reed Collection.

tempest, cyclone, or an act of God'. Isn't that queer? An act of God, as though they believe that God may even smote the bird with his own hand. The flat 'drome and a lazy sun and a pale pink haze – out with a roar and a flash of gleaming silver when suddenly the monster was beside us – the tenseness and excitement and the queerness – 'He's not on it!' 'Yes! there he is!'

But we had to wait till he came to us, for visitors are not allowed past [the] white line. Gushings gigglings and smiles on all our faces, a quick cup of coffee – Oh! the cigs and the lavender and flowers – they're to look at later! No time now, 20 minutes [are] up. Mad words silly as they are inevitable. 'Enjoy yourself!' Yes. 'Write' and away she goes … Heigho! back to city – wishing to hell we're on the plane – 'flying to the sun' as [the] placard[s] say.

It was lovely seeing Nolan but he did look tired and the sun will put some weight on him and relax his eyes – he looked as happy as a kid with a new toy. But what a let-down to come back, to leave that world of 'comings' and 'goings'. Resolutions all the way back to the city. We'll get a little box for pennies marked Brisbane, sell the pot boilers. Perhaps I could get an ex[hibition]. of my drawings here and they might sell … We'll go north just as soon as we can. [We] even came back and enquired about fares. The boat people put our name down – well, we might get a bustle on if they have our name and all.

Thank you Sunday for the lavender. It's so strong that it nearly knocked the girl over in the American Ref[erence] Library – and the daphne. I've been besieged by the tenants for 'shoots' – I haven't stopped smelling the bag.

It's 6 pm and Alannah just called in – What a surprise! She had a huge string bag full of woollies for me. 3 jumpers and one heavy jacket, 2 pairs [of] slacks (one for house and one for street!) and a bed jacket and a navy blue beret!! I've been for the last half hour 'trying on' and screaming with ecstasy. Apart from my overcoat, these are the first woollies I've had – except that lovely French check material you gave me. I made it into a blouse minus sleeves [sketch of blouse] as there was only enough for a sleeveless one. It is the prettiest thing and 'chic' and as warm as toast. You know I got my case eventually which had nothing warm in it except one jacket, a thin skirt and cakes of soap etc. so after having lived in my corduroy costume I feel like a 'queen in wool'.

John asked me in [his] letter if I'd like the postal notes sent earlier than he sent them. I usually receive them on a Monday and if it's convenient for John, it would be handier I could get them on a Friday. Thank you for [the] butter coupons. That's a joy to have them. I feel a bit funny after thanking Alannah for woollies and you for lavender, postals and coupons. I realize what a burden I am on the community and it's high time I either kicked the bucket or married money.

Talking to Nolan and telling him wot all the Sydneyites say about Brisbane and that is that paintings 'sell' there. He said he may even hold a 'Barrier Reef' show and I was telling Alannah and she asked me to tell you to pass this on to Nolan – There is one John Cooper in Brisbane, [who is] very nice and apparently willing to exhibit pictures on a commission basis in his galleries and if no paintings are sold, no charge!! and [it] seems a good lurk as far as John Cooper does apparently sincerely like paintings and Alannah had *already mentioned* Nolan to him and she said, he said he'd like to meet him.[1]

There you are. Here's the dope

John Cooper

c/- Mor[e]ton Galleries

AMP Building

Queen Street

Brisbane

So tell Nolan, will you? Nolan said till he gets an address if I'm to write to him to write to Heide and you'll post [it] on or let me have his address.

This is a very stragley [sic] sort of letter and it's been a queer day and bits of Heide came with the flowers and bits of Brisbane went with Nolan and Alannah with her berets and personality and all sorts of weird things inside and I did some drawings last night and I have to go to McCallum on Friday to hear results of X ray and I feel very well today and feel as though the X rays can't be negative . . .

Love to you XXX

---

[1] Alannah Coleman knew the Moreton Gallery from her own experience, as she had exhibited there in June 1947.

61 Bayswater Road, King's Cross
Friday (July 1947)

Dear Sun

... The days could almost be termed mystical for they are certainly endowed with that shimmering sort of stillness with wonderful red and gold sunsets to complete things – I am much more 'sky' conscious over here. It's a bit like looking out the back door of Heide all the time. The sky is always before you like a veil ahead. That is because one is always on a hill here and they slope so suddenly away from one's feet, leaving only roof tops and sky before one. Melbourne is not like that. One looks up to the sky.

Went to McCallum and the X rays revealed an improvement in my chest glands and he says my neck ones are smaller, too, so that's good news, isn't it? He says no more treatment at the moment and I am to see him in 6 wks time, so that's good too! He's a quaint old world Scotch type [sic], very dandy and sweet and a good face. Although he is not the personality I come to grips with at once – I like him better each time although I feel unsure of what I think of him – but he doesn't grate in any way, so that's really the main thing.

I asked him a few questions about ultimate cure and he said he'd not be prepared to say, but as he said, 'Shall we say, more that the disease sleeps for a period, dormant'. But that period he said can be quite a long time and then he seemed quite cheerful and pleased with me and said it may even be quite a long time before more ray is necessary – I feel quite pleased too – although it doesn't worry me if he'd said otherwise. I am quite happy and do not worry about ultimates or anything for, this is right from the depths – what does it matter? One's time is when one's time is and that's all.

A funny thing about time. A man was knocked down by a lorry in Parramatta Rd the other day and while he was lying on the ground and they were waiting for an ambulance, he was run over by a passing car and killed. It was meant that way – I would have liked to see his palm. I'm sure it would have been there.

I have never cared particularly for Eliot's 'Ash Wednesday' but as it is the only poem I have of his here I have read and reread it and find it now a very beautiful thing, an ever expanding thing. The only other good poem I have is in the same American book and that's E E Cummings' [sic]

'Two Sonnets' and I think except for one line it is equal to anything ever written. It is in the highest poetic form – How I long for my dear Ezra [Pound] though he lives somewhere in me, I know. Every word of his rings throughout me constantly – I see the world his way too or should I say I see his world here.

Went to see quite a good little newsreel made by Geoff Collings called *Whither Japan.*[1] It has some Wellesian and Eisensteinian shots in it and gives a real feeling of Japan and people although one wishes there were more of it. Some superb close ups and the lovely faces on the Japanese are worth seeing, real faces, on old men who look like God.

Gray is writing a story for the *Women's Weekly* or one of those papers. It's such fun and so mushy that I read each page as he writes it, [so] enthralled that I can hardly wait to see what happens. He is a curious boy – he can sit and read anything whatsoever over and over again if there is nothing else to read – be it a women's mag or a philosophical tome – and in the same way seems to be able to write that way too as the mood takes him – his painting is exactly the same. There is a very curious mixture.

His insight is just as curious, turning up the most unexpected depths in the simplest thing – the capacity to see the *whole* of a thing, I think it is – he is also the most complex person I have met, in this way. I don't mean neurotic for he seems to have absolutely none – in fact, I have only met peasants and farmers with as little neurosis and then only rarely. There is always an abstract stillness about him and complete lack of interest in what happens and yet at the same time a very stormy turbulent response to some trivial thing that may frighten him. He reminds me of the god of thunder Thor – terribly quick thunderous sorts of flashes and yet a nerve like quicksilver or the lightning that darts through heavy clouds just as sharp and blinding, and [he] seems to have an earthy mental and physical strength that exudes more than [it] appears. It intrigues me, this personality – also makes me think of Strindberg – and a superb funmaker! All the time – quite [a] unique sort of humour.

This sounds a bit like a 'crush' that little girls get but it is quite objective because I have no crush – and also as I mentioned before, [he has] a

---

[1]   Between 1946 and 1949 Geoffrey Collings (b.1905) was director and senior producer for the Commonwealth Film Unit. In 1954 he and Dahl Collings, his wife, began making a series of documentaries, sponsored by Qantas, on Dobell, Drysdale and Nolan.

very extraordinary head which at first seeing does not unfold itself at all. It is these things that make me feel still inside. They do me good for it also reminds me of Ezra's poems, very much so. Every value I have ever had, I find I have not got now – what is worse I have no values to replace them. I find I no longer have values – it's good – it is stillness – and it is the first stillness I have ever known. In fact I did not know it existed – having no values – they just vanished – I didn't know that till now! – makes life easier for there are no complications – can never be now – it's a bit like being a star. If they were shooting an atomic rocket to Mars today here, I would volunteer for it – Yes I feel that still . . .

Love to you all.

Love to Nolan and S. Let's know latest on the Brisbanite and love to Heide and you – and dear Min[2]

XXX

61 Bayswater Road, King's Cross
29 July 1947

Dear Sun

'Plenty of work here, overtime too', 'Good place. Brisbane no good, no materials.' Just a snatch of conversation [heard] outside our back door. The 'overtime too' amused me. What a heaven to be able to think that way, to walk with the world.

Clive Turnbull[1] is over here and opened [Sali] Herman's[2] show with cocktails, and then took all the artists present to the Hotel Aussie [Australia] for dinner and then to 'Princes' the flashiest night club here and everyone got drunk at Turnbull's expense on champagne no less!! Turnbull himself got so drunk he couldn't stand up! See what I missed. I went the day after the opening!

---

[2] Min was the name of Sunday's Siamese cat. Although Sunday did not breed Siamese professionally, she had many, of whom Min was the first.

[1] Clive Turnbull (1906–75) was the art critic for the Melbourne *Herald*, 1943–48. A strong supporter of contemporary art, he organised the exhibition *Australian Present Day Art* (1945) and was an early buyer of Nolan's work.

[2] Sali Herman (1898–1993) was a Swiss-born painter of Sydney's inner suburbs.

The notorious Clive has written a book on art – 'Art from Bouvelot to Nolan' [sic] is the title.[3] Only had a brief glance at Alannah's copy and could not see much except a print of Nolan's and it came out beautifully too! The gun has a genuine patina. It came out well.

He doesn't seemed to have mentioned Bert's name. As I have not read the book closely I don't know whether it is a compliment or an insult. The former, I presume, but what of the title? Bouvelot to Nolan? It is good – I got a shock when I saw it because I thought Bouvelot was a French word and meant 'salute' and I screamed with laughter when Alannah told me he was a painter. I remembered then, of course . . .

Mrs Sadie Solomon has lent us an iron and (Thank God) a radiator. She's a gem! but I'm not going to her today as gem or no gem, one gets tired of eternal sparkles.

Orchards are planted in my head with grass beneath the trees. Last night I dreamed of a 'golden orchard' and heard all the apples speaking.

Mrs Smith[4] sent us a pair of scissors so we have both cut our hairs [sic]! Gray looks like a monk and I look like an apple tree unpruned – it's very short. Love to Sunday and John and Nolan and Swene and the dream apples. There are lots of honey suckers over here, black with red behinds and a crest [sketch of bird].

Love again

Untitled

Oh, golden orchard
golden orchard
what do you say today?

'apples drop, and apples fall
but there's no one to take 'em away'

---

[3] Clive Turnbull, *Art Here: Buvelot to Nolan*, Hawthorn Press, Melbourne, 1947.
[4] Elsie Smith was Gray's mother. She ran the Aladdin Gift Shop on the corner of Glenferrie Road and Chrystobel Crescent, Hawthorn, which sold pottery and weavings. Behind the shop, Martin Smith ran his picture-framing business. During Joy and Gray's months in Sydney, Elsie regularly sent Gray money.

oh, golden orchard
golden orchard
what do you wish today?

'a pretty maid
a dainty young girl
a basket, to take 'em away'
a moon, a ring,
a rainwashed stair,
please take my apples away.

Untitled

there is a little place I know
big enough for a mouse to hide
beneath the apple tree – one day
when I am young again
there'll just be room for me.

Above poems written on reverse of envelope.

Fragment
61 Bayswater Road, King's Cross
(c. August 1947)

... I have done more drawings and
my impulse is to send them to you as they look better than most I've
done, but I won't, not yet anyway as I would like to see if I can get a
gallery – and the only one is a mad one called 'Gro[s]venor' right down
near the quay. No one likes the place so I may be able to get it.

Gray wrote this 'mush' story for Woman [Women's Weekly] or such like
and in vain we've tried to get [a] typewriter or get it typed – impossible
[as] they want about 9/- to type it! I was wondering if I sent it to John in
town if Miss Uniake could do it?[1] Ask John if this is poss. It would give

---

[1]   Noreen Uniake was John Reed's secretary at Reed & Harris.

Miss Uniake a kick as it's about an artist's model and it's awful! but it might sell – I even think it's bad enough to sell.

We (when the pics sell) are going to try and get a cottage in the country and keep chooks and live in the lovely air for a while. Rent one I mean if we can get one – Pymble is a nice place and not too far from hospitals etc. or Palm Beach – we'll see.

I have felt sad today. I think it's my neck – but I've been thinking of poor Bert and I really could not patch things up there – I think I was mean to him and I regret that, but this world would be a better place if everyone 'found' themselves. I can't find myself, the world's too big. God the world seems so big to me. I just can't look – but poor Bert was so good to me – and I was to him, but Sun what is this demon inside us and outside us who like Judith Wright says,

> only the sound of the clock is still the same.
> each of us followed it to a different hour
> that like a bushranger held its gun on us
> and forced our choice.[2]

This demon holds the gun and forces choice on us – what for? Still we are forced! I feel this bushranger at me all the time but he can't bluff me anymore as I know the gun's not loaded! I could not possibly tell Bert I am alone, he'd want to come to me! I want to be alone – I will never love another man for I know such things don't exist. I can love you, I cannot love men, as I am not capable of it. I don't know what it means to love a man. I love Gray – as much as I am capable but then it isn't love. That's only the name I give it – how can I love Gray when he is me! and I am alone.

Now I've found Gray and he's found me it does not matter terribly to either of us if we should never meet again. He is the 'man' of me and I am the 'woman' of him. Like Caesar said we are part man, part woman, part God but I don't think the God exists in either of us. It's like a puzzle, piecing oneself together . . .

It is funny to grow up and watch our friends grow up – it's painful, too, and sad and one is told this by instinct when one is a child . . . We can't take notice of these things when we are children very much or

[2]   Judith Wright, 'The Moving Image', from *The Moving Image*, op. cit., (1942).

we'd never enter the world of men. I think the beautiful people are those who don't – some exist …

The pottery decorating seems to have fallen thru. Have not heard any more from Guy – so sleep well children of Heide and Min.

May love lighten your life – blow a kiss to the old wattles on the river for me.

XX

61 Bayswater Road, King's Cross
Sunday, August 1947

Dear Sun
No letter from you and I have so many things to say I don't know how to say them – p'raps I talk too much – but Gray and I had a letter from Melbourne which said Bert was leaving for London on 20th August and that he was paying a visit here first – well so far as I know he hasn't arrived yet – though we both quake a bit every time the door bell rings – if I see him I will try and explain how I feel to him.

Perhaps if I see him he will not want to 'talk things over' but until recently I have not felt I could say in words how I do feel – but I could now – then again, is it worth it? Can one convey to another how one feels? I think one can, but the other has to be a sort of receptionist to understand and in Bert's case sort of accept it as a part of me – which I feel he must have known about somewhere deep down, after having been so close to me for so long.

How close does one really get to another person? God knows but words don't mean a thing. It's what goes on in another part of one where the words don't come from that we act on and in this sense I feel closer to Gray than Bert. Anyway, whatever way I look at it and have looked at it, it seems the best for both of us. But there seems there is no end to personal conflict, no end at all. Gray and I came away for the same reasons – to break something we felt was encircling us. The thing was hard to do but essential for each of us personally. We were both in much the same boat – being with someone we loved and yet resenting it somewhere, fighting against it.

I do not know if we love each other Gray and I – or what love is, there are so many sorts of love – but we are being, at all costs, at the expense of hurting each other, we are trying to be honest which is hard. I think we are both essentially dishonest – with ourselves anyway. Ever since we have been here it has not been easy – not easy at all for either of us for we don't know what we want but by a system of being honest and elimination we hope to find it – or somewhere near to it.

Vonnie, Gray's wife, was over here all the time until a week ago and we were dodging trams and things and finally banged into her. Gray did, one day alone. This, of course, and the turmoil [all] over again and left nothing any more straightened out than it had been. Gray was put in a turmoil mentally for a couple of weeks as to what he wanted, what he'd left and finally [he] rang her up and told her as best he could how he felt – she seemed satisfied and has now gone back to Melb. – poor little thing. We both feel so helpless about it all, but I think it's now up to Bert and Vonnie alone. There seems to have been no let up of this sort of tension since we met. God, why did we have to? But perhaps it only speeded up the inevitable.

Now today Gray has gone to the train to meet Mrs Smith, who has come over for a couple of weeks to stay with her sister, the one Vonnie stayed with while over here.[1] It is all very complicated because the sister doesn't know Mrs S knows Gray is with me – but it's funny really. But Gray will be so glad to see his mother even though he doesn't like her sister. She's like my mother a bit ...

I will have to see McCallum again next week for I've been having the most peculiar thing – an electric shock running through me at intervals during the last few days. It is exactly as though I touched a live wire somewhere – it's a bit nerve racking [sic] to say the least – it may be due to the fact I have got a cold – it may be the ray [treatment]. McCallum will set my mind at rest anyway.

Apart from the above dirge there is not much news ...

Sadie and Sollie are OK. Still we're all gems.

I have been thinking – well, it all started from a dream – that John turned Queen Street into an art gallery.[2] Not a bad idea – one where artists could hang their pictures unframed, unglassed if they wanted to.

---

[1] Susan McKay, Gray's aunt, would purchase two properties for Joy and Gray; Gar in 1948 and Cherry's Lane in 1952.

[2] 48 Queen Street, Melbourne, was the office of Reed & Harris.

This is the curse of galleries, they're so stuffy about having frames and really it is a terrific expense for an artist to frame an exhibition, and drawings have to have glass, too! It'd be a revolution. It could also be quite renumerative to have a gallery, Queen St is quite a good place. All you'd have to do would be [to] take down the partitions and white wash the place. Wouldn't cost anything to set up.

The Nat[ional]. Gallery here has a lovely Tom Roberts – a painting of a stage coach hold up.[3] Have you seen it? I think it the most important Aussie painting of that era – lovely and fresh. Nolan would love it. How is he – still 'at sea?'

... Am posting you [a] self-portrait, an emotional one called *Hodgkins*.[4] Love to you all. It's Matthew Perceval's birthday on the 21st.[5] Swene might like to send him a kiss.

Love to you all and Heide in the morning mist and John with his beret

61 Bayswater Road, King's Cross
(August 1947)

Dear Sun

Just a quick note from the post office ... things have been a bit higgley piggley [sic] as Gray has been expecting his mother over and she has arrived and is staying with her sister in Rose Bay and he has sort of left everything in the air so he can go out with them. Mrs Smith is well but arrangements, letter writing have more or less gone by the board and I have written one to you with a drawing but have not posted it yet. I will do so today.

I have not posted it because I wrote it after I had received news Bert was coming over here and had said a few things re that to you in the letter – but as I had [had] no word from you, I decided something was 'brewing' and thought I'd wait before I posted it to hear the low down –

[3]   Tom Roberts, *Bailed Up*, 1890, Art Gallery of NSW.
[4]   When Hester exhibited her 1947 Sydney drawings at the Melbourne Bookclub Gallery in February 1950 all carried the title *Faces*. It is difficult, given their abstracted, masklike features, to distinguish a self-portrait.
[5]   Matthew Perceval (b.1945) is the son of Mary Boyd and John Perceval.

but evidently not. This news of B helped to make the week higgly piggly [sic] as I have been expecting him to 'walk in' every tick of the clock. I told you in the letter that I wouldn't mind seeing him as I felt more at ease etc. but don't tell Bert that as it may send him flying over and I meant I wouldn't mind seeing him if I had to. Still, enough of that. I'll write another day. Also on the higgly piggly [sic] side I have had a cold and a bad cough and have not been able to sleep for about 3 nights, even with APC Veginins [sic] and God knows what but it seems to be on the improve.

Love to you
Joy

Dear Sun
PS   Another reason I haven't written is lousy pen and paper. Will buy some in town *today* and write a bumper tonight as I'm bursting with news and no time or place at this moment. So if you won't worry I'll give you the low down tonight. Saw McCallum yesterday and will tell you all tonight.

Heide
(August 1947)

Dear Joy
I won't write more than a few words till I hear your bursting news! A maddening thing to say to me ... do try to steer through all the turmoil with some sense of calm and strength. I'm no use at all at low downs and brews but as far as we know Bert is sailing on the *Largs Bay* on the 9th [of September] from Sydney.

He has planned a few days there before he goes and I think will definitely be leaving Melbourne at the end of next week unless some hitch occurs in the shipping arrangements. Bert has not said anything at all to John about seeing you. I don't know more only that if you yourself decided you wanted to see him, you could let me know and John could tell Bert before he goes.* But don't feel this is my wish or I am implying something I do not tell. Your life with Bert has been so long and close as you said and I know that you and Bert alone can make these decisions and sense the human necessity that may still be between you both. But I do want you to find clarification and quietness before you are perhaps confronted with some crisis. I'm sure you should look after yourself in this way and it is my particular wish that you should find all your answers from the reality rather than from nervous tension. I don't help I know but I'm glad you write as you do. I understand all that is part of you. Love now from all that is Heide and the spring coming in the garden.

Haste S

Does Bert know your address? We don't.

* I would not pass any of your thoughts [on] unless you asked me to.

S

Rose Bay
Friday (August/September 1947)

Dear Sun
Got your letter today – was very moved by it because it seemed more than ever to carry your 'scent' with it.

Your description of yourself not eating and getting like the old woman of the steps [sic]. I cannot see the affinity there I'm afraid, – but I do feel an affinity (this is a bit presumptious!) [sic] with you and I visualize you at the breakfast table – and your meagre appetite. And I worry – please eat more, Sun – but it is in keeping, for, I think you are a saint, and saints don't eat much do they? You are, you know. You can never die – nothing can really happen [to] you seeing you're a saint – but I think all saints are sad – very sad – in themselves I think, and that is because not even saints can have everything. Their cross is their sadness like little Jesus's sorrows – and Min is also a saint. All saints have an emblem or carry a flower. You have your hand gently laid on Min's head [while] the other hand holds a flower to your heart – and your eyes and Min's are the same transparent blue and as you stand against the sky, your eyes are like little windows that let the sky shine thru from behind . . .

This last week things have been a bit 'upsy' as Mrs S[mith]'s sister got sick, just as Mrs S was to catch [the] train and go home, so she is still here and will be for a few more days looking after the cot case. It has been a bit of a 'try' as it rather takes the edge off the good her holiday did her, and Gray and I have been at her [Susan McKay's] house staying for last week keeping his Ma company but we are both a bit fed up and hoping auntie gets off her back soon – I suspect she's malingering. Prior to that she took us for many trips down the coast and in the country that we otherwise would not have seen. Consequently neither of us have [sic] done any painting or drawing.

As far as Swene goes I do not care to see him – because for one thing in my mind he is yours till the gods say different and I would not wish to trouble him. Let him drink peacefully at the fountain of Heide while he can – it will stand him in good stead for the rest of his life. When he was born, I wanted to take him to Heide at once so he could get his first view of this world from that green hill. He is a lucky child to get so young, to see and feel the things that aged men hunt after and some-times never find, and whatever happens to him later in life wherever he is, he will have that green hill in his mind's ear and eye to return to – to replenish himself at – that's if he is still a human at that time. By that I mean, if he is not de-atomized. Well, if he is, it will be the same. He'll return perhaps a little quicker to Heide, that's all . . .

There is another point – he is part of life, of a life that is no longer mine – I will never have him again. If in a year Bert wants him – if Bert has another girl, I would prefer you to have him sooner than the girl and I will try to work that way. But if Bert insists well – that's too far ahead. But Swene will grow like a plant. Someone set him on course – he will run true to it no matter what you, I, or Bert do. All we can do is set the compass at birth (I set it in the hills of Heide somewhere) and we can't control the winds that blow – no matter how good the craft, or how sure the compass.

Here are some jingles for a laugh.

penny a look
tuppence a feel
threepence a go on the hairy wheel

I had forgotten them, but I like the 'circus air' of the above.

In 1904
The Scotchies went to war

They had no guns
They used their bums
In 1904

Have to go now, love to trees and all
Joy

Fragment
Rose Bay
(1947)

    ... Barrie[Barrett Reid]'s poems – I
love and wonder how such a young boy can be so wise, [have] such deep
observations and still more how one growing up as he must have in this
between-war world can be so pure and simple. The one starting out 'Out
west of childhood' I thought very lovely and contained so much in a few
words – that is his genius.[1] If you write [to him] I would like one day for
you to say how much his poems are appreciated and that one can't seem
to get enough of them – but somehow to convey to him that someone,
well, that he's a good poet. I think it's always good for an artist or poet
to know that his work is not cast into a complete void, that people
respond ...

Fraser Island Looking West

Out west in childhood
there grows a flower
in the wet years;
sometimes it is red
sometimes it is blue
sometimes it is white with tears.

And in this sandy forest
a ganger takes a part

[1] Reid travelled with Nolan to Fraser Island, off the Queensland coast, in September 1947.

of a sprig with a flower
and wears it in his hat,
wears it all day,
a wave to memory setting him apart.

Fragment
Rose Bay
(August/September 1947)

... In telling anyone, doctors or anyone, they ask me how I feel I say a bit lazy but OK – it is indescribable to say how one can feel one's energy gone somewhere else. I know and feel now without being a hypo that this is the thing I have had for many years, ever since I was a child I have had a mad gland that swelled into lumps etc. and no one took any notice including me. I accepted it as part of me – and remember how much energy I got out in bursts and yet I could never make that hill at Heide and felt a prig if I didn't feel like going to the river and how I didn't know then that it was what I feel now to a lesser degree.

But it's like finding a solution to a crossword puzzle that one has never tried to work out. In fact it's not in my power really to describe [it] and at the moment I don't think I have Hodgkin's in me, but I have the effect or the cause if you know what I mean.

I have only one swollen gland under my arm but I have 1 hr's energy at a time these days and then I feel buggered. I feel how I felt before I went to any doctors but because I didn't know it was a matter of energy I didn't know how to describe it because for an hour, I most probably have more energy than anyone. In fact this energy runs away with me, takes control and I am overjubilant and as though I've had a couple of drinks – I'm tops so to speak. I have no control over it. It wells up and goes out in laughter and activity etc. then as one switches off a light it's gone ... When I have this energy it's as though I have an injection of it and I can't help putting it out. Well enough of this but it's strange how one's system works isn't it? Knowing all this I think I now have less nervous output as I can consciously control that a bit and it makes things easier.

It makes me observe other people's energy, such as Gray's which is different again and I think of yours a lot dear Sun and of you in bed and how unsympathetic I always was really about these things – and it almost frightens me when I think of Bert's nervous energy and I worry for he was the most on edge person I've ever known. Even when he was relaxed he tapped his feet – one feels it must burn out sometime and that it's sort of frightening when I think of it in connection with Bert.

Well, dear Sun, I am sorry [that] I make you my whipping post so to speak – but I am so anxious to get this over and get home and paint and paint. I feel I can now – I somehow feel terribly self-centred but I have also found out something conscious about the way I work artistically or aesthetically and hope a new thing will grow out of it. In fact, mentally a new thing has grown there but I have not been able to paint, worrying about all this.

Sorry to bore and tire you Sunday.

Love to you
Joy

Rose Bay
Saturday, September 1947

Dear Sun
No little letter. How are you – how are your old teeth and ears? Are you alright?

Sydney still has my love – I have or rather we have been staying in Rose Bay overlooking the mighty ocean, a lovely spot as we can see old Ben Buckler's Point from here and [can] see all the boats[1] – ships coming to and fro from the heads. It is quite a quaint village here, more like a country town of one's dreams. [There's] a small shopping centre called Rose Bay North. Quaint old world people – women like [those] one sees at [Point] Lonsdale – from another world.

We are making a garden for the aunt – it is all on the rocky slopes and is great fun and [there's] lovely weather although I have no tan yet as I have not yet been exposed.

Saw the *Largs Bay* go thru the heads, [it] gave me a very queer feeling. I wonder about Bert going over to that alien place and foodless. I hope

---

[1]   Ben Buckler's Point is the tip of the headland at the north end of Bondi Beach.

he took plenty of vitamin pills etc. I did not see him of course, but had an odd feeling all day and saw the boat moored in the morning in the harbour from the front windows of this house and then saw it in the ocean. I cannot say how I feel except that I am like the man who goes to the desert to find God or perhaps Bert is more like that than I. I think that is right perhaps. I don't know – Can anyone ever be honest[?] – I have been searching for honesty and I don't think there is such a thing any more than there can be a democracy. What are these words? What do they mean other than more words? It is rather disillusioning to search and find with a jolt that no such thing exists ...

I am as well as a pike-staff with not a thing wrong and really feel I've waved ta ta to Mr Hodgkin's. How's John? Has hay fever descended yet? Poor thing, I hope not. Write and let me know what you are both up to ...

I have no news, taking life pretty much as it comes – a bit of a new experience for me as prior to now have always gone ½ way to meet it. Still it's relaxing. Have done no drawings.

How are the Boyd brew? Have the boys closed down?[2] Have not seen Guy for a long time – too wide a gap between us – could bridge it, what for? That sounds rude but not meant that way – if you see Mary give her my love.[3] I often think of her, dear little thing she is – I should write to her but tremble from doing so, knowing what a lovely mother she is and just how much importance she places on these things – makes me feel really inadequate.

Mrs Smith was over here and had some lovely talks with her. One thing she said [which] impressed me very much was how when she was a young girl and had three babies and an invalid mother to look after and a none too helpful husband, she used to say over and over to herself 'I am master of my fate, captain of my soul'[4] [and] thinking it made her stick to her guns and carry on through 3 attacks of rheumatic fever, too. She said how she looks back and realizes how she misunderstood the

---

[2]   Hester is referring to Arthur Merric Boyd Pottery at Murrumbeena.

[3]   Mary Boyd (b.1926) painter and potter, married John Perceval in 1944. She exhibited *Hands* (1942, Museum of Modern Art at Heide) at the Contemporary Art Society when she was 15. Her work at Boyd Pottery would involve painting ceramics. In 1978, she married Sidney Nolan. See also Joan Kerr (ed.); *Heritage, The National Women's Art Book*, G & B International Limited, Sydney, 1995.

[4]   The last lines of W E Henley's poem 'Invictus' reads, 'I am the master of my fate/I am the captain of my soul.'

words and how she made a mistake as far as she herself was concerned. 'I shouldn't have done it.' Still I'm sure she, well, it's just as well someone does do it. I s'pose Mary is such a one too, I feel – these are the women that make women a reality. God knows what I'm babbling about.

Love to you and may S[weeney] make you laugh a lot.

Kisses

Joy

Chapter 4

October
December
1947

Rose Bay
Tuesday (October 1947)

Dear Sun
Well, it's happened! Yes, we have a
cottage. We put an add [sic] in [the] Rose Bay local rag for [a] flat or
house in return for part-time services – only one answer – and we got it!

It's at Point Piper, a delightful harbour point which is really a high
hill right on the water's edge and it overlooks on one side Rose Bay
harbour (where the flying boats sleep) and on the other side Double Bay
harbour, and out the back is the ocean in the distance and I can, if I
squeeze, just see my Ben Buckler ...

A woman answered our add and said we can have the 'flat' as she
calls it on top of her garages. It has a bathroom, a balcony, a lounge, a
bedroom and [a] kitchen ... She pays gas and light and [it] is right away
from her house and completely self-contained. It is in her garden and
[we] have our own gate even and we are right above the street in one of
the highest parts of the point and are surrounded by big oak trees and
harbour. It is a 'bougie' district like say Toorak in Melb. and the places
are all surrounded with trees and [a] lovely sort of parklike gardens.

This woman wants Gray to stoke her furnace at 7 am, 1 pm and 7 pm
and clean the courtyard which is made of old handmade bricks and has
a big fig tree slap bang in the middle of it. The place itself could (the flat
I mean) really be called a loft – it has a gas bath heater put in and from
every window a view of trees and water – idyllic – we get it furnished ...
it has a lovely old mahogany couch and is very comfortable. We get it
rent free in exchange for Gray stoking her furnace – it really amounts to
2 hrs' work a day with the courtyard – we are mad with excitement. We
have our own little garden, all private too ... We move in on Thursday.
Tell John from now on to post to Rose Bay Post Office – we are so glad
to get out of the city – and the rush. Enough of That.

How is the abscess? I do hope by this time the wretched thing is fixed
for good – fancy being sick when you have 5 brand new Siamese!! Min
will be by now I s'pose quite an accustomed mother – the garden sounds
lovely now with spring there. My love to the apple and pear blossoms
and love to John and S. I'll write no more now dear Sun as am still too
excited – think of all the paintings that will be done now.

Do get better Sun and enjoy the sunshine and the smell of spring.

Love to you all

Point Piper
(September/October 1947)

Dear Sun

Just a quickie as it's about 5.30 pm
and [I] am just about to sit down and eat a lovely juicy steak (does that
make you turn up your nose?) and have just had a lovely glass of claret.
They make nice claret over here, [it's from] a firm named Lindemans.

Had a letter and photo from Nolan – we really are funny. He writes
me the glories of Qld. I write him the glories of NSW.

This is what I saw in an ABC book called *Talk* which is a condensa-
tion of ABC talks. Letters to the Editor column, Australian Poetry –
Heading – Dear Ed.

In his rather narrow survey of Contemporary Australian Poetry, which he
all but restricts to *Jindyworobak* and *Meanjin* – Rex Ingamells refers to
Judith Wright as a *Meanjin* 'discovery'. I do not know in what sense Miss
Wright may be regarded as a 'discovery'. A graduate of Sydney University,
she contributed to under-graduate magazines, also to *Southerly* before
spending some years abroad after which she became a contributor to
Meanjin and renewed her connection with *Southerly*. She is well known
here. signed R G Howarth Editor of *Southerly*[1]

It interested me as it gave me a brief but very brief, outline of her life.
By the way, Robin Boyd has written a book called *Victorian Model* about
the history of a house from the Victorian day[s] upwards.[2] I believe it's
very good.

---

[1] *Talk: the Australian listener's national monthly magazine*, ABC, Sydney, September/
October, 1947.

[2] Robin Boyd, *Victorian Modern: one hundred and eleven years of modern architecture*,
Architecture Students Society of the Royal Victorian Institute of Architects, Melbourne,
1947.

... Let's know what's news of Peter Cowan.[3] I have not heard a thing and has he written more? I liked him very much.

... We are painting the woodwork at this place with watercolor – looks lovely. Nice matte surface. How long we will be here God knows – but it's nice. I have nothing to do and would love a lend of one or two books if you could manage it. I'll send back as soon as I've read [them]. Gray, who is now called by me 'Smoky Stover', is stoking his furnace ...

I won't forget John's tie. But it's a Xmas pressy so he'll have to wait. The ties we decided may not sell and so we abandoned that project – just another! But it's fun and I'm fat as butter really. I'm 9 [stone] 5 [lb] so that's up the doctors – I have not seen them for a while and really will do it before the month's out – Lovell is supposed to be *the* top notch here I found out.

The people in the house, the Wentworths, their son has a station 150 miles from anywhere and he has a daughter of 6 who fell from a horse onto the stump of a tree and would have died except that Lovell flew up there – ordered a special train 4 am in the morning and operated at 8.30 pm and although the little thing is not through the mill yet it looks as though she may live – minus a spleen and God knows what else.

Sun, I must go now and tell me of Peter Cowan and love to you and love to John and his 'come on dogs', 'get out of that, ducks'. Have you heard of Bert? Love especially to dear Min of the slanting eyes

Untitled

Two children dreamt
of long ago
and stood before a darkening tree
not know when who became
or where she dwelt.
Nightfall fell –
and long ago was now
and trees were stone
you and I were there

[3] Perth writer Peter Cowan (b.1914) met both Hester and Tucker through *Angry Penguins* between 1943 and 1946. He was also a friend of the Reeds. See also Chapter 6, p. 162.

we cried – remember when?
for then was now
and we were dead
the woods were dark.
the children stood
hand in hand
and fear was there
for not knowing, who became
or where she went –
but seeing eyelids close
and nightfall come
seeing through the ages then
eyelids close one by one.
and standing there
for you and I to see
before we parted.

murderous tree
outstretched its limbs
the tree asking, in the dark
for caresses
that were more of mine
than yours – and time
was there, Elizabeth too
and we were children
standing. dreaming,
of summer days to come
and years to pass.

The poem on the back I don't know whether good or bad is, in a veiled [way] (to me anyway) about Bert and [me] but I don't understand it. I only wrote it as it came to me, as far as I know it's from the 'core' as you put it – I would like Bert to see it but perhaps he'd respond in the wrong way. I don't know so I'll not send it to him. Somehow I think there is nothing I can really say he could understand in the way I say it or in the terms I mean it to be read at the moment. I understand that and I feel I know what he would analyse it for and I think it's better I don't make any further contact with him while he's sad – I don't want to hurt him more – I think at night, or on grey days, [about] what I did to him and I want to cry but I could never be with him again and I only wish I could not have hurt him but still I s'pose things have got to work out for him one day. I hope they will. Poor Bert, I feel as though I have smacked a child who was too small to know why it was smacked.

Still, I really believe good comes from all conflict. Though if conflict can be avoided, better still but when it comes – one has to go thru it and always there is something to live for better than one ever dreamed was there. This we believe. Everyone *has* to or we'd not bother living. My glands are almost vanished on my neck though my throat is still dry and I have crops of lovely pimples which are due to [a] change of water and diet I think. I feel well and hope you all are. Love to you and kisses. I love hearing from you. Your letters are like being near you and I see your lovely mouth curl in the corners as you speak and your birdlike soft neck on your shoulders again.

Goodnight and love to John – and S

Fragment
Point Piper
(c. October 1947)

... I have thought of Heide for the last three nights – the last thing that flitted through my head has been Heide and then I fell to sleep.

I see Heide as a flat pattern like a sampler, with all the fields, the house, the road and river standing perpendicular and flat, not hilly as it is, but greener in a dry way, as though one has one's back to it and was looking at the reflection in a small hand mirror. It stands up like this, neatly before my closed eyes and in the green fields near the veg garden are your eyes, Sun – and John's hair is always in the gum tree with his profile facing riverward – but it is all flat and arranged in my mirror and your eyes and John's hair look as patternlike as the rest of it. It all fits in like an unruffled jigsaw puzzle, still, green, and very beautiful.

And I know deeply that I'll always hold this little mirror before me, for it is mine and my Heide and it is probably one of the very few things one can ever own, is one's own personal mirror, and there is unfortunately no one in the world who can even glimpse into even a corner of it and see its captured beauty – it is not say of the beauty of my soul or anything. It's an 'internal' external ... It's something from outside that has been grafted, immovable, onto my 'inside' ...

It is a funny thing that every time I look into my mirror it is always the same, not a leaf or an eye bats within the pattern. If I could paint I would like to paint it but I'm afraid it's the sort of picture that I myself could not paint. If we get a place somewhere I may get a shot at it.

[We] were at Bondi again yesterday. I was swept off my feet with the current a couple of times – and the color there is like no other sea or sky in the world. It's different to every other beach in Sydney. And I gaze at my Ben Buckler with far off sea eyes and try to picture the man who had such a lovely name. I do not know ... whether it's the beauty of Ben Buckler's point and its jaggard [sic] rocks gaping seawards or whether it's the romance of the man himself – it's both.

Point Piper, Sydney
Monday (10 November 1947)

Dear Sun
                    I received the books Friday –
Lovely! have had nothing to read. Am wallowing in them – Have read *Ariane*.[1] I liked it although after reading *Pity for Women*[2] by that French bloke whom I forget his name, it seems to fall short or seem too familiar to me – there have been a lot of books written by the French in that manner. Nevertheless I devoured it and enjoyed it.

The Kokoska [sic] [I] enjoyed getting very much as I'd glanced at it longingly on the stalls over here – surprised to see his diversity and his very obvious influences ... I had never seen more than 2 or 3 of his works and I must say I was surprised.[3] He is a very beautiful painter, at times, a very experimental and inconsistent one for his age – I am surprised that after living his life there are so few paintings which show

---

[1] *Ariane*, author & publishing details unknown.
[2] Henri de Montherlant, *Pity for Women*, translated by Thomas McGreevy and John Redker, Alfred Knopf, New York, 1938.
[3] Oskar Kokoschka (1886–1980) Austrian expressionist painter and graphic artist.

the *real* Kokoska if one can say such a thing – or rather I should say the *mature* Kokoska. I feel he still has to know himself – in spite of what he says in his prose – at least he is honest in his painting but somehow I feel as far as a mature artist goes he has fallen short somewhere except for one or two exceptions . . .

I have not really been up to scratch. Am prego and have been vomiting a fair bit and have had a very enervated feeling. I went to the Women's Hospital the other day to see about an abortion. I think it can be arranged on account of Hodgkin's but I have to go back on Thursday and see the medical superintendent as he has the final say. Today I had an appointment with Doctor Ham at Prince Alfred [Hospital] which is about nearly an hour's run from here, to see if I have to have any more ray just yet – and am seeing McCallum on Wednesday [to] see if I can kid him into giving a note to the Women's to have my phelopian [sic] tubes cut at the same time as no matter what precautions I seem to take none seem to work – still heigho all in a day's work but I know I'll feel better in health when I'm rid of the extra strain it puts on me.

I feel as though I've been an awful hypocondiac [sic] but I have really not felt well for about three weeks. I have not told McCallum about the Women's as he's not the easiest man to talk to – I think he thinks anything like that carries some sort of stigma. He'd rather avoid such grovellings. Still I shall be able to ask him on Wed. as I can't go on getting prego – it's really fantastic. Enough of this.

Am living a most sober quiet life retiring early and rising at about 7 am and seeing the best of the day over the 'arbour . . .

I have [done] no drawing or poems as I haven't been A1 although I am not really sick if you understand.

Gray is a very wise person – naturally so and not in what one would say a 'book' way but one of the wisest people I have met and one of the strangest personalities – really he does me a lot of good. There is always a laugh – and I feel in some way his sickness is an intrinsic part of his personality – for when he is sick his whole personality is carried to the complete extreme of what it is in everyday life – it is a strange thing.

John tells me his office is gone – or practically. Miss Uniake is and somehow now I suppose in one way you feel you are back where you started. Only one is never really that because of the years between. That is the sad thing – I really think living is a very sad thing all together.

I am being plagued by mosquito[e]s . . . and after trying everything I think I'll have to resort to a mosquito net over my bed – I have had bung eyes and swollen arms till I'm 'fair fed up'.

This letter is full of groans but after this week of hospitals and wot is over will feel more cheerful but really am not as glum as I sound as I still love and adore Sydney.

Saw a good picture the other day. Not really a great one but a good pro-Semite theme called *Crossfire*[3] which was an excellent study of 5 or 6 modern men and it showed all of them were accepted as normal and to our way of thinking normal but showing them all just a little off key so that they all looked completely abnormal. There were some excellent sequences in it and some good close ups and no music which made the film unusual – but as I say it was very good – but not great although it touched in a couple of places on an extremely high and new sort of level of analysis via the camera.

Well, Sun I must be off. Thank you for the book and love to you all – I've not heard of Nolan – Let's know how the wanderer fairs [sic] and I s'pose your wild garden is heavy with the scent of magnolia – and the frangipani over here is just starting to shed their embalming rags and a green shoot out of the odd stem shows here and there – the figs and passionfruit are not yet ripe – apricots are in here – the place smells good with fruit and flowers.

> Love
> Joy

> Point Piper
> Wednesday, 12 November 1947

Dear Sun

Received a very lovely letter from John and another one from you and a card from Nolan of Circular Quay Brisbane with a big X marking his embarking spot for his further roamings. Really I felt like a princess – 3 letters in one day!

We went to a crazy sort of party last night at Gray's aunt's place. We

---

[3] *Crossfire* (1947), directed by Edward Dmytryk, with Robert Ryan, Robert Mitchum and Gloria Graeme.

mix so little with people and [are] so closed up in our own small but happy life that I'm beginning to believe we'll never be able to 'make' the world again. People somehow look like marionettes, not people in trams but people in rooms that we meet occasionally – they seem suspended on nervous strings and have an incoherence about them. Nothing seems to tie up in any way, with us or with them or with the things we think about. The few people one has a couple of words to say [to] – the grocer, or a man with a dog on the beach, or a tram conductress – all fleeting but lovely as they seem to fit into the stream but when placed in a room with persons, they seem so unrelaxed and they glitter like metal in the sun.

It was a strange night, not really a party – but a party to us, the 2 of us, his aunt and 3 of her friends of various sexes – we both decided our retreat from the land of the living, unplanned and unconscious as it has been, is a complete one. Some wire seems to have been cut – it does not worry me as I am more relaxed than I have ever been in my life – even for a moment. It's rather nice, I feel a bit like a tree that is planted somewhere and people pass and I am still there when they've gone . . .

I was very harsh with *Ariane*. I really enjoyed it, and its subtlety lasts.

I am reading *The Ballad and the Source*.[1] Only a few pages [so far] and am enjoying it very much as she has some of the real qualities of childhood put down – those fleeting, gossamer ones that are so hard to pin in words.

Well, I went to the Prince Alfred and saw a Doctor Flecker or something. Apparently I'm not now one of Doctor Ham's patients – he could tell naught as I had to have X rays taken – had 2 chest X rays and have to go back on Friday to hear [the] results and whether [I] have to have more deep ray. Went to McCallum today and told him about the Women's Hospital expedition and their finding and I really must say he was the sweetest he's ever been and the easiest to talk to, so I mentioned about the abortion and being sterilized and he said, 'Oh but Doctor Lovell and I are quite agreed on that – I'll get you a note to the superintendent of the Women's re. same'. So apparently he and Lovell had talked that over – but he said of course it was not his place to suggest such a thing and was glad I had brought it up. So [I] am going to have both done but have to wait till Friday to see the 'ray' doctor to see

[1] Rosamond Lehmann, *The Ballad and the Source*, Collins, London, 1944.

whether I am have to 'ray' first (if I have to) or go [to] the Women's first or have Women's first and ray after.

Then I have to see McCallum on Monday and tell [him] what ray man says and then McCallum will see the Women's and get me in there for that time. So it's all a bit in the air but there is a marvellous relief to me to know I am getting it [the sterilisation] done – and old McCallum was so sweet and nice about it, and helpful.

I have a feeling that I will have to pay something for my next ray treatments if I have to have them, as the other X ray people (the chest ones) said I only got the ray free as I was an 'inpatient' when I started the treatment and all outpatients have to pay and next time I will be an outpatient although I don't think actually it will amount to very much, as they are pretty reasonable with the X rays. This time I got 2 for 15/- which is very good.

I don't think I'll have to pay at the Women's as I'll be an 'inpatient' there and inpatients are covered by the government subsidy – well enough of all this rigmarole. It takes a hell of a lot of time at these places, there is so much waiting. Hospitals are notorious for that side of things as you know and by the time I get from Point Piper to Newtown [it's] nearly 1 hr's journey as transport doesn't link up – a trip there takes most of the day.

I always seem to write extremely selfish letters all about myself – think of it, 5 pages of 'me' – and having exhausted [the] 'me' side of the picture I can't think of much more news.

Except that we got £2 worth [of] 40 sheets of cardboard strawboard to paint on – the first we've had since [we] have been over here. [We've] been, or rather Gray has [been] painting on all sorts of scraps – even an old glass photo we found in a hundred-year-old house but we managed to scrounge quite [a] bit here and there and when we found (quite by chance) we could get the strawboard we went mad and got 40 sheets – never to be stuck for something again. So it looks as though I may be using some myself very soon – after the hospitals and rot are over – it's lovely to look at it all.

Sunday dear, I *must* stop this ramble and my love to you all

Joy

Point Piper
(November 1947)

Dear Sun and John

... I still have not heard from the Women's. Expect to this week and am seeing McCallum tomorrow. I have not really been particularly well although not too bad but I have not been able to keep my blessed food down for a week and I think this must be physiological, to do with the worry of the prego business – nevertheless worse things happen at sea so –

Gray's wife Vonnie is after a divorce and God knows what and she has written to his aunt. He is also a bit out of sorts as the wretched maintenance business will come up again I s'pose – but he does not earn enough to pay it so they can't get blood from a stone and also he is not well enough to do a job 8 hrs a day so we are hoping that she wants the divorce so she can marry again and that would settle all. Whilst he earns enough for us both to pool evenly and we have no rent, there is never any over so she really can't do much I s'pose. Nevertheless life seems to get a bit complicated now and then.

He seems well and has not had a fit for over a month now – but it is a funny thing with epilepsy how close one can sail to the wind of having one and ... all the sym[p]toms of one coming on for a couple of days and then the depression passes and nothing happens. One feels very conscious of the hidden strings that make up a human system. And just how close every one of us are to some sort of borderline or other. It's really a tightrope sort of business, living – for anyone. We all, even the most balanced (and perhaps the most balanced ones), come closer to borderlines than anyone ...

I was very glad to receive the cheque. Thank you both. The extra £5 will be a great help as one has to supply one's own cotton wool at the Women's and a few extras like that.

... Well, dear Sun and John and S, goodbye now and all sleep well and visit those lost cities of space and time and come back refreshed – dream well.

Love to all
Joy

Point Piper
(November 1947)

Dear Sun

Just a very quick note which I have been intending to write for days. I had two lovely long letters from Nolan describing the tropic[al] haze and the odd types on the wanderer and how it all reminded him of the East and then with a start realized that it is Aussie and nothing to do with the East at all but something to do with us.

I went to the Women's Hospital and they are going to admit me 'for consideration' which I don't quite know what that means so I will have to see McCallum and see if he can enlighten me. They said they'd write and let me know a date to go in, in 5 or 10 days time – what 'for consideration' means I don't know. I asked them if that meant they'd do the job and they said they'd consider it. It's all a bit of a worry because if I do go in and they don't do it, it may be too late to have it done elsewhere – but am seeing McCallum on Monday to see what he says. I wish it was over.

We have been painting a few Xmas cards and made quite a little bit of extra cash.

We have had Melbourne weather here for the last 3 days, [it's] been quite cold and wet and we have [had] an electricity strike and have been [living] by candlelight ...

The rain has fallen [on] the beautiful magnolias here – are yours out yet?

Have done quite a bit of drawing but want to get some paint and use the lovely cardboards we have – drawing no longer satisfies me – but when I draw now I try to visulize [sic] what it would be if it was paint. We have just bought an excellent book on colors and grounds.[1] Very easy to get recipes but of course one has to get ingredients first so I s'pose [it] will be a while before anything is done.

Sunday, I'd love to write more. The CAS exhibition was here and I missed it. I believe there was only *one* painting from Melb. What happened? Didn't the CAS in Melb have an ex[hibition]?

In terrible haste
Joy
and love to all

[1] A ground is the underlying surface on which a painting is made.

Crown Street Women's Hospital
Wednesday, 3 December 1947

Dear Sun and John
Thank you very much for your
telegram and ringing McCallum. It was good as McCallum rang the
superintendent of the W H and as a result I am in here. I was worried a
bit as McCallum had written to the superintendent but I struck a nurse
with a bit of a crab and she just crossed superintendent off the envelope
and sent me to outpatients, when the letter should have gone to the
superintendent in the first place.

Well, being here and seeing McC before I came in this morning it
seems as though everything will be OK. I have not seen the doctor here
yet but McC told me they may or may not do both operations at once.
Sometimes they wait a while and do the sterility one later, although not
always. Anyway it is very good for you to bother about me – but I don't
know what I would have done without you both.

They have not told me when I will be done but I am in a bed right
outside the labour ward and then afterwards they move you down somewhere else, so I s'pose it won't be long and it will be a terrific worry and
strain over when it is. I have spent the afternoon sleeping and I feel
pretty good now.

I have scrawled 2 or 3 poems which I left at home which I intended
to post you. I have *Wolf Solent* in here with me.[1]

It is still wet and humid over here, quite tropical really and this is just
a short letter to let you know how things stand and my love to you both.

[pencil drawing of pregnant woman lying on bed covered with sheet]

I look along a long line of beds with women in various stages of prego.

---

[1] John Cowper Powys, *Wolf Solent*, Jonathan Cape, London, 1929.

Crown Street Women's Hospital
Saturday, 13 December 1947

Dear Sun and John

Thank you for your telegram. Since Gray answered it I have seen Dr McGrath who is Dr Chesterman's offsider and he told me yesterday they will do me next week. Thank God! I am so pleased now I know that they are actually going to do me. I was so upset last night thinking and worrying about what to do if I had to have it if they let me go on too long.

I didn't sleep all night. Apart from worrying there's a great big fat bitch here who snores like a bull. Still it's all OK now so I s'pose they'll do me on Tues. or Wed. Dr Chesterman, who looks like a Methodist parson, is going to do it. He's a woman's specialist, so I feel quite happy about all that.

It is very hard for me to write in this ward as the tarts are all cackling about their operations and one hears bits here and there and it's quite disconcerting. Nevertheless will write to you tomorrow or Monday when they quieten down a bit.

Am sending a cutting from the very top of the front page of today's *Daily Telegraph* – might make you laugh a bit.

Also, David Boyd is back from Tahiti or New Mear [sic] or wherever he was. A bit sadder I believe altho' I have not seen him. Alannah tells me he looks a bit grey on it and is going to Melb. for Xmas.

There is a Henry Moore exhibition of sculpture on here and Gray went to see it but could not get in, I believe there was a huge crowd. I would like to see it – it may still be on when I come out – I s'pose I'll be here over Xmas and wot.

Also Drysdale and Donald Friend have a Xmas exhibition on with a few others – Alannah tells me [Paul] Haefliger[1] now paints little Nolans – God, they're a crew!

> ... Will write later. Love to you all
> Joy

---

[1]   Paul Haefliger (1914–82), was a painter and a critic for the *Sydney Morning Herald*. He was married to Jean Bellette (1909–91).

Joy has received a hamper from
Sunday and John.
Point Piper
26 December 1947

Dear Sun and John

What can I say? Except that it was
all so lovely and that I blubbed profusely. I couldn't help it, but I wished
you had both been there to see the pleasure I got. But I was with you
both so much when I opened it.

Alannah, who was spending her first Xmas without her mother and is
so alone (and underneath a frightened but brave little girl) spent Xmas
Eve and day with us and she was telling us that the only letter she kept
that was written her, after her mother died, was from you, dear John –
and we talked of things past and you both, and Gray had his yellow shirt
on so I hope you felt the rays of our warmth coming to you.

I must say that I have never had a Xmas surprise like that, not even
when I was a little girl and [had] a Xmas stocking full of goodies, as there
was always a 'scene' or something to take the edge off Daddy Xmas but I
felt like Alice in Wonderland when she first saw Wonderland only I felt
so much better as I smelt the lavender and the love and the loveliness
you both sent with it I just can't tell you, that's all. Because I felt like
things Eliot talks about in *Little Gidding*[1] about 'beginnings and ends' and
there being only 'beginnings and ends' joined together – making no
beginning or end – and that is how I felt. Because the day before I had
felt sick and was inclined to give in to seeing things in 'parts' ... and
wishing for ends and not wanting them and then Xmas morning I knew
there was no end or beginning, but one long stream of loveliness, that I
was lucky as I had always 'known' and always smelt that Heide lavender
since before I did, and what's more, is there any completion more than
this? and I knew there wasn't, as I had known, but had forgotten.

I feel very well now, back to normal although my glands are still a bit
swollen due to the 'change' over in the system, the tax on the system of
readjustment to not being geared up for bearing babies – did I tell you

[1] 'What we call the beginning is often the end
And to make an end is to make a beginning.
The end is where we start from.'
T S Eliot, 'Little Gidding', *The Four Quartets*, Faber & Faber, London, 1944.

they were twin males? No wonder I felt a bit on kus [?] during those 3 mths.

But it is of you Sun and John I think and the frock, which is like a dream of a young girl in the Luxemb[o]urg [Gardens], fits to perfection – and I smell now a bit like you, Sun, and it's lovely because I smell a bit like Min too.

And the Lear is wonderful.[2] I do hope you read him before sending it to me as I think his particular and personal 'message' or philosophy is closer to us than Plato or Marx. Such as his nonsense cookery. 'Serve up in a clean dish, and throw whole lot out of window as fast as possible.' And the 'History of the Seven families of the lake of Pipple-Popple' which starts off, 'In former days, that is to say once upon a time, there lived in the land of Granblanche, seven Families' etc. . . . ' The names of these places you have probably heard of, and you only have *not* to look in your Geography books to find out all about them.' What could be better than that?

I have hogged half the cake myself! but am rationing the next and last half to last right over New Year.

How did you discover Mrs Burton again? Mrs Burton with the gammy leg of Jolimont Rd, Jolimont. She sits at my bedside and will forever more. I have never had a *real live doll* in my life, although I knew 'Gethie' we had our differences owing to being friendly and loving one another but being different nationalities, but Mrs Burton comes to me in the 'bat-crossed' hour and I see her earrings pearly in the night and she knows that I know we belong together forever more and no one is allowed to touch her. I love the lines around her eyes which she always had, of course.[3]

And dear vain Gray is vainer than ever and cheekier than ever as he prances before the mirror in supreme self-satisfaction. He has a particular way he winks at himself in the mirror but since the event of the yellow shirt he kisses the mirror. No, this is not a lie! and he does it when there's no one looking which is worse! and today is the first fine day and we are out to 'show off'. G has even developed a 'Point Piper' accent and 'all that, you know'!

[2] Edward Lear, *The Complete Nonsense of Edward Lear*, Faber & Faber, London, 1947.

[3] Gethie (Gethsemane) was Sunday's doll. Faceless and stuffed with lavender from the Heide garden, it usually sat on Sunday's bed, like a surrealist personage, where it was greeted by visitors. Hester did a series of drawings with Gethsemane as their subject (c.1946). See Janine Burke, *Joy Hester*, pp. 91–5. Mrs Burton was another doll of Sunday's.

No, Sun and John, I will say no more. (Tell Swene I have put his letter in my 'Heide' letter box for safe keeping.) I can say no more except I will send back the lovely hamper packed with drawings before long.

Love to you all and Min and give the ducks a special oily lettuce leaf from me

Joy XX

Heide
Sunday night (December 1947)

Dear Joy
You can't imagine how happy we were when your parcel arrived as somehow it had missed the Christmas mail and so we had missed you on Christmas morning. But now everything is here with us and my belt and all John's lovely ties look so gay and just as they should be for Christmas and I don't know if I look as beautiful in my belt as John does in his tie against his white shirt. They are really a wonderful discovery.

Thank you, Joybells, for making things for us when you have been feeling so ill and the beautiful card with Father Christmas's trousers coming off as Swene said. He loves the penny bag. Already it has become one of those much loved small objects that he clutches and screws up in a hot fist when he goes to bed and pennies have become important since he heard about the pieman saying unto Simon, show me first your penny.

I have been wearing your belt all day and thinking of you and how you are. I told Gray not to let you write but ask[ed] him to let me know soon how you are as it does seem a long time since we had news of you. I have not written because I wanted you to be quiet and not feel you had to answer letters or questions. We had a happy Christmas day with Swene and were all completely exhausted when it came to an end.

I put a big Father Christmas in Sweeney's window while he was asleep made out of his red dressing gown and a stuffed head with a long beard of cotton wool and cherries for his eyes, then, in the morning in the middle of all the unwrappings, we gave him a canvas swimming pool (about the size of a double bed) to put in the orchard. It seemed a great success and Swene promptly jumped into it with all his clothes on! I made a tree for the dinner table and filled it with small candles and tinsel[l]y things and we had crackers which were full of little Jap toys which Swene liked almost best of all, [e]specially the blow balloons which I'm sure only the Japs could make and we threw them onto the tree and I felt you were with us, and laughing, and I kept two balloons for you.

Swene has been the most beautiful of Christmas boys. I don't need poetry in books anymore and sometimes I think how perhaps the young poets are only searching back to their childhood to say again the same things that nobody noticed when they were little. Swene tells me everything about the world that I want to know. Why do we live so long, I wonder.

This is only a note quickly for John to take in the morning. I found your address on the brown paper your pressies came in and so I am using it as it would be silly not to. Your mother did ask me once if I knew where you were but I told her you had never given me the same thing again as indeed it is the truth, which reminds me that your mother told me that you were staying on a farm on the river, so you must let me know when you come back and tell me any other tales you pass on so that I can meet the situation when it arises if it should.

I have asked the Murru[m]beenas [the Boyds] to come and have a glass of wine on New Year's Eve and I hope they will come and Mary [Boyd] and Matthew [Perceval] are coming tomorrow to stay a night and have a swim with us in Swene's pool. We will drink to you at midnight and send wishes from Heide. I am sorry that Gethsemane did not send you her love at Christmas time. She went to sleep I think but she has looked lovely since Christmas in a white thistledown hat that John gave me with long streamers of blue ribbon round her hair but still asleep in my rocking chair. I have missed you a great deal and have felt close to you through the weeks [and] I will be glad to know how you are and if you are returning to hospital. I do wish I could make everything happy and comfortable for you and take your anxiety away. Do take heart. It will all pass and you will be well again.

Did you hear from Nolan at Christmas time[?] He is with Barrie [Reid] now but I think is gradually coming southwards. Letters have been scattered and addresses have been so remote over the last month

(left)
13. Joy breastfeeding Sweeney at Heide, 1945.

(below)
14. Sunday holding Sweeney.

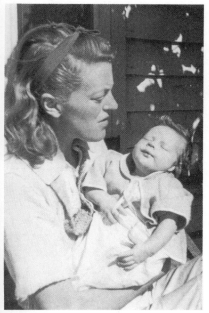

Tuesday.

Dear Sun — Well — the planes' gone and
I've gone, but here I am only half
of me, smelling my lavender bag — I
spose you & John feel the same way
for it was only today of course (I
suppose you did the same) waved
frantically until plane vanished into
the air, and then the inevitable
flatness! — How excitedly we tore
down to mascot — there are no
trams there or so we were told
only one bus to Dolls point a day
so off in a taxi — there was a
tram but we'd never have made it —
bundle out of taxi — we're got ½ hr.
plop! smack bang into another
world of those things and flat
ground and hangers with big shiny
steel beetles poised, with their noses
heavenward as though their not really
shut up but almost looking as they
know its only an interim and off
into their heavens — big notices with
such arrousing statements as "wing
your way with A.N.A" — another curious
little placard about "company takes no responsibility for such things as public disturbance,
tempest, cyclone, or an act of god": isn't
that queer? or an act of god as though
they believe that god may even

(far left)
15. Joy Hester letter addressed to Sunday Reed, July 1947.

(above)
16. Gray Smith, Melbourne, 1948.

(left)
17. Sweeney in Paris, 1948.

(left)
18. John, Sweeney and Sunday at Open Country, 1947.

(above)
19. Gray, John, Joy and Sweeney at Heide, 1948.

(above)
20. Gar, Haley's Gully Road, Hurstbridge.

(right)
21. Joy on the verandah at Gar, c. 1950.

(above)
22. Sunday, Sweeney, John and Siamese cats, c. 1950.

(left)
23. Barrett Reid.

24. Mary Boyd with Matthew Perceval, Sunday and Sweeney, c. 1947.

and I don't think he knows you have been in hospital. We hoped that he and Barrie might walk home, but Barrie is trying to start a bookshop for Mary Martin and Max [Harris] and he is quietly waiting for customers. He sent me a blue hair ribbon for Christmas which I thought was lovely but no new poems to send you as yet.

I expect Nolan will just greet you one day and he talks now of staying in Sydney for a while. You have won him over, I expect, with all your long exchange of letters about the north and Sydney. Anyway it is almost 'the wet' now in Queensland, and so unless he settles in Brisbane I don't think he will be able to move around anymore.

Goodnight and our love to you, New Year love and greetings to you and to Gray. I do wish we were together but it is so, isn't it. Forgive the cake which Swene helped me ice. We only had enough marzipan to make a patch in the centre and couldn't find enough sugar to do the sides and then the crumbs fell all over it and we only had cherry juice to write your name in and I was afraid it wouldn't last the journey and that it anyway wasn't much of a cake but Swene and I had lots of good licks and things and we made a terrific mess bet[w]een us and somehow it has been a Joy Christmas and it still is with our thoughts around and about you.

S XXX

Did Gray collect our note at the post office?

Chapter 5

January
March
1948

Point Piper
(January 1948)

Dear Sun

Just a short note – not much news –
still having treatment and have felt surprisingly well, bit off now and
again but not much ...

Nolan, Gray and I ... went to see *Miracle on 34th Street* the other
night and liked it very much. A cheerful nice happy little picture and
we all came out feeling good.

Nolan is looking around for the most tremendous piece of board. It
will be hard to say whether it's a painting or a mural when finished – so
far he has not succeeded in getting one.

We are still after a cott[age] in the country. No luck so far.

Nolan says Sam and Moya are there with you in the weekend.[1] I
s'pose it is very queer to have them both there at Heide again after so
much has passed. I hope they are not too sad after all the press
comments. It must be very hard for Sam. There's so much of a battle
always in his world.

I do hope you and John are getting through all in your world alright
and that the old Yarra is flowing through the bottom of your garden and
that the willows are just gently trailing their fingers in the water – the
warmth of dear old Sydney to you.

PS Have been reading a lot of Banjo Paterson songs. Am thinking
about their realness and their straightforwardness and simplicity. He
makes Henry Lawson look very tied up and nervous. I feel that perhaps
Paterson knew something when he told the city folk to go bush and
perhaps they will see and know something that Clancy saw and what

---

[1] Sam Atyeo and Moya Dyring, married from 1941–50, were visiting Melbourne after
settling in France. In the early 1930s Atyeo had been an exceptionally talented young
artist experimenting with abstraction, in painting with architecture and design. In 1934
Dyring's first solo exhibition of paintings at Riddell's Gallery was modernist and Cezanne-
influenced. Though Atyeo (1911–90) and Dyring (1908–67) were students at the National
Gallery School in the early 1930s, they were regular visitors to George Bell's studio school.
Dyring's *Portrait of Sunday* (c.1934, Museum of Modern Art at Heide) was probably
painted while Sunday was briefly a student there. By 1948, Atyeo had given up painting
and was attached to the Australian Embassy in Paris. While his appointment as Australian
representative to the United Nations Balkans Commission did raise questions in
Parliament in 1949, press comments in 1948 are unknown.

Clancy knew. Yes, Clancy has become a very real Australian to me. I'm surprised at myself not being more cordial to him before.

Point Piper
(January/February 1948)

Dearest Sun and John
A very short note as we are moving.
I thought it best to let you know not to post to Wentworth Street [Point Piper] – we are moving because Gray has been sick and is in hospital. He fell out of a car and had a pretty bad day of fits afterward and was unconscious for the whole day and is in hospital down at La Perouse.[1] He would have written you but the week following Xmas he had an awful tummy ache – gripes really – and I think it was only nerves but it incapacitated him. Everything turns out for the best. They've X ray[e]d his head in hospital and may get on to some treatment that will do him good. Do not mention this in Melb. as we don't want to worry his mother.

I am so glad Nolan was here to help me which sounds selfish but he was and is a great help and [I] feel I couldn't have managed without him and of course I would have been able to but it would have been harder. Barrie and Charles [Osborne] are here and we all went to see Manly [beach] and had tea and the boys (not Nolan or I) hogged themselves on sweets and pink ice cream and waffles.[2]

I had a lovely talk with Barrie, short as it was – a lot of what he is came through to me and I'll leave that for a later date. There is only one thing I wish to tell you both [and that] is that what I was saying once in a letter to you about seeds being sown etc., Barrie is a result of this. He told me of his love for you both and just what a strength you both have

---

[1] When Gray became ill and their landlady discovered he suffered from epilepsy, she asked them to leave. They went to stay with Susan McKay, Gray's aunt, at Rose Bay.

[2] Barrett Reid and Charles Osborne (b.1927) had hitched from Brisbane to Sydney. Between 1947 and 1949, Osborne managed the Ballad Bookshop, which Reid owned. He was also involved with *Barjai*, the precocious art and literary journal started by Reid. See also Charles Osborne, *Giving it Away, Memoirs of an Uncivil Servant*, Secker & Warburg, London, 1986.

been to him and how he just had to get to Heide for a couple of days to renew this strength, or not renew it, but in some way to contact it again and these are things you have done, John and Sun. This does not adequately convey in any way what Barrie in his own beautiful way conveyed to me of his feelings for you both but you see the seeds grow and flower.

Nolan is well and tan and looks well. His thoughts are with you both as are mine. There is not much for me to say about him except to say it's so good to see him and hear his stories of the north. He has done some drawings even since he's been here but says he's sorting himself out at the moment and trying to masticate his holiday so to speak – or his experiences for them to be of use to him in the deeper sense.

Mad letter but just to convey a little love from sunny Sydney where I have not had a chance to wear my lovely 'gown' – it's too nice to call frock – as it's been raining constantly.

And Dolly Burton sends her pearly love and so to bed.

Love to you dears and S too

PS   By the way the Haw[k]esbury holiday was Crown Street. I rigged up a tale for the old chook [Joy's mother] so I'd not have to write for a couple of weeks. Said I went to stay at a little house away from civilization and [with] a friend named Mrs Francis whom I've no idea who she may be but tell my Ma stories of how she takes me for drives in her car etc. – all lies!

Rose Bay
(January 1948)

Dear Sun
Your postcard today. How lovely it looks the dear old lighthouse [at Point Lonsdale] and all. It's a nice photo isn't it?

This is just a shortie re. the doctor's health etc. (What again!)

Went to see McCallum today and there's not much news except I asked him for some pills to take to pick me up when I felt a little faint. He gave me some phenabarb [sic] as APC don't seem any good, so went to Townly the chemist and got them. Was talking over with McCallum about going into hospital for the sterilization and I have rather gone off the idea in the time [that has] elapsed and Dr Chesterman assured me he could give me a 100% [foolproof] thing 'fitted and all'. Ha! ha! So have decided to try that for a year but have yet to see Chesterman next Wed. to discuss the advisability and workability of such things.

G seems more pleased about this than tampering with nature and Dr McC thinks if one can avoid an[a]esthetic all the better. I saw a letter from Crown Street re. me on his desk and he told me he'd got a letter from them and really thinks that I *must not* get prego, but also thinks if an op[eration] can be avoided, all the better. He's a nice man now I know him better and I would not care to change doctors as I have got myself on a 'footing' with his quaint manners and feel at home with him now. So all rests till next Wed. then after that I have a date to see the doctor at Prince Alfred.

G came with me to McC and as I was worried about his sore wrist (right) I got McC to have a look at it. He's put my mind at rest and says he's torn muscles in his wrist and so it's just a matter of time and the soreness will go and he'll be able to use it again . . . Gray is on to an entirely new drug now, a 'new isolation' as the chemists call it. Seems OK so far but the real test is when he feels crook [if] it can ward off turns.

Nolan must think we are queer fish. It's a pity he did not arrive when Gray was really so well for I'm afraid I seem to have been a very poor hostess to a wanderer but my life is so bound up with G's that I think Nolan must think I'm quite mad as I watch G like a cat watching a mouse. One has to for his system could not take another shock at the moment and after such a day of fits as he had, the system has to repair itself it's all so tremulous. This epilepsy, it has such small beginnings. The doctor told me that it's the hardest thing to know with a person like G just what is going to be taken by the mind and if he is not well can in a sense cause another bout.

Living ten months almost alone with him I've got to know a bit what trifles worry him. Funny thing any sort of big worry he can face at the moment and really [he] has more strength than I have at those times. Still how can one express these things except that we are so close and so bound up in our own small world of love and God's earth that somehow I find it hard to tell these things. All I know is that we are both well in our world – this all sounds cuckoo – but as far as I am concerned I've *never* felt better in my life than I do at the moment.

I am going to make an appointment with McCallum and see him this week and if I have to have treatment will most probably stay here until that's finished as it will suit us financially to do so . . .

Nolan is a dear and is well and we were at Bondi yesterday and we saw a little girl with long hair and brown skin and a white frock and a pink bow (quite old fashioned) standing on the shore paddling and we both thought of you when you were a little girl. Perhaps it was the way she was standing staring at the sea, she looked so much a part of it and had lovely seaweed sea green hair in the wind – we both felt a little queer.

Nolan seems to love our Sydney and says he must have been blind when he was there before – he's staying in Alannah's studio at the moment while Alannah is away staying at someone else's but he'll leave soon as she wants it back[1] and so he's been to see John's Cynthia.[2] He says she's so well and relaxed and Jinx is [a] lovely, chattery little girl who says people stink if she doesn't like them. Cynthia has put him on to a Madame Fifi or some fantastic name who has a room in the 'loo [Wooloomooloo] which may suit him – he did six paintings the other night, all in one night![3]

He seems to be a little worried or not exactly that but seems to be worrying about absorbing the north and not wanting to lose the north. In some way he does want to find himself again in relation to 'his

---

[1] Alannah Coleman lent Nolan her studio apartment at 151 Dowling Street, Wooloomooloo. A rambling old house which eventually became home or studio to many artists, it featured in fashion photography during the late 1940s. The sculptor Oliffe Richmond had the downstairs studio and often worked outside in the small garden.

[2] Early in January, Nolan visited Cynthia at her Wahroonga home. The first of many visits, it coincided with Cynthia collecting Jinx from hospital. A broken wrist had laid the six-year-old up for two days. Concerned about Sunday's response – relations between the two women were uneasy – Nolan wrote to John wondering if it were an odd thing to do, seeing Cynthia. Yet the visit, Nolan felt, was relaxed. (Sidney Nolan to John Reed, 14 January 1948, Reed Collection.)

[3] Nolan's room was situated at the lower end of Wooloomooloo. He wrote to John Sinclair that while it was a shabby, old and bleak part of town he found it somehow attractive. Nolan was impressed by the movement of ships against the lines of the houses and by the water itself, such a feature of the sprawling disorder of Sydney's city and suburbs. The light was wonderful, brilliantly clear as the morning mist lifted. Nolan admitted sadly that relations had gone from bad to worse with Sunday. He missed hearing about her on a daily basis and wished he could reach out to her. However, he felt that it was no longer possible. (Sidney Nolan to John Sinclair, January 1948, Langley Collection.)

north'. Most probably feels a little insecure until he is stabalized [sic]. He seems very much to want to do this before he goes home so he can go home 'whole' so to speak. I think he perhaps feels he will be stronger [and better able] to cope with Victoria if he can do this before he goes there – perhaps I'm wrong. I don't know.

Well Sunday and John dear, write and tell me of yourselves and your own lovely world which is over here very much after seeing Barrie and Nolan.

We are going to dice G's aunt as soon as we can and we don't know what from then on – anyway enough of this.

Love to you two both

Joy

Rose Bay
28 January 1948

Dear Sun

I suppose today is the day you get back from Lonsdale and I believe it's 103 degrees in Melb. at the moment. It's hot here although nowhere near like that – it's more muggy here as we've had so much rain ... Everything seems a little tropical. Nolan says it is just like the north ... [He] seems to be doing a lot of painting and has been to see Cynthia several times and is taking us next time.

We are staying still with Gray's mad aunt until we can get somewhere cheap. Once again [we] are intent on a place in the bush and have asked Cynthia to keep an eye open. Once again [we] are trying to get the invalid pension for Gray [which] the hospital said was no go. There's always a 'niche in industry for epileptics' they say – but have got him a Doctor Stephens. If he is a nice bloke [he] may push it.

How we'd love a shack somewhere! Meanwhile, will be here for another week if we can stick the old bitch as cannot see what else to do as I will be going to the Prince Alfred on Friday to see the ray doctor and pretty certain to have a few rays. Dr Chesterman on holidays from Women's so will just have to be careful until he gets back. Ha! Ha!

Have not been 100% so will be glad of the ray to pick me up again.

Gray's hand is almost back to normal and he himself is better although the aunt would drive us both to the nut house. [We've had] too much of her. But somehow by ourselves we have a neat little ship and we can look after each other.

Nolan has been coming out a few times. He must think us mad as we packed him off before 10 pm last time. But we were both exceedingly tired. I hope he understands, I know he does. But somehow Sun, our lives change. I would have no more sent someone packing than fly once but our lives are small and selfish, with few exceptions, out of necessity. The child has returned and the circle is narrow and if I could convey what you and John mean to me I would only be half pleased. I was thinking today of John madly pruning and telling G of the violet tunnel and the mad cats that live near the chooks' house and I wondered if the little frogs still beat their pulse against the kitchen window?

It is a rare thing to have a place in one's mind one knows is not a dream – and there *is* a secluded wild garden and one *can* go knee deep in violets and there are two such people who walk stick in hand through the paddocks at evening and every chocolate cake was a reality. Yes, Gray and I tell stories to each other. He tells me of his lovely brothers and how they hid in blackberry bushes the three of them and played make-believe, and of the reality of their dreams and of summer nights and I tell him stories told and retold between us both … of John and how he put marzipan on his lap and looked so blissfully at that tin. And of your lovely father and your mother and the lighthouse,[1] of John and his brother in Tasmania and of John at university and there being no hot water. Yes, this is our life. It is from here we dream on and swap dream and reality to make a reality of our own, a small happy life.

… Well Sun I'll ramble no more as it's time for tea. My love to you all and give the ducks an extra handful of wheat for me.
PS   Loved your drawing of 'Gethie'.

[1]   From 1881 James Baillieu, Sunday's grandfather, was the lighthouse keeper at Point Lonsdale.

Rose Bay
Saturday, 7 February 1948

Dear Sun

Forgive me if my letters have been too haphazard or too something – I feel they have and I have felt unhappy after I had dropped them in the post. Some mad frustrated feeling the minute I hear them drop in the bottom of the box, and now this blasted ink is too light and I always find it hard to express myself in light ink as when I am writing I like to see my writing above the level of my eye forming some sort of a pattern or drawing and this all blurs into one and is not the same to me somehow. Perhaps it has something to do with how one's eyes are adjusted and to do again with the way we draw.

I received your letter today, the one in which you said you enclosed 10/- for the books. I could not find the 10/- so perhaps you forgot to put it in or perhaps the postmen are as clever as they say, in that they can 'feel' when money is in a letter ...

HAVE JUST RUNG YOU UP!!

It's certainly strange ringing up long distance. When I answered I said, 'It's Joy here, John'. He said 'Oh, how are you?', I said 'OK' etc. and he said 'Where are you?' and I think he didn't believe me. He said 'Sydney?!' Gray's aunt was out and we hate her so much we rang up and it will go on her account and she won't know as she's always ringing Melbourne up.

She is the original bitch from Bitchland, a very cruel woman. We are just staying here until my ray is over and we can get a place. She has been very cruel to Gray and has blamed him for being sick and 'taken it out' on him if you know what I mean. She sort of takes this attitude – you're a nuisince [sic] always ... having fits and even said to him one day, 'Don't you dare throw one in my house. I just couldn't stand it!' Poor Gray who feels badly about being an epileptic anyhow because the minute people find out that he is they run as fast as they can in the opposite direction as though he is a lunatic at large or has the plague or something – and that's what's happened all his life and in every job he's had. That's what happened at [the] Wentworths, and Mrs Wentworth [their landlady at Point Piper] even wrote a couple of nasty letters after we left saying 'had we *known* we'd never [have] had him there.'

The whole business with the Wentworths was very sordid and nasty.

The moment Gray went into hospital they asked us to leave pronto. By the next day! Nolan was staying at our place and helping with the furnace and I went to stay at Gray's aunt's place when Gray went into hospital and they immediately started on Nolan and asked him to get out. Now the old bitch is trying to claim all sorts of expenses such as £1 for getting the carpet cleaned and the flat cleaned and money for a lock we broke which we didn't etc., etc.

Mrs Wentworth and Gray's aunt are carrying on a barney by letter and they're both the same sort of person so the sparks are flying. We are just sitting back now and letting them fight it out themselves.

Gray is now on a new drug for epilepsy and I don't know. I'm very worried about it all as it's the latest isolation or something. It's called Phenytoin or Phenfoin [sic]. He's supposed to take it three times a day for 2 yrs and possibly it will cure him. Well, it does the most extraordinary things to his eyes. Makes the black part small and beady and the eye is not sort of steady anymore and looks sort of pre-fit all the time. His nerves are almost on their last string and one wonders if it's worth it; whether it wouldn't be better without it. It's too exciting to my mind. He gets so excited with rage on a minute's notice. One wonders whether the system can stand it. His eyes get mad and one feels if anyone who didn't know him was to strike this they'd retaliate and one trembles to think of the consequences.

Perhaps I carry my thoughts too far but I asked Nolan and he said excatly the same – I don't wish you to make a reference to this in a letter to me as G may see it and I'd hate to actually worry him about it as it's best to watch him as Nolan suggests very closely for a time and see how it works. But nevertheless it has me a bit worried and we have so many worries at the moment I don't think it wise for me to worry him about it although I know he's not happy about it himself.

One day Nolan, I and Gray went to see Cynthia – she has a dear little cottage in the semi bush. Nice part – Cynthia herself does not look too well. In fact I'd say she looked no better than when I last saw her in Melb. one day in the city. We had a pleasant day. The boys enjoyed themselves. We went for a long walk in the bush and I am particularly taken with Jinx who is a lovely wild animal. We talked, Jinx and I, about looking for gold in the rocks and about becoming the richest people in all the land and about the sun and the people who live in the sun and about the anaesthetic she had for her arm to be set. It has been broken while playing and is by no means right at all. Jinx bashes it about and goes in for swims and wets the plaster and God knows if it will ever be right, the tomboy way she knocks it around. She is a real person and a very lovely one – a very defiant and humorous person with an alternate twinkle and stare of defiance in her eye. I loved her, really took to the spirit of her.

As far as Cynthia went I was a bit sorry I'd gone. She was very pleasant but I sensed some sort of awful undercurrent. Nolan had told me she was so relaxed and changed and I went and looked forward to seeing her. I s'pose it's some lack in myself to come across to her. We had a short girls talk about this and that and I did not feel very happy about her. I feel in some way she's driving herself against her natural self, forcing things. Perhaps I'm wrong. She kept saying funny things to Jinx about being socially conscious and what would the neighbours think. I really could not tie this up with her at all as I say. It was a pleasant day that left me with a funny feeling about Cynthia herself. I felt sorry that she was as she was and I s'pose [it] is up to me to find something of her [to relate to] but I don't think I would try to.

I loved hearing you say 'hello darling'.

By the way, I was telling John on the phone that Cynthia read of a new treatment for Hodgkie in the paper. Something about injections of poison gas. She has the cutting and is going to give it to Nolan for me (he's taken Jinx and Cynthia to the ballet today). They've tried it on the first two cases in Adelaide last week. Well I say let 'em try on someone else and see how they go and then we'll think about it. At the moment ray seems to keep it in check.

I still do feel queer every time they pack me up with rubber and weight the rubber over my head but when I see all the other poor cows going in with big cancers ... on their face[s] I have a little more courage. I talk myself out of a panic, so to speak. I talk to myself in my head all the time I'm under it. I tell myself it's silly to be frightened. All in all it's better than having Hodgkin's, because before I went for this last lot of treatment I had an awful let down physically and all my resistance went at once and I realised I had no more left and felt happy that I'd be having ray and I'd get some more given [to] me.

You ask me about expenses. I s'pose it's silly to say there are none for at the moment there are. Gray goes to his hospital in the morning and has infra red ray on his wrist and [a] massage. (He's writing a letter to

John. [It's] the first time he's written more than half a dozen words. His wrist is getting better.) While we are staying with Gray's aunt we pay no rent but it costs us food and about 16/- a week on fares to the hospital. Gray's mother has been sending him about £1 a week while he can't work. His bitch of an aunt won't help at all. She used to give him £1 a day to do her garden once a week. Now he can't do that she doesn't give him a hapenny. We have been able to keep the £12 John sent intact as we feel we'll need that to get away from here. So we have a bank account of £14 which we are going to hang on to this month. Then we can tell auntie to stick her hospitality and we'll get a little cottage. But all this is extraneous and beside the point.

I didn't have to pay for Dr Chesterman. He's away on holidays so [I] have done no more in that direction. It is free at Crown Street for in-patients. You only have to pay for outpatients, only about 2/- a visit. I don't have to pay for my ray although I was told it would cost 3/- a visit. So far I have not had to pay. The girl on the desk seems to like me – I have only to pay 15/- for the chest X ray which is just an ordinary X ray. I'm not telling you this for you to send me any money – as I say, we have been able to keep £12 in the bank and it's been there for over a week and we are going to try and keep it there till next month but because you asked about expenses I'm telling you. The chemist business is fine as I've not had to use it except to get phenabarbs [sic] and have only had one lot of them but will get some more soon. In fact I should cut this part out of the letter but I won't as I know you'll take it in the right way. If only we could grow our own veg somewhere.

This is a mad letter. Don't take too much notice of it. I love seeing Nolan and we both have felt marvellous about him being here. He's keeping us normal so to speak [and] kept things in their right proportion for us and [has] been such a feeling of strength to us both as this has been the worst period we've had together. We've both felt a little as though we're a liability to the community and a bit depressed and lost and frightened. Gray feels he's been too much a liability for me and vice versa. I feel that I should not be writing this letter. Never mind, dear Sun, my thoughts always gain strength and momentem [sic] when we think of you both. I feel that once we get out of this cul-de-sac perhaps we can be of some cheer and help to you and John in some way. I don't know quite how but I would have jumped in the lake long ago but for the wonderful feeling of strength you and John have been.

Enough of this muck. The brushes will be put to use as soon as we get a spot of our own. Daren't draw here – Gray's aunt thinks she's the only artist that existed. God! You should see the stuff!

The hamper as I said will be sent back chock-a-block full of drawings, until then I will care for it absolutely.

Love to you dear Sun and John

PS   This is the last letter of this kind I *will ever write*.

Rose Bay
Tuesday, 10 February 1948

Dear Sun and John

Just a short note in a much more cheerful frame of mind – forgive my last tomb [sic] (one of those letters one should never post) but felt very depressed having just had ray treatment and having rung you up in the middle of the letter and had my pain and all seemed very flat (not the phone call) but the sun is out [now] and it's warm and cheerful and I feel well. Gray looks his best since New Year. His eyes look their lovely soft selves today for the first time. I am no longer frightened or afraid. Gray has been drawing for the first time and he's happy, too. Nolan, whom we see almost every day, is happy and painting and doing lots of lovely drawings of Sydney.

Sydney is smelling its sweetest, just like I imagine Europe smells at the first sign of spring as the sun's on the damp grass here. It smells good . . .

I have not used the brushes and kindly tell me again how to make the Chinese ink as I don't want to mess it up this time. The last lot was good but it sort of separated a bit on the paper.

Have put adds [sic] in about 6 papers and started the ball rolling to get out of here so that's good.

Nolan is coming and he and Gray are going for a walk on the cliffs here tonight as the sun goes down.

I had a note from Barrie, a note very much like the feeling I got from Barrie when I met him. I cannot say I quite caught on to all he was saying but I got a feeling of Barrie in the note so it doesn't matter about the words. I liked the second verse very much of his poem to Sweeney and the last.[1]

I do hope I can send my happiness a bit to you as I am thinking of you now at sunset in the paddock and the Dandenongs in the fading haze of color. I feel happy because that's where you are and that, dear Sun and John, is also where happiness is. And then to the veg[ie] garden for dinner for the dinner veg[ie]s and perhaps a little bit of ironing and perhaps it's warm enough to go out and have dinner on the piazza? As the light fades the beauty of you both is shining through the golden hour now and there are 3 little Sydney hearts beating in the little rose at the window of the kitchen with love and cheer for you all at Heide.

Sweet dreams

I cannot take myself to the Archibald show. No, I can't.

Sydney looks like Cezanne this evening, all solid and all so light and breezy.

Katoomba NSW
8 am, 3 March 1948

Dear Sun
It's no use describing these wonder-ful hills except to say that it is so blatantly God – that it's almost unbe-lievable when one looks for miles and miles across the deep valley rock, walled and foreboding. We left Sydney at 8 am yesterday and feel as though we might have left it one hundred or more years ago with D'Arcy, Wentworth and Lawson and Blaxland. What men they must have been and strange we should have lived with his [Wentworth's] grandson [their landlord at Point Piper] and felt the decline of a family so much when we come here and the mountains look absolutely impen-etrable but for the few settlements such as Katoomba which stop very abruptly on the rock's edge.

Gray came into a tenner unexpectedly and so we took the bull by the

[1] Barrett Reid, *Sweeney Egotistes* (1948), now lost.

horns and away. He was very sick on Thursday, was unconscious all day and stayed in bed all the weekend and seems pretty fit now. So here we are and there are no shacks at all here so we are getting the mountain puff puff on to Bathurst where we'll try for one there ... Then later on today we go from Bathurst to Orange where the cherries grow and it's 200 miles or more from Sydney and we'll stay the night there and come home I s'pose tomorrow or the next day.

Life is very sweet not knowing what is around the next hill and a 'Clancy' on every rail station and one night in a cheap pub. Yes, these are the longest loveliest days of one's life. In the bush the days seem so endless, one day gently folds in on another – in the city it's more harsh, the beginning[s] and ends of days, and they seem to pass much quicker – and before you know it a month has passed. Here every day is a month. I really do not think there's much hope of a shack anywhere – even at Orange or Bathurst – it seems in the bush if a man builds a house, he lives in it ...

Nolan gave Gray the complete works of Banjo Paterson and we all sat down and read them aloud the other night. Saw the photos of Nolan's show in Brisbane and the easels are a very good idea for Nolan's paintings in that particular gallery, I think. I love the picture of Mrs Someone or other bending over.[1]

Goodbye Sun and John and our love to you both and warmth for the coming winter to you Sun.

Joy

Fragment
Rose Bay
(March 1948)

... It is a bit disconcerting writing this letter as G is reading out all the fuckie bits from a very spicey [sic]

---

[1] Sidney Nolan, *Mrs Fraser*, 1947, (Private Collection). Exhibited Moreton Galleries, Brisbane, February 1948. '*Mrs Fraser*, 1947, straddles on all fours in the bush, naked, defenceless, and androgynous: one thinks of Shakespeare's "poor, bare, fork'd animal". It is a shocking and unforgettable image.' Robert Hughes, *The Art of Australia*, Penguin, 1977, p. 222.

autobiography of Robbie Burns[2] – it really is a good book but it's funny –
John would scream –

I have not slept for 4 nights running – despite every drug in creation.
I have had a hacking cough which only comes on when I lie down. I
went to see McCallum and he gave me a mixture and some linctus so I
hope for a night's sleep. I feel I can hardly keep my eyes open in the
daytime and so I think I'll take 40 winks but I start coughing – sounds
phsycollogical [sic] but McCallum says I've got bronkitis [sic] – but the
electric shock things I told you about have almost stopped and
McCallum says that's nerves. So there, I thought the end had come but
no such luck. It's only 'noives'.

This is a bit of secret news for you only. You and John that is – Gray
and I are coming to Melb in about a month's time or 3 weeks. This is
our plan. We want a cottage in the bush not far from Melb. and Gray is
going to apply for the invalid pension. His doctor told him, or rather
Vonnie his wife, that epileptics were eligable [sic]. This is £1/12/6. But it
would be good if he got it and we had a shack in the bush and could
grow vegies. So dear Sun I hope it comes soon.

. . . Dear Sun, forgive this letter as I feel tired tonight and not exactly
in a writing mood. Been a bit introvert with this blasted cough as it's
distracting.

I will love to see you again but [it will] be a while yet and more letters
will come and go – so love to you and all the things you are and J and S
and Heide.

---

[2] Robert Burns (1759–96) was a Scottish poet.

Chapter 6

August 1948
February 1949

In March 1948 Joy and Gray returned to Melbourne. After nearly a year of illness and worry, Joy had entered a period of remission from Hodgkin's disease that would last until 1956. They stayed briefly in a flat in Dandenong Road, Caulfield, before moving to Heide. They were still determined to find their cottage in the bush and begin a new, healthy life.

Susan McKay had agreed to buy them a small farm. To Joy, Susan might have seemed the 'original bitch from Bitchland' when they stayed with her at Rose Bay but she would not only finance Garford, their property at Hurstbridge, but a larger one at Avonsleigh in the Dandenong Ranges where they moved in 1952.

Joy and Gray moved to Gar in July 1948. Gar was an old weatherboard house on less than a hectare of land in Haley's Gully Road. It had originally been built as a billiard saloon and transported to Hurstbridge from the city. There was no electricity or sewerage. The house had two large rooms and a smaller one that was used as a bedroom. Joy sometimes used the back verandah as a studio. A small apple and pear orchard attached to the property had to be pruned and a garden was started, with help from Heide. Gray built a dam.

In August, the Reeds sailed to France. They wanted to settle Sweeney's adoption with Albert Tucker, then living in Paris. They also planned to organise an exhibition of Nolan's *Ned Kelly* series in Europe. It was to be a holiday, too, with trips to Italy, England and the south of France.

> MS *Tournai* en route to France
> August 1948
>
> [Dear Joy]
> Here we are are on the sterniest part
of the stern watching the albatrosses. [Sketch.] They are like angels following the boat. I think they are. About an hour after we sailed, Sweeney got the top of his right hand middle finger squashed in the hinge side of our cabin door. John shut it hard and it is unbearable to think of. Poor little boy, it was the most dreadful squashing and the nail was lifted quite out and we do [not] know yet what has happened to the finger itself! We think it can be hardly be anything else but broken! The captain and the first and second officer[s] came straightaway and we

bound it up together as best we could and I do not know who took the ship through the heads.

Swene managed to come through it all without fainting away although I think we have all been fainting ever since and Weeney has been wailing at night like a migrant bird and it was a great shock I think and he was very sick for two days, not able to eat or drink anything and I expect we were seasick although it is hard to say what we were, we were so upset. I will be thankful to get to Fremantle tomorrow to a surgeon and we will hurry to Perth as soon as we arrive. Fortunately, we have three days. The wound, the poor little mashed finger, is marvellously healthy anyway. Two of the passengers are nurses, not that they could do anything but one had a tube of sulpha ointment which may have helped. The ship's carpenter made a little splint, too.

Today has been our best day and we have been sitting most of the morning on the hatch near our cabin watching the Aussie shores as we near sailing round the corner to Fremantle. I still feel the boat is going the other way and Heide is ahead. Swene has been on his bike, too, and is able to do most things in spite of his enormous bandage. Our Rockbye has been rockbyeing in the Bight. I felt the Nullabor Plains under us, not wind and white horse but a tremendous landscape of heaving sea. You could feel everything coming up from under it and great mountains pushed up and then deep deep down into the iron. I hugged Gethy looking through the port last night, frightened, expecting to see what one always sees – the sea, the sky – and finding nothing there but a wall. No air, no sky we were right down deep in the valley.

Later, night

I thought it was the best day but it turned out to be the worst. We have been battling with storms all afternoon and it still goes on. All sorts of old Norwegians have come from goodness knows where in oilskins and souwesters fighting their way round the rain soaked decks and young boys in woollen caps climb up ladders. The wind lashes and the rain hurls and the sea heaves and a wave came in our port [hole windows] which we hadn't closed in time and soaked the bed while Sweeney was tuckbyes – but he didn't mind. It all seemed quite beautiful in the movies but it isn't really and I can't be a sailor's daughter any longer or even my father's.[1] The thought of land in the morning is like

---

[1] Arthur Baillieu was a keen sailor, owning a yacht he sailed in Port Phillip Bay.

heaven and I can't write anymore with everything slipping and sliding in the cabin and the scream of the wind and sea down the ventilators. I have long since got my sea legs but my spirit lags.

I did not like leaving your tears, darling, and Gray's streamer yet I seemed not to leave you [a]nd I slipped out of my new white shirt and had my arms round you looking at myself sailing away and perhaps now it is often that way, that I am somewhere I am not and you will find me still with you and in and out [of] the herbs and sitting by the kitchen fire just as usual – if only you can see. And I know I am at Heide, too, and Min knows, she knows more than anyone. Since the storm began I have been thinking of her having kittens. I hope we will have news tomorrow. I will write again before we sail and let you know more about Swene-o. He has been more than marvellous. I don't know how any of us could have stood what he did without an injection. Strangely the wound does not hurt him anymore but the shock I think, has been quite a big one.

The going was just a dream with kisses that were not long or fast enough, my arms waving. I hope I did not look as horrible as Queen Elizabeth blowing kisses I thought afterwards. John had his glasses and we watched the last moments of you all but I could not find you or Gray. Love to you and [let] quietness take possession of you both and all that is yours and to be, God bless you. The waves are hitting the boat with huge bangs. How you would hate it. Already I secretly plot to get off at Genoa. Could the Bay of Biscay be worse than this?

S

Fremantle
Anchored all day. Unable to get a berth.

Gar, Haley's Gully Road, Hurstbridge
September 1948

Dear Sun
You poor things – no one could say that you have had a good start – I hope that poor little Weeno has survived the shock and that by now all is well – and that Jesus has walked the restless sea ... You assure me it's not as nice as the movies

but it makes me feel as though every film and sea story I've ever heard have passed and somehow your storm seemed very real and I almost felt seasick — so I would say that you must be a good letter writer! and here we were all saying 'Yes, they won't feel a storm, their little Rock-by is so well in the sea and pretty heavy' and we all sat smugly back and felt comfortable about that thought.

My mother got her field glasses and went to the end of the street[1] and saw the little thing very clearly and also remarked how well weighted it was and she watched until it was only a dot on the horizon and was surprised she saw it so well. We were glad to get your letter as we thought perhaps you hadn't written and were a bit worried as it seemed as though it was a long time since you went.

We have planted more lettuce, carrots, Chinese cabbage, butter beans and leeks and turnips and our broad beans are well up and we sprayed the trees with 'cuprot'. The leaves and flowers are beginning on all the trees and we had for about 3 days torrential downpours and then sun and warmth ever since and God is here and everything seems bewitched — and we have quite a veg garden now! We have not been to town since you left and our little house was glad about that — and tell John the rose at the back door near the blackberry has tremendous shoots on it.

Florence [Noonan]'s back is better and she looks very well again now.[2] We laugh a lot as she drops in for a 'cuppa' on her way to the village and the other day Gray called me out and said 'Can you hear what I hear?' and I listened and above the magpies and birds was laughter, great chatter but no one in sight. I said 'Yes, Flo will be here soon, I can hear her down the road' and about five minutes later she came chatting and chortling and we said, 'Are you coming to have a cup?' 'No, I won't have time, I have to go and look for Trilby [Florence's goat].' Well, she did and she stayed for about 1½ hrs and off she toddled for Trilby. She told us yesterday, 'Just as well I stayed and had that cup of tea. I didn't find Trilby for 3½ hours. I wandered over the hills and found gold mines and all sorts of things but no Tril'. Finally the bitch turned up over the hill and the exhausted Florence started her long journey home!

---

[1] Dawson Avenue, Elwood, ended at Port Phillip Bay.
[2] Florence Noonan had once worked as a cook for the Baillieus and was now a neighbour at Hurstbridge.

Tomorrow we are invited to Florence's for lunch from whence we proceed to explore the old gold mines and nooks and crannies beyond Florence's which she found on her 'Trilby' expedition and she can't wait to show us. So as it's a lovely day today we feel quite excited about tomorrow's adventure.

Martin [Smith] had a letter from Johnnie Yule who is in Brisbane and who has 'found' Mary Christina! and Mary and John are due in Melbourne tomorrow.[3] A rare pair no doubt they will make! Tell John at least he has the same name!

Roy Sharp [a neighbour] was horned by his bull and badly bruised and just escaped and the bull went so mad it couldn't be caught to be taken away by four men and so it had to be shot. This same Sharp bloke who is the taxi driver too has not [had] any sleep for four nights as one cow has chillblains on the udder and has to be massaged and the other cow got lost and was found alive in the creek caught under a log and was so weak she couldn't stand up so the garage boys had to go down with their truck and crane and lift her out and take her home – which touched my sense of humour and sounded like Banjo Paterson.

Tell Weeno his plant is still 'intactus' as he planted it – which is one bottle buried deep with a quart of tin around same. When he was on the boat he asked me if I was going back to Hurstbridge and I said yes. He said 'You won't dig up the flower I planted, will you?' I promised not to. The post office woman told me he was the sort of child she would like to adopt – he went in and asked her if she had any money to give him and she said 'I thought his father was such a lovely man.' She even sounded as though she would adopt John at a pinch also.

I loved your little Rockbye drawing because that is exactly how it looked from the pier. I felt also as though I was up in the air like a bird, quite high and remote and sort of disinterest[ed]ly looking down on it like you drew and focussing very personally on 3 little heads that hurt me to look at so I turned around and ran past the old darling Wolsley

[3] John Yule travelled to Sydney in 1947 to work with Guy and David Boyd. When they went to Brisbane seeking new markets, Yule travelled with them. Here he met Mary Christina through Barrett Reid. Mary Williams was an Adelaide poet and Latin scholar who had changed her name to Mary Christina St John of the Angels. She published two volumes of poetry, *The White Hind* and *The Blue Gazinta*, and was also published in *Ern Malley's Journal*, vol. 1, no. 2, March 1953. She worked as a prostitute in Brisbane and Melbourne. She also collected dolls. Later she lived in England where she became a headmistress of a girls' school.

[sic] parked on the pier and didn't look at the Rockbye again. I couldn't. Still after your letter I feel again as though you are here and not me looking at you 3 from somewhere else watching you all vanish into a line called horizon.

And a gentle sea breeze kiss to you all and today I found the penny-royal that you planted.

MS *Tournai*, Fremantle WA
16 September 1948

Dear Joybells

Just a quick note before I go tuckbye to let you know that our little boy is better. We contacted our old friend Marshall Sumner – p'raps you don't remember him. He sometimes gives concerts in Melbourne and teaches the piano here at the University. Anyway, he put us in touch with a children's specialist and surgeon and we spent yesterday in a private hospital. A horrible day in one way but we were so cheered that the X ray showed no bones broken so that everything was really much better than we expected. Swene had an anaesthetic and a needle stuck in his arm and all the usual awful things that happen to us on these occasions but he behaved like an angel and Crisp the surgeon cleaned the wound and removed all the nail which was hanging by a thread and he is confident it should be right for the journey.

We have to dress it of course and are surrounded in bandages gauze adhesive tape ointment antiseptics cotton wool and goodness knows what and it is all very difficult indeed to do without hurting him. Anyway don't worry. The sad part is that the nail, the new one, may not grow normally, at least Crisp seems doubtful, but somehow I feel hopeful and I will take great care of it when once it begins to show signs of life.

Swene is in grand form today and Marshall drove us to the hills this afternoon. I thought of you and Gray and Martin too because the wildflowers are just a dream and I wished we were seeing them together. We had Peter Cowan with us this morning.[1] He has a mad little

---

[1] Peter Cowan recalls meeting the Reeds at the boat and driving them, with Sweeney, in his secondhand 1929 Riley round Canning Highway, along the Swan River and through King's Park, and on to the University. A few days later, he drove them down to his house in Rockingham. (Correspondence with the editor, April 1994.)

Charlie Chaplin sort of car, hand painted and no running boards but it goes and we toured around the Swan River through the park where in places the bush is still untouched and the wildflowers even more beautiful than in the hills. If only you could see the kangaroo paws growing everywhere under the gums. How Nolan would love them. They are waiting for him to paint. Goodnight darling.

John is on the wharf picking up stones to put on the bottom of a flowerpot we bought for your four leafed clover. It is quite well so far but we think we will have to take it into the sun when we set sail again. Gray's vegie garden letter arrived today with news that beds were dug and waiting and I hope letters will greet us in Paris and tell us that you are just about eating the first lettuce. Kiss yourself and Gray from us all three and greetings and all else and lots of rain be yours.

> S
> Expect to leave this afternoon.

Gar
1 October 1948
PHENOMENA LETTER

Dear Sun
We had a phenomenal phenomena today! In fact I think we *may* be the only people in the world to experience it!! I don't know, but I have not heard of anyone living ever finding it before!

Yesterday it rained all day and G and I went to Florence's for lunch and when we came back to Gar there was a rainbow in Bingly Ave! Starting at the corner of our place and ending further along, about near our dam, on the other side of the road, so, hardly believing our own eyes we tore across the road to stand under the end of it, to find the pot o' gold. And so to prove no myth I stood on one side while Gray ran into the *very* end of it, and yes, there it was, yellow, green and blue all down his shirt and we both stood right on the *very end* of the first rainbow I have ever found the end of, and we wished, and our first wish was for you both and the second one was for us and then the rainbow went very suddenly and we had no time for more wishes.

Whenever I have endeavoured to find the end of a rainbow before, I discovered or I *thought* I discovered that it was all a myth because when you get to the place where it appears to end you see the end is actually a bit further on – a sort of optical illusion – well, I would not have believed it!! and I really felt or we both did that the Lord had picked us out and that we were standing in the light of the Lord and it all seemed very special and very holy and today when I look at that spot over the road, I sort of said to myself, that's where the Lord was. Do you know anyone else who has ever found the end of a rainbow? I have never ever heard of it!!

... Then some news from Brisbane that Mary Christina is on her way to Melbourne with Johnnie Yule, but Johnnie wrote to Martin an urgent letter to say he's following later and Martin would *have* to meet Mary at the station and find her somewhere to live because 'many a time I have found her on the street corner crying because she was lonely' said Johnnie in his letter and 'goodness knows what would happen if she found herself in a strange state alone' ...

My mother was very thrilled to have got a letter from John and told me about Swene's finger etc. which of course I knew.

I have been doing a few 'candle light' drawings or 'lamplight' series. Ha! Ha! No, but it's lovely how a face, feature or some part of a personality gets isolated in this old light and the edge of the shadow is the only blackness, and personality or feature ends where the light ends and seems so emphatic on the edges of the light and the blackness seems not black but volume.

At the moment it is absolutely teaming! [sic] like the tropics, heavy heavy rain and unceasing for about 3 hrs now and we are wondering if our veg garden may not get flooded out and float down the Gully. Anyway there's always the broad beans up here in the front of the house and a bit of spinach which is now ready to eat! We have 7 veg gardens now in flats. And by accident we sprayed the walnut tree with Bordeaux mixture[1] and burnt all the tiny just-opening leaves to a cinder, or at least we think that's what must have happened as they have all gone black and died and *The Australian Gardener* says walnuts are not much susceptible [sic] to pests or disease so we can't imagine what else has got to it.

---

[1] A fungicide consisting of copper sulfate, lime and water.

I have not been the best and am off to see your little Doctor Sewell tomorrow.[2] I must say when I glimpsed him in The Oriental [Hotel] I was agreeably surprised.[3] From your description, Sun, I'd imagined something short of a toadstool or what not!

Florence and I were reading John's horoscope and it says he's going in for 'public affairs' next month or so – so needless to say Gray roared his head off and I have been seeing John at UNO [United Nations Organization] meetings ever since. Write as soon as you can and let us know what you are short of, but I believe around Xmas, parcels take somewhere in the vicinity of 4 mths though that's for England, France may be a little better.

I think of you three on the little Rockbye when I go to bed and it's so still and quiet and Aussie smelling, and I look at the stars and wonder if they still shine on you or have you now changed stars? And what smells are you smelling – and Haley's Gully hides its gold and its legend and I start to think I'm on the Rockbye – I find it's morning again and I wonder if it's night then where you are.

Wish I was on the telephone to the Rockbye and could ring up and say is it night there yet, Sun? It seems so distant where I am writing to because I suppose this letter may be in Paris before you are there and the words will be talking to no one and then I can see you all going up the stairs of Lloyds for your mail and you don't seem so far away.

Sometimes I panic and I think perhaps you won't come back here again and you'll be walking down streets that I have been a long time ago in dreams. And I see you Sun in a brown dress walking in your Sun way and John in his John way and I see us all walking in a gully in an old Aussie town before we were born.

Dear Sun and John and Weeno I send all my love to you and wait each day for news of you and you, Sun, having a birthday I think, on the Rockbye[4] and love to your birthday and all the rainbow wishes to you and all the herbs are flowering now for you and the borage and another yellow flower to go with the little blue borage stars and kiss the stars in the Rockbye world for me to you.

---

[2]   Dr Erskine Sewell, Sunday's doctor, had a practice in Collins Street, Melbourne.

[3]   The Oriental Hotel, Collins Street, where Sunday and John stayed in the weeks before their departure.

[4]   Sunday's birthday was on 15 October.

Gar
14 October 1948

Dear both

What are you doing? What strange things are happening in Paris far away? What four walls support three breaths breathing and closely hold you there from all the people there must be living in France – I can feel those walls with your breath warm.

... G and I have kalsomined the bedroom a pale-blue-white come [sic] ethereal color and G has made the most elegant bedside table for me and a wardrobe. And we have put butter muslin on the window and tied it with Sun lace from Heide and it looks very simple. It is pouring outside and we have more floods again and the moon again came in on its back and it has been raining ever since – and little Gar is happy and everything is growing. We have already eaten *two* lots of silver beet and the borage is very tall and blue. The herbs are all increased – and we have strawberries and gooseberries already, although still green. All our pumpkins are up – and the columbine greets us now, with five ladies on a stalk, all so dainty, all so formal.

We went to see Sartre's *The Die is Cast* which we enjoyed very much – see it if you can – it may be on somewhere in English, as the dialogue is very important. It is a very adult film, contrary to what we had heard about it, 'too intellectual!', 'left me quite flat!', 'old fashioned', 'bad photography'. As usual, it seems, we found it just the opposite! The photography, well, it was suitable and not at all bad or old-fashioned, although not the latest, as far as 'tricks' are concerned. It is well done and in quiet taste. The story, I thought, [was] excellent and the content stimulating – as it unfolds each phrase and sentence [is] very illuminating and the symbols employed become richer and stronger ... The cross references seem to be so various, subtle and complex that a formal interpretation would seem clumsy. It is precise and to the point, the implications deep and moving – strangely enough the story skims round and about with incidents on some sort of a parallel with our own lives, although incidents in the film were used in an allegorical sense. One came out of the therter [sic] stimulated and a little sad as it seemed to ring too true to life – it brings up all sorts of things, such as the time element, and the stress on the space and stretch of time and on the time of love and reminded me of Eliot's last poems ('Little Gidding' etc.)

From this angle [there was] a deep nostalgic stress on 'time beginning' and 'time ended'.

Our pup, who is called Egypt, as you were there or nearly when we got her and our catems-puss 'Bella' are the best of pals and play all day together, one chasing the other and they trick and tease each other. Our catems is growing into an elegant self-contained female with very becoming habits. I am writing this letter in bed and puss is trying to crawl right down the end of the bed under the blankets – and this I put a very firm stop to as I am frightened she'll smother . . .

I found the nephew Sewell very informative and quite at ease.[1] It seems I will go on till next February without treatment if I am lucky. So that's not too bad, is it? G is well too. What can one expect seeing we are on Hay most of the time, except for a few minor diversions!!

I think about you a lot and how much I learned during the time we came from Sydney and when you went abroad in the Rockbye – unfortunately I feel much wiser now than I did and wish I could have been as wise when you were here and with us. Both of you come to me clearer than ever before and I tremble at the way I behaved on occasions. For since I have known you I have never felt a subtraction, only an adding and enriching of love. I wish I could have been more at the time, and not been split when I should have been whole, and perhaps one day when I am a hundred I will 'know' at the time to 'know' and my pieces will be collected and my actions and thoughts will not be broadcast but will be needlepoint sharp at the time they should be. I am staggered sometimes when I think, if you should not come back but live in that Paris land forever, a picture as frustrating as the picture children play with of [drawing of an empty rectangle]. An aeroplane flown out of sight comes to me and I can't function as to what things would be, I only see the frame.

We have a mopoke who calls mopoke, mopoke, mopoke at about 11 pm every night and I fall asleep usually answering him in my mind's eye through the night, mopoke mopoke and it's truly a music and one dreams pleasant dreams.

By the way how did the seasick[ness] medicine work or did[n't] you have need of it? (Have not received a letter since Fremantle) so by the time you read this you will have already answered my question before you read this – isn't that funny?

[1] A doctor and the nephew of Dr Erskine Sewell.

Mrs Smith had a letter from Jack and Pauline [McCarthy] who are living in Adelaide with Pauline's parents and they have let their library.[2] They have not seen much of Max whom Pauline says, very wittily, is very 'Harris' tweed these days.

Neil Douglas won his divorce case which is not absolute for another two months yet.[3]

Graeme Bell is playing at Legget[t]'s Dance Cabaret, a very low sort of dive where all the girls get dressed up to the nines in black satin and what and dance together.[4]

21 February 1949

Found these in Gray's pants when I was taking them to the cleaner's yesterday!! God knows how many letters were written you with that fate befalling them.

In November 1948 Louise, Joy's mother, died. Louise and Joy had had a painful, combative relationship. Joy thought her older brother Neville was the favoured child and regarded him as an ogre, allying with Louise against her after their father died. Louise was mean with money, harsh, unsentimental and argumentative. Joy would often arrive at her uncle George Bracher's home wearing old, ill-fitting clothes and with bare legs. Mrs Bracher implored Louise to be a little more generous with Joy.

As a teenager Joy began to run away from home, often to the Brachers or to sympathetic friends. Her home life at Dawson Avenue was disruptive, punctuated by violent fights and secret schemes for escape. When she finally

[2] Pauline and Jack McCarthy ran a secondhand bookshop and library called the Kismet Bookshop in Johnston Street, Fitzroy. It was at the Kismet that Joy met Gray in 1947. Pauline was an old friend of Hester's. She had stayed with her immediately after the birth of Pauline's first child, at the Martin Street, Elwood, flat in February 1947 while Tucker was in Japan.

[3] Neil Douglas (b.1911) is a potter, painter and environmentalist who worked on the Heide garden with Sunday.

[4] Graeme Bell (b.1914) is one of Australia's most influential jazz musicians. In 1941, Graeme Bell's Jazz Gang had played for the third CAS Annual Exhibition at the Hotel Australia in Melbourne. A friend of the Reeds, and of Sidney Nolan, Bell regularly played at Heide parties. Leggett's Ballroom was a popular dancehall in Greville Street, Prahran. Bell had been a student of Max Meldrum's. See also Andrew Bisset, *Black Roots, White Flowers, a history of jazz in Australia*, ABC Books, Sydney, 1987.

left home to live with Bert, Louise continued to pursue Joy. Even when Joy left Melbourne with Gray in 1947 she remained frightened of her mother.

However, relations between the two did mellow. Louise made one spectacular trip to Gar, a visit that was received with great dread by Gray and Joy. After she caught the train to Hurstbridge, Louise refused to be met at the station and instead walked the distance to Haley's Gully Road. Her arrival was announced by the clank of bottles for Louise insisted on bringing her own drinking water.

After Louise's death, Gray wrote to John, '[Louise] had told Joy that had she been faced with the same set of circumstances at the same age she would have done the same! (that's about me and Joy). It has all had a rather severe effect on Joy, she has been upset – wondering if maybe she had been hard on [Louise] in the past – this coming from the softness her ma had shown in the latter stages of her life.'

November 1948, Reed Collection.

Gar
14 November 1948

Dear Sun and John
Just received your first card from Gay Paree – a lovely 'very French' one. Your card took ten days to get here which is not bad is it? I see it cost 57 francs. That sounds a terrific amount for a letter even, but for a postcard it's exhorbitant [sic]. How much is a franc worth? Is it still 40 francs to £2? In that case, it cost you 20/- odd – that sounds quite mad, we'd better not write anymore and let's go in for telepathy, it's cheaper!

You say you are just north of the map on the postcard – how the hell do we know what is north in gay Paree John? Where is the Rue Passy? Remember Julien [Green], [Louis-Ferdinand] Cèline and [Georges] Duhamel all wrote from houses in Rue Passy? Are you near there?

. . . I'm glad to hear veg are so cheap and good and I can imagine how expensive it must be to be living in a hotel and I do hope you'll be able to find a place that is good, also cheap, of your own. Are places hard to get or are they all exhorbitant? [sic] I s'pose it's much the same as here. Is it snowing yet? Can we send anything? *Let us know.*

... We are back at Gar after three weeks at Elwood, where Gray and I had the harrowing job of cleaning out every corner of the house, going through every drawer and paper and making way for tenants – I did not like it. I found love letters from my mother and father to each other of a most moving nature – I am more upset than I can say, as I did not see my mother conscious and had no chance to bid her adieu – she knew she was dying although she was not ill. Why does death have to shed such clarity?

Something like birth, the first day after birth a child looks like it is never to look in childhood, but it seems as though it will look like that when it is an adult. There is some clarity of intention and personality that takes death to regain perhaps – I don't know.

It has been raining here for about two months and the grass is at least without exaggeration 3 feet high! We have strawberries 1" in diameter and [with] very sweet, rich flavour. The silver beet is going to seed. The herbs and iris are all in flower. Not one thing has been lost, even in the cutting bed – we also have lettuces and Chinese cabbage to eat – butter beans and peas nearly ready – the dill got washed away in the flood.

Mary Christina has been a lot to Glenferrie but we have been too bust to meet her.[1] She seems to be a bit lost in Melbourne. As far as business is concerned, she can't get a madame to take her. They are all full up so she has had to solicit which is a bit precarious. She is selling everything she had in Brisbane and seems to be living with Johnnie Yule ...

Gray and I are both very well and happy to be back at our darling Gar ... Puss is prego and Gyp about the size of a fox terrier. John Perceval is having an exhibition on Tuesday I think – he sent us an invitation to Glenferrie.

We've seen none of the Boyds although Rosemary and Mary Boyd see alot of each other, and Yvon [Yvonne Lennie], too,[2] as Yvon is having another, and Rose is having one – they all put their heads together and discuss their future family. I think it would be nice to be such a girl perhaps – things most probably seem much simpler.

Love to you three Parisians. Let's know *all*!

---

[1] Martin and Rosemary Smith lived at 35 Chrystobel Crescent, Glenferrie (now Hawthorn). Mary Christina was introduced to the Smiths through John Yule.

[2] Yvonne Lennie (b. circa 1920) painter and former Gallery School student is married to Arthur Boyd.

Grand Hotel Haussmann
Rue du Helder, Paris
23 November 1948

Darling little Joy
My heart has been with you. We are
both so distressed to hear the news of your mother. I know how deeply it
has marked your days and I wish that I had been with you and that our
letters from the boat had not reached you just at that time.

It is strange isn't it, that we send our thoughts away not knowing just
how or when they will fall, writing in a moment that spontaneously
seems quite mutual – but it isn't so and once our letters drop through the
mysterious little hole in the wall, worlds divide. How then do we ever
catch hold of time that isn't in ourselves? As you say we are always on
the threshold of learning, then it seems too late and sometimes too soon.

I understand your letters with my heart because my own little gentle
mother died too, crying, and I would like to speak of it but it is painful
for me and would be painful for you. Only this, darling, that perhaps it
is not for you to grieve for the changes. Believe me when I say that I
remember and think of you walking down the path at Gar, your arm in
your mother's, leading her down the hill to the roadside where the old
jeep was waiting and I remember so clearly the *way* of your face and the
incline of your body and all the implications of giving and acceptance
and the whole *quality* of time then proven in you and the magpies in the
old gums around you were singing of these things. How then can you cry
against the singing of the birds? Is it that moments pass in this way from
life to life? Experience will mark you but change is only understood, I
think, not in its own moment but in the moment that it is *included* and
lived in your next moment. And it seems to me that death throws its
light on us, as well as on those who have died for us, so that one's adieu
is forever unceasing and measured. Or so it is for myself, I cannot tell for
you. I only know that as my life continues and to the end I am saying
goodbye to my mother and my father, at least I try to in my own way –
and fail I know.

For myself I will always remember all that you have told me of your
mother's life, travelling up and down through the years in the Heide
train and by the fire and all the places when you have spoken truly of
her heart and courage with tenderness and insight and I have felt the

love and love's suffering implicit in you both and these are the memories I carry for her within my life. When we left Melbourne I thought of her a great deal, feeling that she would miss Sweeney in some very real way and wishing that the strain in my own life had not come between them, as I feel it often did; when weeks would pass without a meeting for them both. I wish that I had said something to her and I hope she forgave me for whatever failure in myself she may have felt and I hope too darling that you will accept now, for her, these thoughts. So many places I do not cover. I know it.

I dreamt of her and the news of her death unfolded the dream suddenly like lightning, that I found her lying beside the roadside. I was quite young and driving my loved old Packard car in the night alone as I often did. Sometimes in my nightie I would get out of bed and drive in the night. And I just found her, that's all, and she had died and I carried her into the car and drove on and on and there was nothing else in the dream. Nothing.

I hurry to send you my love, to kiss you and hold you. Your letters have only taken six days to come. It feels almost too quick for the thousands of miles of sea that we crossed as if indeed you may yet travel in an aeroplane fast enough to find me beside you both in your little kitchen. If only it were so. God knows how homesick I am. How lovely is Aussie. We are still here in this little hotel quite unable to find anywhere to live. It is more difficult than at home and sometimes I wonder just how long we can go on looking and what is the alternative? How long will we survive in this world of ours in one room. And the budget always exceeded just eating one's food in restaurants.

How happy I am to know that you are back at Gar. I only hope you will find it again and be at peace and I think of you with all the veg[ie]s ready to pick and just what it means to have a garden and a kitchen I don't know. I have been feeling very strained and forgive me that I cannot write enough or bring you healing, if only I could. I can only say how much your love means and how since Nolan left me, when in the buses and the trains and walking down the street I often think I am dying and the blood drains from my face and pours out of me then your love and Gray's comes into me and so with John I try to go on my way, on your way. May I learn the way.

Dear Weeno. He often repeats your letter to him. Dear Weeno, it is raining now. I'm afraid he is already tired of Paris. Why did we come to

Paris, Sun? Why don't we go back to Heide? He has had another bout of bronchitis as he had at the Oriental but I try now not to be alarmed and I can almost tell the moment it arrives and what to do and when he will recover. I hope if we stay on in Paris that we will find him a kindergarten, a French one. I daresay I could find him a place with the American children but I don't want to as I'm anxious he should get to grips with the language.

Already he is able to ring up in the morning for our breakfast. 'Trois petit dejeuners complets avec thé s'il vous plaît, Bonjour' which is not a bad start, even if his accent is like John's! I would not say we are exactly talking ten to the dozen but at least we are absorbed in the language as one has to be if one lives here. We read nothing but French which improves as the days go on and I have just started Julien [Green's] Mont Cinère and think of you all the time and wish I were reading it to you.

... It is lovely to see all Julien's books and I will of course if we have the money, collect them all. At least all the ones that are not translated. I have just read Sa[r]tre's Les mains sales and enjoyed [it] I suppose mostly because I read in French fairly easily. Did you I wonder see his film, the other one, in Melbourne? I've forgotten the name. But I read somewhere about it and think it dealt with two lovers who loved and died and then after death met and loved again or perhaps something a little like that.

Beli[e]ve it or not, we still live in our suitcases. Not that I have anything in the trunks that I need or could wear but we have no room to put anything else and our food is still in store with the paintings and maybe we will come home with it all untouched! The weather is not yet snowing but shows signs of doing so soon. John keeps on saying it is mild! but I always seem huddled up in my big coat which I am so thankful for. There are plenty of the same sort. All the old hags and funny people wear them, poor things, but never mind, mine is different, isn't it? Weeno has a beret and looks just like a French boy. His coat too has been a great success and looks lovely. We haven't worn our fur caps yet. I only hope that we are somewhere else for Christmas so that we can give Weeney some fun.

Goodnight Joy Joy, no there is nothing to send, only your thoughts, darling, always all of them. We have all we want except butter and today got our issue of tickets for Swene milk (I hope enough for my tea) butter and cheese, etc. I think we should get enough butter to last us for breakfast. I long for tea which I haven't had since we left and so I'm just indifferent to the tea here and have ceased now to worry if it's good or bad. It's just a hot drink in the morning with Hovis or Russian bread that we buy and honey. Lunch we buy tomato[e]s and apples and milk and cheese and eat it on the bed and dinner we go out. Swene, as often as not, asks to have his dinner in bed and has a raw egg and orange juice and tomatoes and mayon[n]aise and apples and glucose and there you are. And we buy figs and raisins and a cake for arvo [tea]. Two cakes to be exact. They are madly expensive, and chocolate, too.

Give my love to Florence and keep in touch with her as she wrote and told me how glad she was to have you and Gray near, that it had brought something to her life she missed and needed. I do hope she will come through it all. Kisses and kisses. Forgive me and to both of you. Take heart. Keep strong. Think of Min for me with her darling belly.

Love to Gyp. Thank you for Barrie's poem. He had not written so it was nice to have it.

Gar

Monday, 20 November 1948

Dear Sun and John

I hope by now you poor things have found a *chez* Reed – when I think of you there in your little hotel room trying to write with Sweno and all I wish I had been able to fly over and mind S for you and let you have some peace, for I can realise what a terrific strain it is when you are both tired and exhausted after a day's tramp and only hope you don't have to take Weeno on the tramps as well. And that by the time you get this letter Lady Luck will have shined down on you 3 little Aussies . . .

You seem to have been cooking some veg or have you been eating them raw? Has your hotel a little stove or is [it] a hotel in the sort of way we know hotels – just bedroom and meals supplied?

The other night Martin and Rosemary went to a send-off party . . . Warwick Armstrong and, I think, six boys are all leaving for England this week or next.[1] It makes me sad somehow to hear of everyone going

---

[1] Warwick Armstrong (b.1919) is a Melbourne theatre designer and teacher. He helped form the Melbourne Theatre Guild and, after travelling to England, designed sets for film and theatre.

'abroad' for it is not like the old days when people went away it was for a 'holiday' and they enjoyed themselves but now it seems something different and the boys go away disliking our old Aussie land ... They go from one city here on our litttle Aussie coast to another city there and they never want to go beyond the city here but go all over the country and farm districts of another land. I don't like to think about all these boys going away from one of the few realities left – still it would be nice to feel the air that Van Gogh felt and see Turner's sunsets.

By the way, according to some lovely photos Arles looks, but for a few minor alterations, just the same as Van Gogh saw it and this makes me happy and I hope you will be able to go to Arles and see the crooked trees and feel the warm mistral and see Van Gogh for me.[2] And if Lourdes is not far away, will you go to Lourdes for me?[3]

John Perceval's show went off with a bang.[4] Martin Boyd from England, Merric's brother who writes mad books is out here and opened it – Arthur [Boyd] and John sold him a painting each for £50. The Shepparton Gallery, I think, has bought a drawing. Daryl Lindsay has been in to see the show and apparently is considering buying one. We did not get down to see the show unfortunately as our goat arrived on the day we were going – it's a billy goat and we got it to eat the grass. We would need a herd of goats really to make any impression on it but we are very fond of [the goat] and it has a face just like Bac[c]hus ... He looks sacred and untouched and sprays himself with a beautiful musk-like perfume all day.

I have been terribly well. So has Gray ...

The herb garden is all flowers and the iris and the cuttings bed has pinks out and all the bellus pereus[5] [sic] are cheerful and our own little apples are on all the trees. We have had whopping big strawberries.

---

[2]   The mistral is not warm but a cold, dry, northerly wind common in southern France.

[3]   Lourdes, in the French Pyrenees, was where, in 1858, 14-year-old Bernadette Soubirous claimed to have see the Virgin Mary in a series of visions that took place in a shallow cave on the banks of the river Gave de Pau. Lourdes has become a site of pilgrimage for the sick and its water is supposed to have miraculous healing qualities.

[4]   John Perceval's first solo exhibition was held at the Melbourne Bookclub Gallery, 225 Collins Street, Melbourne, where Hester would also hold her first solo exhibition in February 1950.

[5]   *Bellis perrenis.*

Hurstbridge and us seem to be interlocked with love and warmth and there are many stories to write of this quaint little place. I will write them as soon as I can get all the painting (house) done and we have a bit more control over our long grass.

I s'pose you have seen Bert and will see him over the days there. I feel very strongly about getting the parenthood of Weeney settled as I think it should be settled once and for all while you are over there. Bert should either give him to you holus-bolus and if you feel that would be more than you could cope with I will take him holus-bolus. But if Bert wants him I don't know. I think perhaps we should talk it over by letter for naturally I would sooner take him than let Bert have him, and I suppose Bert would sooner take him than let me have him and I am incapable of talking to Bert and should feel frightened if Bert came back to Australia and it was unsettled and I should have to meet Bert. I don't think I could.

But also I feel that I should be fair and seeing how I have been unkind to Bert I would not like to be doubly unkind and if he really is interested in having Sweeney for Sweeney's sake and *not* for *Bert's* sake and he does not want to *use Sweeney* to fill a gap in his own life, well then if you find also Sweeno is too much for you to cope with, I would feel alright about Bert having him. But I feel it would be too precarious a life for Weeno, really. Perhaps Bert getting a girl and Weeno having yet another mummie, no, I would sooner you have him. I'd feel happy and content about it if you did have him and if you want him that's what I want but *if you don't want him* my only thought is what is the best *and most secure place for Sweeney.* I think a child needs a mummie of some sort and not a mummie of *any sort.* If Bert could think it out clearly from *Sweeney's point of view,* I think he might be better back with me than with Bert. I am trying to think only of Weeno. I hope I am not too biased but as far as I can see Bert will have to be very clear about it too and be unbiased and give him to you if you want – but as Weeno is getting older now I think it essential for Weeno to know one way or the other where his security is. He cannot go on indefin[i]tely having ½ a doz[e]n parents. I am not pushing you both but I thought if I made my thoughts a little clear, it would help all concerned if the subject should crop up between you over the [next few] days.

I hope you'll forgive this intrusion at a time when I feel you must feel very insecure yourselves with no house and strange things about you.

My love to you 3. My thoughts are with your tired feet and Gar sends its sweet summer scents to you.

Joy

Write to Bank
Grand Hotel Haussmann
Rue du Helder, Paris
10 December 1948
John's birthday

Dear Joy
It is strange that your letter about Sweeney should have reached us yesterday as we have been thinking about him so deeply over the last weeks and we are both glad you wrote. But I can't help wondering if my postcard saying – if I remember – that I couldn't write with Sweeney in the room had hurt you in some inside way, making you feel too that perhaps I had suddenly become overwhelmed, and that you were a long way away.

I could only love you for being vulnerable but even so you must trust me beyond it – always. It is true that all of us make each other tired sometimes but that is only what living and loving each other brings, and we come through and love more, not less, because of it. As you know there is nothing that I would not say to you about our life with Weeno – if I say I am tired because he roars like a bull or has measles, or because [of] anything at all, it is not because he is *not* my child that I say it. I would say it just the same if he were. It is just something that I tell you about myself and Weeno, in the same way that I might tell you about myself and the man in the moon if I lived with him.

I know you understand these things as I do but I understand, too, that words often change their reality and I could not bear to hurt you in this way. John and I have been thinking of you so much and before anything there is just one thing that we must ask you to tell us – if perhaps you have been feeling that you would like Wene beside you again. Your own life has secured itself in so many ways. Now that you are at Gar with love and warmth around you, and the Aussie hills, and under your own little apple trees, is it, I wonder, that your thoughts move around him deeply and feeling, as you may, that you have sufficient strength now to meet your life together? If this is true of you darling then you must indeed say so now and we ask you to tell us so that together we can seek only the deepest springs in each other in order to bring Sweeney permanence and peace.

For our own part in answer to your thoughts I can only say that we will always enclose Sweeney in our life and love for as long as he is in our life. Please, you mustn't feel this obscure since it is so real in fact. I could not detach myself from yourself and say to you 'I want Sweeney, yes'. I could only say I want Sweeney forever if finally that is what you want of me. You must not think this *excludes* our love for Sweeney himself, it is the only way we know of expressing it truly both in loving him and loving you. I agree with all you say that Sweeney should now know where his security is, his home, and all that home is or isn't in his life.

We have always thought about it and wanted it for Wene as you know and when Bert left Melbourne we talked about it then and he said he wished for a year to resolve his own thoughts. But he said nothing of it at all and so a week or so ago we felt we would have to lead the way and we talked for a long time. It was not at all a happy talk and ultimately I felt too tired in myself to continue it, so that nothing was resolved – not that my tiredness was responsible for nothing, rather the other way round. And so the matter was left.

Since then of course your letter arrived and we feel more than ever a resolution must be reached. Bert as far as I understand feels that Sweeney's position is so to speak sufficient unto the day and that it is unnecessary to force anything further on himself. Factually, he is living alone in a hotel on the left bank and his living as I see it is unchanged. This being so it is at present not in any way possible for him to have Sweeney nor do I think he wishes it, nor do I feel he would willingly take Sweeney away from us were his own future resolved but it is clear he wishes to maintain the concept of parenthood, I think, for two reasons.

One, that he feels any concept to the contrary would be some kind of renunciation for himself and two, although he has not specifically said so, that he wishes to be in a position of control, should, from his point of view, any contingency arise. While understanding his thoughts, for myself and John they do not in any way establish Sweeney's future peace and security and if in our life Sweeney is to move forward out of love towards love within it, it is impossible to contemplate that it should become a battleground at any given moment and I am sure were it to become such that psychologically, even factually, it would endanger the whole position of my own responsibility and trust, quite apart from Weeney's security and your own fears.

For ourselves, it is Sweeney we are thinking about now, [for] if it [the adoption] is to become real, then we must be free to see it as real. Darling will you write again as soon as you can – I will not present your thoughts as you put them to me, to Bert, as it is useless to present or rather to provoke conflict so you may write as you wish to me, though we will of course tell Bert that we have had a letter from you and that it is your deepest wish that Sweeney's life should be settled and secured now.

I will not go on tonight. We are still here in this little hotel, three beds in a row against the wall, a dressing table, a desk and a chair on the other side and three feet of carpet in between. A bathroom, thanks be, where I am now, straddling the bidet. A table with a little petrol stove we bought in desperation and where some nights just to make it like home I cook a cabbage for John and Swene. We cannot cook much [as] it is too difficult and anyhow the hotel wouldn't like it but at least I get a hotty every night and we make tea in a big saucepan for arvo [tea].

When I said I did not know if we would be happy in Paris, I just meant that if we couldn't find a place to settle and live we might decide to change our plans and perhaps move off to the south and then Italy in the new year. House hunting is an exhausting pastime although we have, as John puts it, absorbed a great deal of the French scene and seen a great deal more of Paris but I need not tell you what living in a room is like. Paris or no Paris. We are still exceeding our budget too and live in a constant state of frustration and cannot buy *anything* other than necessities. And we see so many things we would like to send you or to take back to Heide and as we walk down the streets we get window-looking cramps in our heads turning from side to side! Imagine being in Paris without even a bottle of scent.

We have just about and practically bought a little Peugeot car which on the face of our budget sounds quite mad but apparently it isn't as it just means we have to sell it at the precise moment so its price on resale provides the last months of our year's budget and for some reason the reselling price is higher to the French than the original sale to a foreigner. Everything is terribly complicated and really one needs six months' training before you can live comfortably.

We think if we can't have an appartement we might as well have a car so that we can move off if we want to. Every morning I say, no more of this house hunting. At night I say, let's wait for the miracle, and I suppose, really, that we don't want to leave Paris. Our trunks are still in store, and also the food which I daresay will come home with us, and Ned Kelly is still in customs. The French are quite mad on the question of bringing paintings in and we have got quite a guilt complex with all the goings on and backwards and forwards to place after place.

No, the little hotels are not like ours. In this one as in hundreds of hotels in Paris there is no restaurant and all one can get is tea or coffee or petit déjeuner (breakfast) in the morning sent up. Bread with half a teaspoon of butter and one teasp. of jam. We buy honey and we buy rye bread and we eat the scrap of butter supplemented by our ration which amounts to a piece about the size of a walnut a day. We are a bit the worse for wear I think through lack of butter and fats which I get a mad lust for, rather like wanting a cigarette and not being able to have one. Jonny has had a cold, the first for years and years, and Weeno got his usual bronchitis and I just tottered around like [a] scarecrow but we are beginning to feel better though I expect we are so toxic now that it doesn't matter much.

Goodness how lovely it would be if you were here to do and see everything with us. I always long to share all I look at and feel. Tell Gray I don't *look* for 'happiness' in Paris, I know it is everywhere just as he knows it. Somewhere my thoughts must have lost themselves in the post but I do hope you are not cross with me about anything I have said, or disappointed.

Weeno is still at school and seems very happy about it though I don't know why as we have discovered the French don't have kindergartens. I think he just sits on a little chair beside a table and writes in an exercise book and sometimes has blocks or a sewing card but they work the children from the moment they can walk. You know what I feel about schools but I feel that over and above that, Swene needs to see children and that as a temporary arrangement it is good because he is contacting French all the time and as long as he is happy that any influence is too remote to be harmful. Language is a long story and one needs to be at peace and to have French friends in order to talk. We have gradually assimilated quite a lot and we are reading fairly well and beginning to hear with more confidence. Weeno surprises us by knowing lots of words which he says out of the blue and he enjoys it enormously and likes to think he is a French boy. He looks lovely in his little beret and his coat has been a wonderful success and there is just no boy in the whole of Paris who looks anything like Weeno.

My coat is a great heavy old thing and I think I must look like Stalin in it. All the French coats, the fur ones, are so soft and gentle. But it is marvellously warm and keeps Jack Frost away. I had to buy fur boots, I simply couldn't stand the cold on my feet. They cost five pounds and knocked the poor budget sideways and took a week off our year perhaps but still I had to have them, and fur gloves.

Love to you both and Gar. Do tell me about the painting in the house and what you are doing. . . . Love to the apples. Your little silver circle is with me. I have not worn it yet because the clasp is so uncertain that I'm frightened of losing it and we have not found the right place to take it. I have also broken my pearls and so they are together in my jewel box. But I shall have it ready for summer when my arms are free of my old coat and I can see it on my wrist. Kisses.

It is not yet snowing but John remembers that on the 15th Dec. Napoleon's ashes were brought to Paris from St Hélène and that there was a terrific snow storm! Sweeney and I are still clutching little bags of roasted chestnuts. We can never pass a chestnut man, and we put the bag inside our coats to make [a] warm spot over our heart or against our faces and then we can't wait any longer and eat them madly they are so delicious. John had a lovely long letter from Gray which made us feel that you and Gar had just landed in the Rue [du] Helder.

Helder is only a little rue between two boulevards, Italien and Haussmann, and our hotel is just five windows high and across. We are only a few moments from Place de l'Opéra where all the buses go everywhere. It is the hurly burly of Paris – banks, business, cinemas. It's not at all a chichi part but the rue du Helder is quite quiet and we were lucky to find ourselves in a hotel that is French, but clean and modern enough to keep us warm and comfortable. They are rare in Paris at this price and everyone says how did we find it and we did, just by going one day into hundreds of hotels, up and down, and asking prices and looking at rooms. And goodnight again,

S XXX

[Sketch of SR, JR and Sweeney holding hands.]

*(Re: Weeno letter of yours which I
rec[eived] today. You wrote it on the
10th so that means it takes ten days.)*
Gar
20 December 1948

Dear Sun
I received your lovely 'very Sun'
letter today and I feel so close to Paris and the little kero stove (Is it like
ours? Remember John saying, 'You ought to take one' like ours to Paris
and you saying you couldn't take everything?) and your 3 little beds in a
row. Is it a large room? Is it furnished with any sort of taste? I feel so
close to the rue du Helder at the moment, I wonder if you are thinking
of me at this precise moment!

First of all, I will write of Weeno. You say in your letter, relating to
where Bert lives that it 'is not in anyway possible for him to have
Weeno with him, nor do I think he wishes it' to quote your letter *'nor do
I feel that he would willingly take Weeno away from us, were his own future
resolved'*. To me, that is the important part of your letter – that is all I
want to know, and if (for Weenie's sake) Bert will confirm that, I will be
quite happy – my only worry when I wrote you before was that Bert
would take Weeno from you, and I would worry then. I *do* feel for Bert,
I *do feel* that in some way I understand him not wanting to 'renounce
the concept of parenthood' but I do feel too that he need not renounce
the concept *in himself* if he feels it necessary, but for Weeno's sake it is
necessary that he renounce something. I have forced him into this position. I know, he, Bert would not have had to do this had I been a different person, but I am *not* a different person and his fight is really (in
regards to Weeno) not with his own renouncings, or feelings, and not
with or over Weeno, but with me.

I evaded this fight perhaps in *actual words* with him, over this *particular issue* and now I feel for him being forced, by me, into some sort of
position he had not thought would arise – And this I am sorry for –
about my own weakness and I (as one always seems, in these things to
revert to) have to have some peg to hang my hat on – in reality, as far as
my knowledge of myself goes I would have been incapable of doing so,
and still am – and I feel quite seriously it's something to do with my
particular glandular set up that I am unable to face Bert. I do not know

(above)
27. Sunday and Sweeney.

(right)
28. Florence Noonan at Heide.

(far right)
29. Sweeney in the Heide garden, c. 1955.

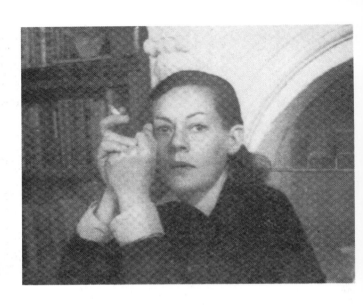

(top left)
30. Joy in the Heide library, 1958.

(left)
31. Peregrine and Fern at Avonsleigh, c. 1956.

(above)
32. Joy, Charles Osborne and Gray at Joy's solo exhibition at
the Melbourne Bookclub Gallery, February 1950. The *Faces*
series hangs in the background.

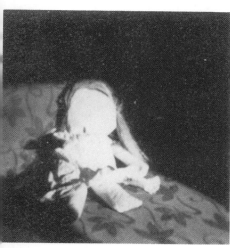

(top left)
33. *Gethsemane V* (c. 1946), Brush, ink and gouache, Collection Museum of Modern Art at Heide.

(bottom left)
34. *Love I* (1949), Brush, ink and paper on board, Collection Pamela McIntosh.

(above)
35. *Face II* (1947—48), Brush, ink and wash, Collection Janine Burke.

(left)
36. Gethsemane, Sunday's doll, 1953.

37. A Heide Christmas card.

quite about this yet but I think it is. I'm not referring particularly to Hodgkie's but to what is *me* and what I can face, and what I can't. Nevertheless out of this sorting ground ... I feel if Bert will leave Weeno with you, I will be happy and it is for you and John to find terms that are suitable and happy with you.

For me I feel that he is a little boy who will grow up, and the only thing I wish is that his growing up is not too painful or that his growing up will [not] undermine him as a man and that is my only wish. If I thought his security was at stake I would be worried. With you I do not feel this. I do not mean that I have no inner peace, for as far as that goes I am quite blazé [sic], I feel so peaceful it makes me wonder – I am happy – but I am not as good for Weeno as you and John, but I love Weeno and I want him to be a man. What sort I don't care, whether he be an artist or a pick and shovel man, all is that he be complete – I can't say anymore.

... I have not seen any Boyds. I wrote Mary and told her to come and see me if she felt like a day in the bush. I have seen a dear little table in the Primrose Pottery Shop made up on top of handpainted tiles and glazed in an oven made by Mary Boyd.[1] It was very sweet and looked like Mary in some way.

Yes, Gar has been painted inside and is more Ned Kelly I think now, more by accident than design. The kitchen is a pleasure. Another pleasure to come in the new year is – for the sum of £20 we will be able to have a septic tank and believe me 'burying it is fun' for a while! But when one has a poo or two each day it's a positive menace!! and every blo-fly [sic] has significance, or to me anyway – and then there is only the poo to pee in and each day I wonder where the hell can I tip the poo today? It doesn't take tons of everyday living to run out of pots to find.

The soil is dry and cracked here. We were unable to get it ploughed and we water by running from the dam to the veg garden with numerous buckets of water that always seem inadequate under the Aussie sun and the dam will be dry by January, I should say. We mulch and mulch in concentrated spots only, our lettuces (which I wish I could air mail to

[1] Edith MacMillan opened the Primrose Pottery Shop in 1929. It sold ceramics by the Boyds and others, as well as fabrics, art books and reproductions of modern paintings. It ran until 1977. Though Primrose Pottery would take over the premises of Cynthia Reed's Modern Furnishings in 367 Little Collins Street, eventually it moved to an arcade off Bourke Street.

you) and peas and beans which are lovely and our herbs and strawber-ries. I have made loganberry and gooseberry jam, nice too! But we are too late what with going to Elwood and various interruptions to really get stuck into it! Besides which it has been a lovely lesson in how to plant and just what will and will not grow in our awfully 'Aussie' soil. I'm sure the 'red heart' could not be as parched as we get here so quickly.

I am going to post you a remarkable little Aussie book, not a work of art but rather a work of life called *On the Wool Track*[2]. I found every minute of it intriguing. By the way, did you get my poor little Xmas pressy [of] three little hankies? It would have cost at least £5 to mail air mail any food to you and to send by boat is precarious as I do not know whether you'll be surviving a Paris winter or not . . .

Weeno's school sounds good but as you say not quite perhaps what we would pick as far as schools go – but what of the Aussie kindergartens, they too are not quite – so what? If he's happy there I think it's good. His blue pinafore sounds very sweet and like him. I bet he's very proud of his pinafore.

I am writing this at 3.40 pm and it is hot and there must be a million blo-flies in the kitchen and DDT seems no good now as the flies I'm sure have developed a resistance to same . . .

My poor mother's little estate is clearing itself a little now and I'm afraid by the time Weeno is twenty-one the little house in Elwood will have depreciated so much that it will not be more than the income of a cottage in Moonee Ponds to him, but if social systems allow I suppose it will be nice for him but money will have a different value then.[3]

Gray's Ma has sent you some books but I'm sure you won't get them by Xmas. When I think of my lovely hamper last Xmas I could cry that I cannot send you one this Xmas. A lovely hamper packed with goodies. It was fun! I am going to wear my Xmas frock this Xmas. I will be with you both very much and Gray and I only wish you'd be with us but our

---

[2] C E W Bean, *On the Wool Track*, Charles Scribner's, New York, 1947. It was described on the dust jacket as 'A lively account of the vast Australian frontier and the fabulous sheep ranches which parallel in many ways the romance and rugged atmosphere of America's old west.'

[3] Louise Hester bequeathed her house at 21 Dawson Avenue, Elwood, to Sweeney to inherit when he was twenty-one. When Joy left Tucker and Sweeney, Louise cut Joy out of her will. Under the terms of the will, Joy received the interest on the estate during her lifetime. She also received £200.

love goes to you both and all the fun with snow men and jingle bells I hope you'll have. Perhaps by then you'll have your little Peugeot and will go for a lovely Xmas car ride.

... I have seen Jean [Langley] and [John] Sinclair on the two occasions I have been in town.[4] They are well. Joyce Good is still scrubbing floors in Brisbane.[5] I have not heard of Barrie for a while now. Charles Osborne was in Melb. but we did not see him.

Our love to you both again and Weeno too

Joy

Grand Hotel Haussmann, Paris
16 December 1948

Darling Joy

This is a Christmas and New Year letter and I have been sitting on the bed reading all your letters since we left so I can feel more than ever close when the day comes. I have been thinking of you both standing on the end of the rainbow just as you told me about it and how you must be the only two people in the world to find the end or was it the beginning because you never know which side God starts it. Perhaps no one will ever believe you except me and I do and I think with Gray you may walk up it one day, as Sweeney and I do sometimes, but we have to shut our eyes first.

We wish we had a million pounds in Paris to fill the hamper once more, to send it flying to you with all sorts of froggy things and surprises but I can only send a tiny handky [sic] so that if you weep with disappointment you can blow your nose on a Christmas tree and find the kiss in it. I can't help remembering last year and your lovely letters about Christmas day from Sydney and I wonder if you still have the mad little

[4] Artist Jean Langley (b.1926) would marry John Sinclair (1915–91) in 1952. Sinclair was a friend of the Reeds, and of Nolan's. He lived at Heide intermittently during the 1940s. In 1946, with Jack Bellew, Sinclair worked on *Tomorrow* (1946), a short-lived broadsheet that was the last publication of Reed & Harris. Sinclair would become the Melbourne *Herald*'s long-serving music critic. Introduced by Sinclair to the Reeds, Langley became a close friend of Sunday's.

[5] Joyce Good, a friend of Hester's, was Rosemary Smith's sister. Joyce was married to Malcolm Good who stood as a Communist Party candidate in the federal and state elections of 1940 and 1943. The Reeds financed his campaigns.

dress and if it is a warm summer's New Year's Eve, perhaps you will wear it and think of us in Paris. Perhaps Gray will wear his yellow shirt (unironed) and we will drink to you both in vin rouge and will you drink to us in tea!

We can make our own now in a saucepan with Aussie tea that fortunately we had with us in our suitcases but it is never the same. Never. We don't know why. John thinks [it's] because the saucepan lid has no hole in the top as a teapot has. Oh, to be beside your little stove in the lamplight with the big moon coming up behind the gums, or to be at home with Min in my arms beside a summer fire with the marzipan cake and you all on the sofa. And here we are in Paris, as you say, three little Aussies and in three days in a flying boat.

The weather is as cold as the south pole tho' the seasons take three months to change in God's time and often I feel very mixed up between aeroplanes and God and wonder if the world will ever change the clocks and why not. Thank goodness we have had a beautiful rain today to clean the Paris streets which are always so dirty you dare not look and yet you must and I'm afraid we are always thinking what a dirty old place Paris is. I can never keep my clothes clean and even sitting in the métros the dust and fog seem to penetrate even my coat so that my panties are black at night and unless you know the right soap (which I didn't know for weeks) you can't possibly wash them because the water is so madly hard that ordinary soap just makes mud. And so in desperation we are always taking things to the laundry and so we spend more money and it seems impossible not to and we get very angry that we cannot save a penny.

Well we are expecting our little Peugeot before Christmas day we hope so that we can drive somewhere and have a picnic with ourselves in the snow, not that it has snowed yet but we do hope it will soon. I know Weeno will love it, and then what? We make up our minds every day to leave Paris early in the New Year and then we feel sad at the thought of going away. I'm not sure whether it's because we planned to stay or whether it's because we want to be in Paris. Life is always so complicated that we hardly know what we think or if we think at all. Yet somehow we don't want to move. Our house hunting we have really abandoned now and so unless the miracle happens I do really think we will be making off somewhere about the middle of January. But don't worry about addresses. Always use the Bank and our mail will be forwarded wherever we are.

We went to the rue Passy for you to find your corner. We walked up the long winding street which wasn't as I expected and is a very busy market street with lots of small shops and veg[ie]s on the little stalls and 'tout le monde sur le balcon' as the French say which means all the world is on the balcony, and for some reason of their own is also a vulgar expression for a woman with big breasts. Anyway it is a very crowded winding street with markets and there were lots of corners but we couldn't make up our minds if we recognised yours and so I suppose we didn't and we never found anywhere to live though Passy itself is quite a lovely part of Paris where it is residential and quiet on the hill.

I have thought of Julien [Green]. We wish he were in the telephone book so that we could go and stand outside his house and wave to him and Weeno might say 'Bonjour Monsieur, ça va?' as he does now with everyone and anyone in the street charging around Paris, with all his engines going as he puts it.

I sent you a little book the other day which was meant to arrive for Christmas but I forgot about the price of stamps and how I couldn't send it air mail so I don't know whenever it will reach you and I have put lots of seeds in it for Gray to play with and I think you wanted chervil, that lovely ferny frail salad that we used to have at Heide. It is called cerfeuille and you will find it in the pages. Grow it in a shady place and [plant] lots of it. If I remember it doesn't like hot tough conditions. And there is a little salad thing called mache that we eat a lot and you will find it, too. It grows rather like a little bellis perrenis and you have to pull up the whole plant as lettuce. I should think you would need about 12 or 14 for a good salad so grow it thickly. It may come best in the late summer or autumn but it would be fun to try it when it comes and keep extra seed for later on in case it's not a success. As you know all seeds are forbidden and if they open my packet they will surely confiscate the lot. John says if by any chance you should be asked any questions just say you know nothing whatever about it but it might be best not to give the seed away to anyone else.

Goodnight to you both. It is bedtime and once again I sit in the bathroom while John reads the French papers from end to end and Swene builds an Arc de Triomphe with the blocks Mrs Smith gave him. His most treasured possession and I don't know whatever any of us would have done without them.

Kiss yourselves for me and may our love be active and with you in some way and jumping about and around you when Christmas comes and New Year's Eve at midnight. Love to all at Gar and all the farm and Gyp and your beautiful goat and bless all for us and a thousand wishes for everlasting peace on your loved heads.

S

Weeno chose his own Christmas card for you. In fact he just got it for you from a girl in a shop while we were looking at something else.

Gar
Wednesday, 5 January (1949)

Dear Sun and John
All the lovely 'tres equisites'!! [sic] and today the photo arrived of that very seasoned looking little traveller. He certainly looks 'tres continentale'!! and very illusive [sic] around the eyes – a beaut little boy he looks in his beret. What an enormous forehead he seems to have! A real enfant terrible! – a genius no doubt!

We put the magnifying glass on the little black dots on the photo on the cover of Swene's photo and lo! the ladies of Paris all hurrying hither and skither. I have John's beautiful rose card with the silver stars all over it on the top of my cupboard and when the lights are out if there is a moon we have the stars inside too – in the form of a rose – and Weeno's little card beside my bed. If we get any more breaths of Paris, little Gar will certainly have to take to foreign language to cope with it all. I'm not very good at writing small to fit in these air mail things. I hope it's not too much of a struggle to read same. We loved your gay letter, John, about the Café Montaigne and I can just see the girl pleading with Sun for a dance. Gray and I feel as though we were really there giggling with you both that evening. We screamed with laughter as we read your letter John! It reminded us of that song of Maurice Chevalier's – 'Eef you 'appen to bee a stranger in Gay Parree, Wee, wee, cherieee!' Is old Maurice still singing there?

Florence has been madly trying to get the creases out of the print you sent her Sun – you really crazy optimist! 'Do not crush'!! Nevertheless Florence treasures and nurses it daily and peeps to see if it's any flatter per hour. I'm quite sure had the pilot carried it personally Florence would not have enjoyed it anymore and my 'joyeux noel' han[d]kerchief I certainly will not cry in! I feel as though I should pin it with a safety pin on my bosom like mothers pin the[ir] little girls' hankies – mine not for blow, only for show – so everyone will say, 'look it's French!' ...

Gray has not been well. Poor thing had a fit on Xmas morning and we were having Martin and Rose and Gray's ma and unk here for Xmas dinner. Anyway to be completely marvellous Gray was up out of bed by lunch time – he didn't look himself at all but managed to keep some sort of consciousness going. He has been really not too good ever since. It was really too much effort for him so I hope a couple of quiet weeks will see him right again. He has been painting a fair bit down in our wood shed and we got a great kick out of having them on the wall ...

Did I tell you David [Boyd] is making pottery in competition to Guy and that David married his Hermia and it looks as though Guy will marry her sister Clyte [sic]? They are both flooding the market with ashtrays – very slick Sydney-looking things.

I am posting a couple of copies of a kids' newspaper called *News Way* – we get it every week – they are really for the school kids but we devour them madly.

Our little garden would look really poor I suppose if you saw it at the moment but we have had and are still having lettuces, peas, beans and have leeks coming on and our carrots are just over but we have more coming on, and dahlias, gladioli (which shine in their glory 'neath the apples) and cornflowers and marigolds, calendulas. The bellis perrenis are over. They shrink from our sun. Pink-white and a cardinal color ...

We, or I, haven't any news except that my brother has another little girl. We live so much into our selves – not so much from choice but it just happens that way – nevertheless we do not miss not seeing people as our life seems very full and complete but it makes letter writing hard in one way as I feel *too* much of [one] thing can be a little tedious, even to the best people.

... There are no good pictures on here, all revivals of hash[1] for the Xmas holidays I s'pose. We've not been to the pictures since about 3 months. Have you seen any good ones by Cocteau or the boys?

Well the little aeroplanes still sound lost as they trundle across our Gar heaven and we plant by the moon now and have seeds up in 3 days,

[1] Hash is slang for second-rate.

fair dinkum. We love little Gar very much and we love the shadow of the hills in the darkness and Gray still looks for gold in every pebble and we both wore our [Christmas] hamper shirt and frock on New Year's Eve and drank to you in claret in the stillness of those little hills and the shirt I forgot to tell you irons as easily as anything. In fact it is the easiest shirt that I iron and my little frock I love and feel I look very pretty in. Gray says I do anyway. Our love to you both this New Year and from Gar comes the love and kisses to you

Gar
Monday, 24 January 1949

Dear Sun

Well they arrived!! the seeds and 'Paris through the ages' – all intact! What a thrill. We felt quite like smugglers when we received them and opened up the book. A lovely little book and we've looked and looked at your corner street where the Haussman[n] is until I nearly believe if I look long enough that [I] will see you three turn the corner and wave to us from the pages ... Will we ever see you again? When we look at Paris I wonder how you could ever leave such a lovely place. How splendid the Versailles Palace looks! I think I love that best.

We are going to be very very careful and plant the seeds, some in seed boxes and some in a bed and watch over them like little mothers. Did I tell you we have had one loss of the things you planted in the herb garden, the balsam – the thing to cure Gray's fits. I don't know why it just died but the herb garden is really beginning to look formal and a weeny bit like a medieval herb garden. Sounds odd in Hurstbridge but there you are ...

I don't know if I told you Yvon [Lennie] had another child and Mary [Boyd] is 4 months with her 3rd and Rosemary is 4 months, too ...

And did I tell you Neil Douglas got married last Friday? Rosemary and Martin went to the registry office as witnesses and then Neil told Rosemary he had a readymade family! A little boy 2 years old! and Martin has known for 2 years!! No one even knew Neil had a girl – a very unusual one too I believe, quite a radical in her own way. As gossip has it so Neil and wife and child then proceeded to Bayswater to pounce on mama and produce the family of which she knew nothing about. They are now living at Bayswater and fixing up the garden. Flo and I had a lovely laughing day the day we heard the tidings ...

I have sent by boat some Persil. I hope you are allowed to get it. Did Swene get the mad dollie wood I made him for his birthday? I have not yet [seen] Mary Christina and have not heard from Barrie for a while. It is very hot here now and the days are dreamy and little Gar doesn't mind the heat as she has plenty of mulch heaps. Did you meet Peter [Bellew] and his Kirsova yet?[1]

Well my love to you three little Parisians and a dream or two to you of our little fairy hills

Joy

Grand Hotel Haussmann
Rue du Helder, Paris
19 January 1949

Dear Joy
It must be a month or more since I wrote about Weeno and I'm afraid your letter hardly meets the reality because we have been so continually anxious and it doesn't seem possible to resolve the position in the simple way you suggest.

When I said 'that I did not think Bert was in a position to take Sweeney or that even if he were that he would willingly do so' I covered very little ground and at the time I wrote my thoughts, [I was] really deeply concerned in asking you to tell me if you had been feeling that you would like Weeney back in your own life. I do feel that you are happy that he is with us but at some much deeper level I don't feel you answered my questions. In the days following our letters and after talking again with Bert I had reached the feeling in myself that I could not say or do anything that might seem only to push further into Bert's suffering and that if Bert himself were unable to give direction that we must attempt just to live through our time with Sweeney.

[1] Bellew's first wife was Hélène Kirsova, prima ballerina of the de Basil Company. They married during the company's Australian tour.

But I'm sure that this isn't wise even if it were possible as it is evident, and has always been evident, right back to the days when Weeney first came to Heide (and you will remember I told you in letters to Sydney) that Bert's intensive personal relationship with Sweeney is quite incompatible with the circumstance of Sweeney's life and the security of his future and peace with us.

Since we came to Paris it has been a period for us of tension and continual anxiety so far as Sweeney and Bert were concerned and I have worried terribly trying to resolve some way that would bring peace for everyone. John I think has felt that if we adopted Sweeney it would be the happiest thing for everyone. Following a day with Sweeney that seemed to bring about some sort of crisis in Bert he put forward ... proposals. He said the proposals provided were in order of preference.

1. That he should take Sweeney.

2. That we should continue our life with Sweeney, his background and environment ...

... In response to the first proposal, what can we say darling? It is not for us. You must know my thoughts and the anxiety I would feel as I know your thoughts. Bert is not in a position to take Sweeney. It is true enough that I don't think he wishes to take Sweeney away from what he has said is the 'best possible environment' which I think is the only concept he has of us.

However, that is only half the picture. I do not know if Bert could arrange to take Sweeney or not but it is possible, of course, that he might be able to and if he decided there was no other alternative I think he might do so. I am sure Bert desires Sweeney's happiness, of course, but he does not take the view that Sweeney's life is the only one to be considered and I think views the situation as a totality of lives concerned in which his own salvation and realisation is of equal measure, neither more or less. I have not told you before as I felt it was unnecessary to make you unhappy but from what Bert has expressed to us I do not think he would consent under any circumstances to Sweeney being with you. I do not know if he will change his mind and I have not put any such thought forward as I felt it might provoke further tension which in the circumstances would be very unwise.

So far as Bert's relationship with Sweeney is concerned his concept of childhood and parenthood is, as I think you know, quite incompatible with our own and I confess inevitably repugnant to us both (forgive the word) but I am sure Bert thinks it is instinctive and good and in consequence it would be best and normal for Sweeney to live with him if it were practical. In response to the second proposal, that we should continue to provide a background for Sweeney, I can only say that as far as I know myself and John that the nature of our lives and our living make it impossible for us to build Sweeney's future with us in those terms.

It seems then if Sweeney is to continue life with us under conditions harmonious and of peace for us all that it will be necessary for Bert to give us affirmation that he desires Sweeney to live with us permanently and that he will agree to do everything possible to direct Sweeney's future life with ours in a way that is compatible with one world, and that in his own relationship he will do nothing to split Sweeney's childhood or disrupt his home and all that word implies in love and responsibility.

Both John and I feel very strongly that we do not wish to put this forward to Bert before hearing from you. I am most anxious to maintain a sense of quietness in order to await your deepest thoughts and consideration and advice as it involves so much anxiety in the possibility perhaps of Bert deciding to take Weeno. If there is anything more we can do or be or protect I know you will tell me and do please write as soon as ever you feel able.

It would be impossible to cover in a letter the whole situation emotionally or detailed and I hope you will forgive me that I do not attempt to do so and [you can] somehow fill in the gaps. Perhaps I should say, as we seem only to be dealing in the factual side that as far as Sweeney is concerned I think Bert has a very powerful influence on him while they are together but I have no evidence in Sweeney that he needs him in a real sense. I am sure that in the very confined life the three of us have had, to live in one room, that he finds release in being with Bert and I could not interpret his reactions and normal warmths and enthusiasms in the way that Bert does.

I cannot write any news tonight, everyone in Paris has had the Grippe and we have all had it too. John was very fragile and ill and had to go to bed but we are all gathering our strength and have just come back from a few days in Normandy pottering through the farmy country in our Peugeot. The lovely beech forests and the church bells were too much for us and we went to mass in the old old Norman church in a place called Le Newbourg where the Abbé was dressed in [a] sparkling green and silver robe and Sweeney thought he was God.

Our love to you Joy and thoughts. Thank you for the lovely little Christmas hanky and from Swene too, we loved our hankys and they helped make our day a happy one.

Your last letter just arrived. Please tell me if Gray is well again and take care of him and take care of you.

S

Gar
1 February 1949

Dear John and Sun
First of all – there is nothing that would make me feel more at ease than for you to adopt Swene. As for my own 'inner feelings'; they are as I have just said.

When I went away with Gray, I went away leaving Sweeney with you in the knowledge that he was safe and happy. I would never have dumped him into the world for just anyone to look after him, and from the day of Swene's birth, and before he was so very bound up in my life and yours and grew with you and love, I had asked Sun before I made any decision to leave Bert defin[i]tely – 'if anything should happen' would she look after Swene as I knew my love, Swene's love, and yours, in a way that love is when it's close. I was happy in the knowledge that your thoughts re Swene's life were as mine. Also I could not have taken him with me nor could I have looked after him *at that time had I been home*. I did not feel capable or well enough.

I really started my life with Gray *after* my hospital session was finished, and I had a rest and our love grew *from there without Swene*.

During my road of rest and recovery, the knowledge that I had so defin[i]tely been given from Lovell that I would not live long, spurred me, with my love to live, and in those months of mental and physical rebirth I started on a new road within myself, without Swene, but it was *essential* for my recovery to have the knowledge that Swene was where he was, *with love*, and I began to build and repair my glands. I can say that the process has taken a year of hard work and control, with many slips in my faith in God and myself and my own capacities, it has meant hanging on very hard – and Gray has helped me fight these things but naturally, he has been a minor part in the sense, that these things *come from within*. Unfortunately, during my life with Bert, these strengths were not in me and I wished to die for many years, I prayed I might, not because of Bert but because of myself. The continual thoughts in one direction over a few years I suppose gave me Hodgkin's – and it is only natural that it takes time and labour now. Had I not changed my life drastically, I would not have had the strength. I had to stop my own particular brand of self-indulgence.

Then came Sweeney, and within a year things had got beyond me, and in the second year I went to Sydney, and with the confirmation of my condition I had to face God and I *started with your help* and *because of it* and your being a mother and love to Swene when I could not be, with that wonderful aid of love from you I have nearly I think regained myself and this is without the little boy my life began anew.

As to Bert's propositions, I will be quite frank – in answer to the first I say I want you to adopt Swene.

In answer to the second, it is, I think, more to do with you both than with me, for if it is – as I gather it to be, that you look after Sweeney, but do not on paper actually adopt him, it would have, I imagine, to be for your satisfaction and for Swene's life, to be drawn up in some way as to give the three of you some feeling of permanence and certainty. That could be done, I suppose, and as you know I have implicit faith in your decisions and will help toward them all I can . . .

. . . That is about as far as I can take [it] from this side of the ocean and my faith and my love is with you both; as regards your proposition I would prefer a straight out legal adoption but in the event of no other course being open to you, my faith and knowledge of you both and my love for you make me give your proposition wholehearted support. As far as Bert being able to take Weeno – can he? I did not desert Weeno, I placed him in your good care – I would fight any attempt of his to do that on all grounds.

> My love to you both now from Gar
> Joy

John and Sunday had the adoption papers drawn up and Bert signed them while the Reeds were still in Europe.

Gar
20 February 1949

Dear Sun
Somehow as the days go by and days go lived and letters come and go and I try to remember when you went away and now it seems as though I have always known the letters and you. When I stop and think 'Sun' you were always in Paris and other days it seems you are not in Paris at all and how silly of me to go to the Post Office as you and John have never been in Paris, what am I thinking of?

And then I remember the days we madly stuck herbs in and I look at the herb garden now and try to remember what it looked like when we put the Heide herbs there. We seem to now for the first time be able to see Gar as a whole and can visualize what it will eventually look like. I have not been able to do this until yesterday when Gray suggested we draw a plan and we drew Gar together and with all the geranium cuttings grown into geranium bushes and trees grown full and big and ageratum in bushes around the door . . .

We had Jack and Pauline McCarthy who are back from Adelaide here for the night last week and Pauline is about to have another baby and they were saying Max and Vonnie have a really beautiful child[1] and that Max was doing very well in Adelaide . . . and they had a lovely veg garden . . .

Gray has done a lovely painting of Sugarloaf Mountain at Kinglake and he has been painting a lot and nobody likes his paintings, and what is more they don't even say they don't like them, there is just silence, and we have put one or two of them out on our little Gar wall and now we've taken them down as Martin and the McCarthys said 'I seen you been painting' [sic] and so that worried Gray and so he has put them in a little stack behind the door, but I like to look at them so gradually I pull them out again.

I went to see nephew Sewell as 'Unk' was not back until yesterday and he is most surprised as last time I went he said, 'I give you until Feb. and you'll have to have more treatment' and so I went to see him in Feb. and he gave me a clean sheet and he makes all sorts of questions to

[1] Samela, Max and Yvonne Harris's daughter.

me as to what I do? do I work hard? how many hours sleep I have etc. What do I eat? and I say 'I'm on Hay' and he asks me how many pounds of meat I eat a week and he said I am very clever and I ought to be proud of myself and I am quite.

We got the lovely jewelled Montmart[r]e postcard from Swene and the very exquisite Ingres postcard from John, a painting I have never seen before. To me it seems to suspend all thought for the moments of beholding it and it is on the shelf in our Gar bedroom and I look at it every morning and am duly astonished by its static qualities ... Swene is quite an expert letter writer now, I see, everything is on the line. And he only puts two cross bars on E instead of the Xmas one [capital E with 5 cross bars] which I suppose was just to emphasise the point.

Our life with Florence is very rich and full and we are very fond of her and we all have happy days which alternate between tramping the wilds of Hurstbridge, exploring the mysteries of the infinite and bawdy laughter with the crazy gossip of Hurstbridge. Yes, our Florence days are good ones ...

I was horrified to hear of the customs stamp on the Ned Kellys – I do hope it's not plonk in the middle of the paintings and am anxious to hear what becomes of them ...

I wonder if old Alice B Toklas is still in Paris?

... Dear Sun, I hope your trials are not too harsh re Swene and that you are not too tired and I think continually of you all and hope that God protects you and love smiles at you ... And if I can send you anything let me know. What about tinned milk? Is milk short? Do tell me if you want any food or things ...

Love and quietness be with you
Joy

PS   The whole of Cooktown was flattened by a cyclone the other day. Only 8 buildings left standing.

Gar
Late February 1949

Dear Sun

Your lovely long letter I received now since a week ago, [and] I have made two attempts to answer it and somehow my thoughts won't collect themselves enough to do justice to those expressed in your letter which moved me very much – so I won't attempt today.

Our lives seem to have been filled with days of work and heat. After our floods and all the rain a few weeks back the grass has grown in Hurstbridge to waist high – and then it's been too wet to burn and the local council have just had to leave it. Then we had two scorching north wind days which dried it all out completely and it was then too dry to burn off as they were afraid of starting bush fires, and they forbid residents to burn off at all – so we've, or rather Gray, has had to scythe it all and then we've had to rake it up into heaps. We have at least a million mulch heaps, but they are dangerous as they are as dry as a bone – I am not exaggerating. The grass is waist high all along the roads here, and we've had two grass fires already – fortunately [brought] under control by our local fire brigade.

Then we had to sell our goat as it was far too strong for me to manage and he broke off his tether and broke 3 thick leather collars we put on him and I had visions of Gray being sick or me being sick or us being in town one day and the goat breaking loose and getting into someone's paddock and completely damaging everything and everytime we had to move him it took the two of us to hold him while one put his stake in the ground as he would butt us, so you can imagine the pandemonium he could cause . . .

This is a very Aussie little place – the longer we are here the more we realize the very 'Aussieness' of the land up here and the climate and the look of the stringy bark hills. We could be 900 hundred miles outback here, the dusty roads and the heat and the dryness and it's very picturesque and has eaten completely into our hearts . . . The people up here are very beautiful, very rough hewn from a long time back somewhere when this Aussie sun taught them how to squint and how [to] know the meaning of the word individual and they have not much respect for much else than that one word which gives them the right to be themselves. And the people here respect that right more than I had ever dreamt [of] from city people ...

We have discovered that we have a Chinatown here too and they all live over the other side of town in the original gold rush humpies and [it's] very picturesque as the place up there is littered with mines and ghost stories from the roaring days. I have been given a deepness of feeling for this place which I shall never lose and will make me not want to leave it for any long periods. It's too close to me now to ever part from. It is the most real part of me that I have ever known, and I can look into me now as though it is a still pool, and see the reflection of the stringy bark hills of my heart ...

Charles Osborne is in Melbourne and he and Johnnie Yule and Mary Christina told Martin they would be coming to see us but it is so long now I think he must have returned to Brisbane.

I have not had time to look in my crystal yet but I feel its life in my drawer. One has to keep them dark as they contain 'odyle', a substance found in things such as the human body and especially magnets and if this is exposed to the sun, which is charged with negative odyle, as the moon is with positive odyle, exposure to a heavy charge of this source upsets the sensitiveness [sic] of a crystal for a long time.[1]

... Love to you three. Am going to the village now and hope there is a blue envelope for us par avion.

'Direct sunshine, firelight, electric light must never be allowed to enter the room while the crystal is being used – if sitting is held in the daytime, the gazer should sit with his back to the light which if possible should filter into the room from the north.

'One of the best times of the day for crystal gazing is just before the oncoming of twilight, an hour which, incidentally, is one particularly favourable to occult manifestations of all kinds. An attempt to read the crystal should never be made shortly after a meal.

'The crystal must be placed in front of the observer on a stand or table, the surface of which should be covered with a black cloth. A black cushion may be used to advantage. [The crystal] must be screened from the reflections of

---

[1] Hester wrote two pages of instruction titled *Divination by Crystal Gazing*, (c.1950), Peregine Smith Collection.

extraneous objects by means of a dark handkerchief wrapped partly round it.

'... The ideal position is that where the crystal ceases to reflect any object whatever and its depths, though appearing darkened, are quite clear and pellucid.

'The gazer should first close his eyes and keep them shut for 2 to 3 minutes so as to exclude all disturbing visual images from the retina. He can now begin to look in the crystal, calmly, steadily and with interest. He must not screw up his eyes in a determined fashion and transfix the unoffending globe with a fierce glare. On the contrary all feeling of tension and exertion must be carefully avoided, and the eyes should be blinked at normal intervals ...

'It is most important for success that the student should not overtax his powers. For this reason he should begin his sittings with a short sitting, gradually increasing the time until the space of an hour or more can be spent gazing without fatigue.'

Chapter 7

March
August
1949

Gar
1 March 1949

Dear Sun

... I find I am changing these days and I have not done much creative work except in the garden. I seem to be becoming much more quiet and composed you'll be glad to hear – or I feel I am ...

We still have no visitors – I wrote Mary Boyd and invited her and kids to come up some day in the jalopy and Gray wrote and asked her to make him a little pottery jerry[1] in her own Mary way, for a pressy for him to give Rosemary's baby ... We've not heard a word, not a simple reply, so I fear really that Mary does not approve or some funny little thing she's thought up. I don't care really that no one comes to see us, but when one puts out in some way to someone I suppose it's natural that it leaves one feeling a little empty when they don't trouble to reply. Still, perhaps it's for some reason and perhaps I have changed and it would really be better for [me] not to see Mary as I may upset her in some way and I would not like to do that ...

I went to see nephew Sewell and he says I'm top hole – I don't feel it but nevertheless I am apparently – I never seem to feel top hole for one solid day. Every day at some time or another I come to the end of my tether – this annoys me when I'm s'posed to be OK it seems mad that I should feel like that. He tells me it would be unwise to get prego and if I get into trouble he will help me which I thought was nice of him and gave me a feeling of security. Not that I will but, you never know, accidents happen. Did Swene ever get [the] dolly [sic] wood that I sent him? Well dear Sun I eagerly await the mail and news of you all.

Love and goodnight to you three 'walkabouts'

Joy

[1] A chamber-pot.

Gar
31 March 1949

Dear Sun and dear both of you
... We've had lots and lots of rain
and the other night as I was lying in bed and it was about 3 am I became
aware of a dim reddish light on the wall. G was asleep and I lay wondering
and thinking of someone being outside with a small lantern or a torch –
so I gathered my fears and leapt out to the window and a most peculiar
thing as I've ever seen! The old sickle moon lying flat on its back – low in
the sky and the color of burning bronze a long way off and very spectral
looking and menacing in a quiet gospel way and God told me to tell
everyone that he was giving them time to prepare, and that the dying old
sickle was his symbol for take heed and he'd be doing awful things like
floods and weird gales soon. 'Dig your trenches and runaways to your
water holes and dams and warn the sick not to be afraid.' I wondered if
Florence was peering out of her little attic, thinking of all her sick and
poorly. The next day I read the papers of the terrible floods in Queensland
and of all the cyclones and gales and earthquakes in the Pacific for two
hours and earthquakes [in] Canberra and I knew we would not be too
badly off for a couple of weeks anyway and I wanted to tell everyone and
I asked everyone if they had seen the moon and no one had.

We have lovely sprouts, cauli and brocoli, but my, it's a business
keeping butterflies, cabbage worms and all the pests from their lush
green leaves – they all want to make lace of them but so far we've defied
them ...

Love to you dear travellers and
XX XXX XX

Gar
3 April 1949

Dear Ones
... Martin is well and so is his Rose
who is about to produce herself a child in less than a month – you ask
how they are, and together? I don't know, they seem like lovers, they
hold hands and goo at each other – it embarrasses me even – I suppose

that is love. I don't know, I haven't loved like that – they are so looking forward to their baby, which already has an enormous trousseau, so large, I am afraid to say the word baby for fear I shall hear of babies, and babble babies. I see them both very sweetly and hopefully of a world that belongs in a world that is not mine – a world I would fear for myself for I fear that is the world I may have been born in. I don't know, nevertheless they are a pretty couple in a pretty picture.

I don't know either of Mary Christina. Mrs Smith tells me she is going to England, where she intends to go on the stage if she gets a chance. She has sold nearly all her treasures and Mrs Smith was offered a beautiful dinner set for £30, which she is debating whether she would be able to sell in the shop ...

I have heard no more on the bush telegraph of the Perceval family ...

We met Woof Woof Matthews in town on a tram and he told us he was running an art school at the top of Collins Street and made us roar with laughter when he said it was a synch [sic][1]. All he did was chew a peppermint and go round the old ladies' easels once a day. Dear old things, he said they ask him if their work is good, and he said 'How can I presume? I would never dare say to another man, you will never do any good, for who knows?' He has got very plump and looks gay – he has a gentle face.

Today we went with Florence over the hills and far away and we saw kangaroos, perhaps 8 in all pad, pad, padding their soft way thru the bush and heath which is out in abundance, pink and white. The darlings did not even hurry to be off when we crossed their path. How anyone could cut them up for soup! ...

... Excitement! G was looking thru a magazine and a page of new French cars! the baby Peugeot was there with its funny headlights behind a grille. What a little character she is! Will there ever be room to take us for a drive in her! ...

We are having a false spring up here, what with all the rain we've had everything has decided at the first bit of sun to flower – wild flowers, heath, orchids and violets everywhere – and even our silly old plum tree, which incidentally has not borne this year is budding even though its leaves [are] gold and red and dropping. The strawberries are blooming

---

[1] Howard Matthews (1910–1980s) was a contemporary of Joy's at the Gallery School and a friend of Nolan's. His cleft palate made speech difficult and earned him the nickname Woof Woof.

too! This is rather odd isn't it? Nature has tricked nature it appears. Florence predicts a dry summer and I a wet one.

Florence and I between us interpret each other's dreams and everyone else's and predict all sorts of joys and catastrophes for the seasons, people and animals. Nothing is sacred and all is in our hands. Between the two of us we [are] even fairly normal I think. I really think we let our imaginations [run away] with us at times and thank goodness we are often quite wrong ...

Well dear ones love to you and England and the island of summeries [sic]. God bless you all and our love to you ... Yes it is funny about Sweeney's face isn't it? I find sometimes, odd times, his personality is so strong and close but without a face then I think that is something to do with being a child.

XX

Gar
April 1949

Dear Sun and John
Every time I write I have to start off by telling almost the same thing – your lovely postcards arrived! By the million! All the lovely Chartres Cathedral ones. Puts old Roulalt [sic] on the spot 'don't it?' The stained glass – it's curious to note the difference a century made to the conception of delineation of facial features – and the seeds!! Already we have French carrots up, lovely little seedlings from the last lot of seeds you sent. And wot's more we know just wot films are on in Paris at the moment.

... There's no doubt about it, G and I will have to learn French! and we would decipher more about the Cocteau film *Terrible Parents* ... We have a deciphering system of first picking out all the English words and then all the French primer words and then adding our interpretation. The Picasso Man[1] – I agree with you John, and I imagine to see it standing at the entrance to the exhibition would bring tears, [t]he amalgamation of man's cherished 'being' in the deepest sense and it reminds me of Eliot's lines

[1] Probably Picasso's *L'homme au mouton* (1943).

I am moved by fancies that are curled
around these images, and cling:
The notion of some infinitely gentle
Infinitely suffering thing.

Gray has been very sick. We went to town on Monday and he was alright except I thought hè seemed a little extreme but put it down to the excitement of town. He felt sick coming home on the train so he said and was very abstract by the time we arrived home. We went to bed and he tossed and turned all night only to get up at 6 am saying he was going to vomit and promptly had a fit – and he didn't come out of that fit but went straight into another and then another and had six fits before 10.30 am and didn't regain consciousness until midday the next day. This is the worst he has ever been and I got worried when he went from one to another and his pills wouldn't work and I could not quieten him. So I had to send an SOS for his ma and we got the doctor who gave him some deadly dope and it is a week now and he is today for the first time again his normal self. But still can only remember very scattered bits of our day in town and is trying to piece the week together in some way for himself.

What was the cause of him being sick I don't know as we have been pretty strict[ly] Hay now for about 6 mths but the enormous void of Monday still exists for him and, poor thing, he was walking around town apparently quite happy and didn't know he was sick nor did I. Still the doctor has given him some different sort of dope now to try and we are very pleased with him so far. He is a local boy from Diamond Creek who is our age and reminds us very much of Ronnie Savage and is also coincidentally a league footballer for Melbourne.[2] But he seems to have one distinct advantage – that he can be talked with and [yet] young enough to know what we are talking about – and he may be of help. It is not so much the fits but the road back – to some sort of piecing [together] of days and time for Gray, some placing of himself into the days and time again that is so difficult.

We met on Monday Mary Christina, whom I though[t] you had met in Brisbane.[3] Still she says not – and I was surprised at her simplicity and liked her.

[2]   Ron Savage was a Carlton league footballer, 1938–45.
[3]   Barrett Reid had introduced Mary Christina to the Reeds in Brisbane in 1946.

Neil Douglas is going into partnership with Arthur Boyd[4] and John Perceval is going to the Gallery again[5] and Mary Boyd and Rosemary are going to have their babies in the same room with the same doctors – too bad if they both come out at the same time!

Still we have more rain and once again the grass seems almost beyond coping which makes us glad.

We bought a book called *The Reprieve* by Sartre because we loved his film *The Die is Cast* so much but the book is quite a different matter. A rather poor war novel with no apparent redeeming features so far.

Florence is well and beaming and madly saying how right I was about the sickle moon and there were 40 people drowned in a cloud burst in Persia just to prove my point!

Easter is at the weekend and Gray and I send all sorts of hot cross kiss buns (symbolically!) to you all and an Easter bunny for Weeno and love and softness to you and hope you will go to a beautiful cruxiafiction [sic] service with candles and crosses for us and it will be lovely springtime for you all.

Joy

Gar
19 May 1949

Dear Ones
     … We had a letter from Barrie which sounded much more cheerful and gay and he sent us some photos of old colonial bushranger pubs now extinct from Queensland and a mad secondhand shop of the early days with a big notice across it 'We buy anything from pins to policemen'! …

He had been to Judith Wright's and had read a lot of poems which he said didn't stay with him but which he loved because of where they came from. He also sent a small poem

---

4   When Peter Herbst went to England, he sold his share in the Arthur Merric Boyd Pottery to Neil Douglas.

5   In 1949, John Perceval was a student under Alan Sumner at the National Gallery School.

touch my eyes now
cover the burning land
or I will go where the rivers go
under the desert sand

Hold my hand.

Also sent a catalogue of Laurie Hope's exhibition which had good write-ups, so he says, and he [Laurie] sold £60 worth of paintings which is really good as they are all [at] pretty low prices, £5 and so on.[1] Barrie said they looked lovely all together and 'went beyond the bits and pieces we'd been seeing here for 4 years.' Barrie wrote a very poetic and beautiful introduction to the paintings in the catalogue ...

G has been sick again on Sunday and the young doctor up here is really a bit of a 'find'. He is putting him on to a new drug and doing his utmost, writing to Almoners to get it for him cheap, as it would run out at 11/- a week, which he argues is ridiculous.[2] He is very good – he comes promptly. Not what you'd call imaginary [sic] or visionary but seems to be most practical and helpful – it was a bit of a blow it following so soon after the last bout, but G seems himself again today, Friday, and cheerful as ever.

Gar is gently coming along but my word the frosts up here are devastating!! Things [which are] not usually sensitive, you find quite dead the next morning – [they] look as though they've been sprayed with poison! Our neighbour in the plaster palace next door madly has everything under hessian bags but I'm afraid I like to see a garden so we will just have to pick what will and what will not take our mad frosts and plant those things. Did I ever tell you of all the things we put in we have lost only the holly and the Judas tree – your little rose, John, is very sure of itself.

[1] Laurence Hope (b.1928) is a painter who studied at East Sydney Technical School, 1943–46, before exhibiting in Brisbane.
[2] Almoner was the contemporary term for hospital social worker.

Gar
May 1949

Dear Sun

... I wonder what you will think of
little Gar when you see it again. I wonder if you'll think we've done
marvels or have not done what we should have – but it looks different
to when we arrived but it is by no means a jungle yet. It's surprising how
long it takes to get roses and things to be big but still we plod on doing
a bit of garden, a bit of resting, a bit of creating and a bit of thinking. I
have thought more than I have ever thought or rather my thoughts
seem to have been clarified here [even] more so and the stillness I
mentioned I had in Sydney keeps coming more and more and I do love
little Gar very much – and we think about it a lot – of what she is and
what she will grow into and I don't think we have taken from her in any
way – in making our little rooms, painting them etc. In fact, I feel we
have given to what was already started 80 yrs ago or whenever a man
built with wattle and clay ...

We have been reading some mad Aussie books, Frank Clune etc. and
enjoying them. Also Max Brown, whom John will remember has
published a book called *Australian Son* about Ned Kelly and Martin has
read it and it's reputed to be the best Kelly book yet. Martin couldn't put
it down and we are dying to read it. This is a funny land. I read of a
foreigner asking someone the other day who our heroes were and the
answer he got was Ned Kelly and Phar Lap. The foreigner said, yes,
everyone has told me of them but haven't you any other ones, I mean
real ones! Ha! Ha! It must be mad for these people to understand that
we have a horse and a bushranger and that anyone else who may
become famous here, such as painters or cricketers or else, are regarded
with the greatest of sceptisism [sic] by the Aussies and when one reads
The Red Heart by Frank Clune, one knows why. I like Frank Clune and
he's very natural and put out something good and in a very Aussie way
which I imagine to a foreigner would be ideal if he 'wanted to know'
what we were.

Still that's another story and it's raining again and I am wondering
where you are now and what is happening with you.

Love from me and G and Gar and
Gyp

Gar
2 June 1949

Dear Sun

While you are gathering little cowries and I can see the three of you all brown and striding along and together in the morning sun, perhaps tracing your silhoettes [sic] in the sand – we are doing a magnificent shiver – it is still raining. Every time I write [it] seems to be so and I feel glad we are on a little hill, for I fear we might go sailing down Haley's Gully, such is the weather.

And these days our little kitchen is so very dark and we say we'll put another window in it and then we think of what we would find if we cut the tin lining to put a frame in. G says we should find nothing, not even a post to nail it to and then we would just have a great big cold hole in the wall and we look again and think well, if we put another window in, all the Kellys would fly out, and after all it will soon be summer.

We have not made our bathroom yet. The weather has been so bad the ground is sodden and too wet for work and it's too dark really to paint – that sounds a sorry state, but not really as these last 3 days have been the worst and we are getting near the shortest day – which is the day my father died. Which reminds me of an odd story my brother told me the other day, and somehow it sent the 'idea' of my father strangely off its keel.

It appears when my father was manager of the London Bank in town and the ES & A [bank] were taking it over or something like that, instead of the money being kept in the London Bank it had to be taken every night by my father and another man around to the ES & A ... They were, of course, armed as was the way then before armoured cars – and it appears my father had had a few drinks in the afternoon and had brought a live crayfish and during their progress from one bank to another the cray had got away and was waltzing down Collins St. My father, being well fortified, just started to fire at it from across the road, which apparently caused much amusement and naturally the traffic pulled up to watch the scene and of course [a]mid roars of laughter and consternation a policeman put a stop to the game and shepherded them both plus the crayfish across to the ES & A. It certainly would have looked a funny scene to see in Collins St.[1]

---

[1] Robert Hester was appointed manager of the London Bank's Flinders Street West branch in 1908. The truth of Neville's story is anyone's guess, though it reveals the drinking which would lead to Hester's sacking in 1930.

G is better again now, and as I think I mentioned the doctor has put him on yet another drug – and this time the latest isolation from America – which is unfortunately hopelessly expensive [at] about 11/- a week and the young doctor had suggested G try for the pension again and he'd sign it up and fix it for him, so G filled in the mad form in which one has to mention the income of one's ancestors almost and remember every relation one ever had. Nevertheless he filled it in and sent it to the pensions board and they sent back a note that G was to have an examination from young doctor Cordner's father, who is the local health officer at Eltham. So we tried to see the young one before setting off but he was late and our train was due to leave so off we went to his father who asked all the usual questions they do in the most impersonal and uninformed way. Anyway how one gets the pension rests on this man who has to give his OK and the blighter went against his son and apparently didn't OK it.

G got a most rude printed form back from the Gov[t] to say he was not eligible for same. The son was so sure about it he'd written to the Almoner of the Melb. Hospital saying G was receiving the pension and that they were to supply G with [the] drug at cost price – so another form filled in for that only to be returned saying they had been given to understand G was receiving the pension and the form did not state it so would he please fill in another form and state why he had not given [a] correct a/c of his financial status . . .

And we can't even get the phone on until we get another neighbour within ¹/₂ a mile to agree to have one too. The doctor visits here 3 times a week at set times and one has to queue up in the village for him – but still things are on the mend and all is going well at the moment but we were so wild about the forms and G even had to go to Eltham Courthouse to swear before the blanky judge – and I don't know whether I told you or not but we did all this once before in Sydney and the epileptic specialist sat in his great big chair in the Royal Sydney and said to G, 'So you want to get something on the cheap do you?', which seemed to be the old man Cordner's attitude as well. It's not so much not getting the thing but the attitude of all these bloody old baboons who sit well and comfortable behind chairs and desks and tell G to try hard work or writing or drugs or self control and all the rot under the sun so they won't have to think of these nuisances anymore. And one goes thru these contortions to prove to the old dodder[er]s that one is an epileptic and then they say, oh well, buck up old man, you['re] not the only one. So much for that – G says they can stick the forms up their arse for all he cares now. So there!

... I won't write more as the rain is pelting [down on] the roof and drumming words out of my head – so love to you darlings and hurry up and come home now,

Joy XXX

This sounds an awfully doleful letter when I read it thru but we are not at all doleful and we have a lovely warm fire and it's very snug in here hearing the rain outside. Tell John his little best loved rose is a small tree now.

Did you hear about the kid at school who was kept in because he'd brought no lunch. So the teacher asked him some Geography questions and said, 'Tell me, Bobby, where is the South Australian Border?' and he said, 'At home with mum. That's why I got no bloody lunch!'

In June, Sunday and John were staying at the Ile de Porquerolle. The largest of the Iles d'Hyères, the Ile de Porquerolle was a beach resort on the Côte d'Azur. It was a short ferry ride from Hyères, between Toulon and St Tropez. Sunday wrote to Gray,

'I don't think either of us wanted to come back to Porquerolle as John felt so ill last time and has been a little ill again and is better now and we are doing what we have wanted to do for a long time – nothing. For the first time since we left home I have been unfaithful to Aussie and you must forgive me. Here in this azure Mediterranée where there are no sharks and no tides you cannot imagine such bliss and we have never loved the water more – one floats infinitely in pale crystal. Sweeney, too, goes with us to the deep, unafraid, kicking legs, beating arms, laughing yet sinking much to his great disappointment and ours ... He is gloriously brown and fair and such a Joy boy since he came back to us that I think it is you when you were little, squatting on the sea wall ... [Sweeney] will not go back to Tours and says the French people never open their windows and that Papa used to bang the table with all the food on it and break the plates and Maman had to go to bed and I suspect that all these things are true but not as true as the real reason. Anyway I would not like him away from us again, it is too soon.[1]

'... The days are slipping past and soon I hope we will be with you. It is a worrying time with shipping news and all else (we must certainly leave in August as we will have no money). We have been offered passage on one of the new Dutch boats on the 5th of August and another on the 30 July [on the] Melbourne Star Line, whatever that is. The Dutch boat we would have liked but it touches on Karachi ... and if we take it [it] will mean about 5 different sorts of vaccination, the thought of which revolts me, however as we may be stuck we have not altogether abandoned the idea.'

Sunday Reed to Gray Smith, 30 June 1949, Smith Collection.

Gar
(c. June 1949)

Dear Sun
It seems ages since I wrote to you, even longer since *last year*!! when I watched the Rockbye go out – or rather when I didn't watch the Rockbye go out. I couldn't. Ever since I was little I could never watch a boat go out without something funny happening to me, what, I don't know but I did know when the little *Tournai* finally pulled up its safe little anchor that the lines of a little Dutch poem kept going on in my head, 'The last slender quay of wood in sand ...'. I often think I'm a little mad as my life or my thoughts on life always seem to be prefixed by someone else's thoughts and I seem to live from one scattered trail of someone's poem to another.

For some completely mad reason just the act of writing that little line reminds me of 'sleep with the darkness, woman, sleep with the night ...' maybe because they are the only two Dutch poems I know except a mad little thing I had to 'recite' to my great aunt every time I saw her

Little mister baggy britches, I love you,
I'll patch yer' me pink, me green and me yella,
If you'll be me Sundie fella, I love you.

---

[1] John and Sunday placed Sweeney with a French family at Tours.

Yes, this crazy aunt had 12 nieces and 21 great nieces of whom I was one and she must have have [had] some secret desire to be on the stage, because she had a stage in her front room – 'the music room' which also had an organ and a 'peeiano' as I called it – and all the nieces, great and otherwise used to assemble there with the male members of the family – and perform no less, each in turn, for the edification of the males I presume – for which we received the magnificent sum of 2/-. 'Mister Baggy Britches' was my contribution on every occasion, being the only suitable thing my memory would hold – and not being a pianist or a budding soprano – that was it. And great aunt used to sit at the side and draw with the long tassels the curtain for each 'item'. She was the old Spaniard who had three hairs on her head and a huge ornate comb!

I don't like bats and that is the one thing that worries me about our little hills. At evening and now the autumn is here especially, when these glorious evenings of frailest hue come and everything looks so peaceful and dear old Sugarloaf settles down heavily in the distance and the distance nestles into the mist and the 'jackies' have finished their heraldry of night – then come the bats! The other night G and I walked into the evening and I was thinking of the peace and watching the lamps being lit in the little houses in the hills and the smoke hardly seemed to be rising from the chimneys, it looked as though it was part of the chimneys. Yes, it looked so very much part of the gentleness and peace, when 'swoosh' – 'swoosh'. Slowly, darkly, came the bats. They are so distinct in their darkness that I cannot rid myself of the thought that they are an omen – of what, I dare not think! My better senses tell me that if bats were an omen, then surely the world would have vanished by now, for all the bats there have been!

And there you are on your little island again [Ile de Porquerolle]. I feel I know that place. Remember how you used to tell of it . . . sitting by the fire many years ago? . . .

And when you mentioned bringing home the Peugeot I screamed with delight and more so when you said you'd be staying until September. Do you mean this year?? then you'll be home at Xmas!? Very selfishly this would be lovely but I hope for you that in a way you mean the following year as you said in your last wonderful letter you hoped to stay 2 summers and 2 winters – but I say 'in a way' because I think that would be nice for you but the other side of the world, from here, seems to be so filled with terrors that I would prefer to know you were coming home *this summer, our summer.*

How I hope that when this letter reaches you John's face will be rosy again and his apple cheeks smooth and he will feel better and you will be able to go to London on a little Channel boat and John will be looking for nightingales in Berkeley Square. My love to John my very best love to his gentle face . . .

. . . Tenderly I think of you both over there and I cannot write of these thoughts, that remain always with me in the network of my brain, and when I think of what I think of you both, I see a lovely jewelled cobweb suspended in the autumn between apple trees and all shimmering there and I can see the world on the other side of the jewels, and that is what I see when I ask of myself what do I think when I think of you both. I see the sun shining making the jewels glisten.

Untitled

So I may return with you
to our beginning
following love
crossing the threshold
of your oneness –

hold me a flower
within the night
tremble my thoughts
divide my passion
deep in your heart
collect the moisture
from my tears
distil me an hour
reserve the perfume
following love.

Goodnight dear both of you and dear John get well for us quickly.
All the love of Joy Gray Gar and little fox Egypt who is on heat now

and is a terribly gentle thing who cries when we go out and sits still and quiet as a mouse as we devour your letters.

XXX

Love to Mrs Smith and all
MS *Torrens*
30 August 1949

Dear little one and Gray
We are due to arrive at Capetown tomorrow, thank God, so a quick greeting to you both. I do hope there will be a letter from you to prepare us for the long journey ahead across the Indian Ocean, the roaring forties they call it and apparently it will be just luck if we get good weather though how I will survive any more storms on this little Rockbye goodness knows.

I confess we haven't had one since I last wrote but even so there has been one long swell ever since we left Takoradi[1] (after having been there a week) and we have been pitching up and down like this [drawing] for days on end all down the coast. This evening for the first time the sun came out and we are now in a calm sea just trotting along like a small horse. I count the days, I even count the waves and John fears I may really go mad.

I read somewhere, sometime in Paris, that often one's relations and friends are unable to recognize those that have been travelling for a long time – they are so changed both physically and spiritually, and so I wonder if you will know us when you see us again[?] Should I wear a red carnation in my buttonhole, should I write John's name and pin it on his back? Swene surely you will know, to me he is always the same but for you, I wonder? He has grown lots more fair hairs on his arms but what else is longer or shorter I don't know. The shadows, I know, have marked my face. Will you find me? Sometimes I seem to *carry* myself, as if I lived outside of myself and so if you see a strange light over my head you will know it is me.

Weeno has retired to bed with the snuffles, overwhelmed with the toxic diet and much cake and I have been showing him pictures of

---

[1] Takoradi is on the coast of Ghana.

Groc the clown and telling him what clowns are. For some reason I remembered driving along in the old Wolsley one night just before we left and you said it would be fun, wouldn't it, when you come back to have a box at the Tivoli! Swene will be just the right age to enjoy everything. Do you remember? And now we are coming back and a box at the Tivoli, the thought of it, makes me feel really happy and as if we are almost home. Believe me in this little boat I begin to wonder about Davy Jones's locker and we hear all sorts of dreadful reports through the wireless about the storms at home and two freighters lost, one on the rocks and one without a propeller. Well, perhaps all will be well by the time we reach Aussie.

Our captain has never been a captain before and hasn't even got his captain's clothes and wears sports clothes and gave a party crossing the equator that nearly killed all the passengers and he the captain did not appear the next day at all! What a mad gloomy letter, darling. Too long at sea, far too long and it will be lovely to touch land tomorrow and hear from you. I enclose a very beautiful drawing that Sweeney did in Paris that I meant to send ages ago but mislaid it. Swene said it was 'Gray laughing' and so it is. Hang it up or keep it, won't you? I have a funny little picture of Gray, too, taken from the top of the pine tree that cheers me up. We have taken to Julien again and have been filling odd hours translating his last book for you, *If I were you*. Hardly translating but putting into English words, si j'étais vous.

Our love to you all and Gar

S

Capetown

No letter from you. I hope this means that you are busy and happy. All feeling terribly depressed after a terrible night rolling and tossing round the Cape. My father was right. He always said don't travel on cargo boats and don't go round the Cape. I hear the air[mail] takes 10 to twelve days from here so this note will probably reach you only two or three days before we reach Adelaide, I think the 14th.

Chapter 8

1949
60

Not long after the Reeds returned to Heide in September 1949, Gray wrote, 'Do you remember saying before you went to Paris that it would be a good idea for the four of us to live together at Heide? Adding as a rider that Joy and I would have to conform more or less with your way of life. Well, I suppose it is from here I get the idea of Gar being a place to wait . . .'[1]

Soon after Gray wrote again, 'I know the enormity of this suggestion but could not rest until I had put it out, whether you would take it as it is and we all find a way to live and work together, working out our lives as I feel they must be worked out.'[2]

John replied, 'Although I know we *spoke* together of all living here I do not think I ever put it forward as a positive idea. My own memory is that Joy (and I think you with her) said you both had come to feel that this is where you wanted to live, and I was very moved by what you said and welcomed the love that prompted it.'[3]

After a holiday together, Sunday responded.

Heide
(Late 1949)

Dear Joy
     We took the little blue flower to the [Botanic] Gardens and its name is *Dampiera stricta*, it doesn't seem to have a pet name other than Rusty Dampiera – the picture in my wild flower book [of it] I recognised but only just. The Parsley is the wild parsley parent as I thought and is of course perfectly edible and the Eggs and Bacon bush is *Pultenacea gunii* – Golden Bush Pea and the other with light droopy pink flowers all the way up the stem (the flowers rather orchid like in form) is *Tetratheca* – Pink Eye. So there you are.

I hope you are both happily home again, everything looked lovely when we arrived and only the thought that Celtic [Hester's dog] had gone made us sad and we felt for you both. We loved our week with you even though we had no fireside for you and Miss Julie was so depressing and my cooking [was] surely worse than usual. These things I hope you

[1] Gray Smith to John Reed, (late 1949), Reed Collection.
[2] Gray Smith to John Reed, (late 1949), Reed Collection.
[3] John Reed to Gray Smith, (late 1949), Reed Collection.

will forgive and for the rest I hope your thoughts will move peacefully. As you know I have always felt that you and Gray should have your own world around you and perhaps I feel you are still in someone else's and have not yet found together the *nature* of the responsibilities that truly belong to you. All living is anxious yet I believe anxiety to be deeply personal and related and when these things are clearer I think you may discover the kind of simplicity in your living that will solve practical and working issues more easily. I do [not] know at all that Heide is an answer or that we can talk or think about it in that way. I don't think I believe in answers but rather in the search for some kind of truth in identity.

Well, for the moment my love to you both and to your poems and all else.

S

Joy had three solo exhibitions in the 1950s, as well as contributing twice a year to Contemporary Art Society exhibitions. She also exhibited in Melbourne's great public art institution, the *Herald* Outdoor Art Show. Barrett Reid wrote,

'Your drawings at the *Herald* show were so lovely, the loveliest of all. Have you seen the show? Not only were they the loveliest, they shone out. Most drawings would be lost out in the open air among all the colours and the hard wire netting and the crowds but these don't; the black which holds the heads like a pillow is so deep and black, soft and resonant – the faces come through the crowds like stars. I only wish there were hundreds of your drawings, books of them like the French publishers make – with your poems on the other pages. I think your drawings should be shown more often now, they will be guarded by hearts that love them and will never get lost.'[1]

Joy's first solo show was in February 1950 and it was held at the Melbourne Bookclub Gallery, downstairs at 225 Collins Street – the 'little show' Joy refers to on page 224. She showed the *Faces* (1947–48), *Sleep* (1947–48) and *Love* (1949) series, several untitled drawings and probably about a dozen poems. It was the culmination of the work Joy began in Sydney. Though Joy priced the drawings modestly between 4 and 7 guineas, none sold, and she gave the entire show to Sunday. The critical response was negative.

[1]   Barrett Reid to Joy Hester, (1950s), Smith Collection.

George Bell had never liked Joy. He had warned Tucker she was not a suitable companion. Politically, he assigned her to the John Reed camp – John was his old foe from the days of the battle for the control of the CAS – and John had written Joy's catalogue introduction. Writing in the *Sun*, Bell classed the drawings 'for want of a better word' as 'expressionist'.[2] Expressionist was a derogatory epithet as far as Bell was concerned. The *Age* art critic, A Cook, regarded the drawings as obscure[3] while Laurie Thomas, writing in the *Herald*, felt more comfortable assessing the poems. He deemed the drawings 'amateurish'.[4]

> This appears to be the 'lost' letter
> Joy refers to in the following letter.
> Gar
> Monday (early 1950)

Dear Sun

It is a long time since I received your letter and longer since seeing you and John – and I have thought and thought, and find we are not at the place we all were. I don't feel sad about this at all but I *do* feel sad that I, anyway, did not recognize the *journey* that has been taken and I have hurt you and John in my lack of realization – this makes me very sad – I am staggered at my *lack* of understanding and breadth.

But, dear Sun, I am weeping as I write you and see before me your face and John's and all *we know and love together* and these things are indestructible. But it is sad that our consciousness or our awareness does not keep some level and things become mysteries and confusions and the balance of love is upset. But I feel this is more my fault than anyone else's, as I know myself now, some drive always in me, a constant nagging inward drive which becomes out of hand, as I do not recognise [it] at *the time it drives* – perhaps I do only partly, and I misdirect it.

That is what I wish to learn – to keep knowing all the time I can – for it destroys me in my hurting [of] you and John, whom I love. Sometimes

[2] George Bell, *Sun*, 9 February 1950, p. 15.
[3] The *Age* art critic (A Cook), *Age*, 7 February 1950, p. 2.
[4] Laurence Thomas, *Herald*, 6 February 1950, p. 8.

I feel so stupid with this lack of knowing – and suddenly the minute when one should have known is past. And there is only the future, and so many minutes that have gone already when, had 'knowing' been there, those times would not have been lost. Looking back over the past, right back, I find the things that remain with one – out of it all – are the moments of love and knowing – and I realize how precious few these are.

. . . I cannot take from you what pain I have caused you both – I wish I could! and transform them into acts of love. I can only hope and to try to see more clearly those precious minutes in the future and to know them at the time they are there, so I can be some help and love to you instead of otherwise and when we meet may I know more of you and less of me.

Gar
(February 1950)

Dear Sun
A week or two back I answered your letter but did not feel satisfied with it and consequently did not post it – now it has completely disappeared with my answer as well. It is a thing I never do – mislay letters – it's all very disturbing because I cannot remember it sufficiently now, to answer, my memory being as it is, and the interval with the show coming on and my thoughts necessarily being scattered during that period.[1]

Anyway I had tried to answer it point to point or as near as I could – and also that is not really my way of reacting to the world and that is the reason I did not post it – and after that, during the show I thought over my inability to answer or say what I felt [to be] adequate. I thought about it a lot, and about us all, and the more I felt the less capable I felt of speaking. For words can have a life of their own and complete their own cycle in the reader and in themselves, quite apart from the writer, and this terrified me and I decided then not to say anything.

Also there is in me now the thought that once we communicate, or attempt to, and a lack of communication results, it creates an urgency.

[1] Joy's first solo exhibition was in February 1950.

And urgencies disturb me. I think that is why G and I went away together – because we felt such a pressure – we released the urgent and just existed and this has been good for us both.

I have felt that our (all of us together) wires have not been communicating properly lately and I have felt that for myself I would say nothing and as the feeling is deep and that does meet, it would flow and naturalness would come.

I don't know what I can say Sun dear, except that God tells me to relax and all will be well – and that all manner of things shall be.

Gray and I are probably fairly inadequate people in the world. But God says again that this is not bad, for we are not inadequate here at Gar – and some day that shall place itself in a peace for us all.

Thank you Sun, for all your patience and your thoughts for the little show, and all your practical help and enthusiasm and my love goes to you with this letter and I'm much better at sending love and drawings than saying these things.

May peace and love be with us all when we are together and may all be well with you both now and your birthflowers shine as always.

Love to you
Joy

Heide
Sunday morning, (February/March 1950)

Dear Joy
Graeme [Bell] rang and asked us to come along on Tuesday night as it seems their contract is depending on the success of the opening night and how much supper everyone can eat and so we have taken tickets. I remembered the late train is on Wednesday but if you can only think of some way to arrange things then will you both come? Charles [Osborne] is returning to Brisbane on Wednesday and I think may be with us, too, on Tuesday night so that if you can come we may need an extra ticket and could you ring us either Tuesday morning early or lunch time?

Thank you for writing and I understand of course what you said but I can't help feeling that when things are not right you run away from me and Gray too and that is always a lonely experience.

I know that words can have a life of their own but is that frightening – why – and *no words* also have an equal reality which perhaps you have not thought about. It is true, I'm sure that we can adjust ourselves to all sorts of gaps in relationships but if we do it does not necessarily mean that we are becoming natural again with each other. But never mind, peace be with you both.

S

Gar
Sunday (1950)

[Dear Sun]
Ultimately, I have always believed that one cannot force a relationship.

The deepest thing one can do is express oneself – then we see the flowers. We select, out of an intimate yet indefinable – recognition.

Give a tree a hormone, it will produce a 'show' flower – the plant will not withstand the sun. The tree will blossom too quickly. Its naturalness will be used up in trying to produce the thing *we want* of it.

Left alone, it may die, be it so – the possibility is remote – but its progress will be slower and perhaps less satisfactory. But the time will arrive – the tree will erect its pristine elucidation for us – and we shall select the petals for our bouquet. But we cannot create the flower – we can only hope and wait for it to shine, and the hidden things we know to appear.

I don't think there can be a purpose which we can create – the purpose is there – is always there – and in due time we shall see it.

In my last letter there was no rejection of any part of you, by no means, all is too dear, but an attempt (admittedly not very well) to put forward some part of how I think discords between us occur.

Perhaps you feel there is an inadequacy in our relationship and it fusses you because 'it goes nowhere' – and my letter was an attempt to quell what I thought was impatience in you, and dear Sun and John, is this letter any clearer? Do I hurt you again? Forgive me for that was not my intention – you see how clumsy my words are? I believed I was sending some understanding, some love.

I started this letter with the intention of trying to describe to you the garden at Heide the other night – I shall never be without that image of you both I saw there – and tears came to my eyes as I see its beauty now.

I have seen no other garden – it is consummate poetry. I love it.

Love
Joy

Heide
Wednesday (1950)

Dear Joy

I thought at first it would be best not to try and add anything more to your last letter but as I always think about the things you say to me it is probably more natural to say something, even if in the end it doesn't mean very much.

You say the deepest thing we can do is to express ourselves and I agree, but it could mean two things, couldn't it? It might mean that the deepest expression of oneself was the development of some kind of 'pure' individual, relative I suppose only to God. God tells me to relax – your words – and God tells me to do this and that and all will be well. Or it might mean that the deepest expression of oneself was relative or related to others. And so it is the expression of yourself [which] might be different of course to myself although in the first place we agree it is our deepest responsibility perhaps.

I don't know that this gets us anywhere in particular but I feel it's had something to do with the rest of your thought, that we cannot force [our] relationship. I suppose I agree in the sense you put it that the tree is best if it can grow naturally but at the same level and using the same analogy there are sorts of obvious answers such as trees needing attention and needing nourishment and natural conditions and so on and (forgive me) the 'forcing' of plants is now the most effective way of killing the *weeds*. I don't know about analogys [sic] but I do know that I really don't live my life in any way like a tree or any other plant though they explain so well why I bother to live at all.

Words then can't be just words, they move and have their validity *within experience*, at least for myself – and so when you speak of not forcing [our] relationship I can only test its truth in that way. As I see it [a] relationship is continuously under pressure by both active and passive forces of all kinds at any moment and even then there is no relationship if you like, humans have a way of scrambling over the top of each other. I feel John's life is what it is because he has accepted the inward flow of life and given to it – that he has been *used* – is to me most beautiful. And then too the changes in your own life, the sudden placing of Sweeney into mine, the responsibilities, readjustments, and involvements of love are all realities that seem to throw light on the process of life over life and the pressures that bear down sometimes arbitrarily from one to the other.

I feel some clearer understanding of what is happening to us all, and what has happened out of which too it is quite certain that our own relationship has lived and had I think very little to do with the Lord. I have wanted to follow you within experience, to live as closely to you [as] to life itself as I know at the time and I think if I had asked God what to do my life would have been another story – not that that counts a button.

But don't whatever else feel a sense of right or wrong. These are, after all, thoughts and rather reluctant ones knowing your own feelings and differences and how all these things are the very 'urgencies' you speak of. But I will know more and learn to intrude less in the peace that is yours. That will be my job. When will I leave my loves alone I wonder? Go quietly into the earth and be as dead as a doornail.

Gaps in time confuse now the real starting point between us when I wrote a few hurried words in the hope that you might send me a few clues as to why, what you call the communication wires, were behaving so badly. Out of tiredness I sought in some way to mend the breakdown and when I said that we must not live together in vain I don't think I meant more than just that, although in your letter you mention that perhaps I am fussed because we seem to get nowhere! On the contrary, I feel quite otherwise and that our relationship is always moving through the landscape to many places. And anyway, where is Nowhere? Only one thing more I remember – your first letter thanked me for my patience, your second speaks of quelling my *im*patience. Which is it darling or is it that you never know?

Well, what a stuffy letter. It might have been better if I had told you the story Sweeney told me yesterday about a rosebush he knew that was three miles high and lived with another little rosebush beside it which was a cutting and the cutting went away and when it came back the rosebush door was shut and it couldn't get in so it went away again and lived with the bees in a French hive.

There is something in the air about me having a holiday week at Sorrento, at Merthon, alone?[1] I might take Sweeney and Matthew [Perceval] and I meant to mention it to you in case you too could run away from home for a few days. I do hope you are safely home by now. I can't tell you what a moving sight you were when you went away. Gray's bald patch like a mad old monk and you. If you could have seen yourselves, this lovely back view, you too would have been moved.

When will we see you? I wish the phone was fixed. Thank you for writing. It is always warm to get letters from you, but rest. All will be well.

> Love
> S

Though Joy had been warned that pregnancy could precipitate her symptoms, she had two more children.

Peregrine was born on 6 May 1951 and Fern on 22 October 1954. Perhaps Joy felt more prepared for motherhood at 31 than she had at 25. She regarded it as a 'heresy' that artists should not have children. In 1955, she firmly encouraged Barbara Blackman, Charles' wife, to go ahead and have the children she wanted, despite the fact that Barbara was inexorably going blind. She did convince Charles who saw how well Joy coped, despite her illness. Joy spoke to the Blackmans with great sadness about the twin boys aborted at the Crown Street Women's Hospital in December 1947, though she treated the news merely with relief in a letter to Sunday.

Joy spoke about the abortion with such feeling that Charles and Barbara thought it had occurred only recently, rather than eight years before. Joy said she wanted to replace the babies she had lost.

---

[1] 'Merthon', the Baillieu family holiday home at Sorrento, was built by Sunday's father, Arthur (1872–1943). A spacious stone house with a large garden, it is set on four acres facing Port Phillip Bay at Point King.

Heide
Tuesday (October 1951)

Dear Joybells

I missed you both but your little parcel with its ribbon of blue roses greet[ed] me on my birthday morning. I had a glorious shower streaming with the warm smell of Chanel 5. I carried the lovely handky [sic] in my pocket all day and in the evening at Doodie's.[1] I smoked your beautiful Black Russians and so you were never far away. It was a peaceful warm day and I thought I would just like to lie in the sun with Micetto and so we curled up and I went to sleep and that was heaven.[2]

I am sorry darling that this year we couldn't arrange the day together. Somehow I felt that you would both understand our pilgrimage to Doodie's and when she rang me and arranged an early dinner I felt what with the moos and all the pussies that it would be best to have the day at home and I would have worried if you and Gray had scrambled to Heide for such a short visit. Now you have Peregrine all these things are really more difficult for you than us. But we will plan a celebration some night when we can deal with the babies. In the meantime my love to you.

In the pussy world there are all sorts of happenings. Ev[erard] rang me to take Sylvie again because their dog threatened to eat her and they could not cope and so here she is again sleeping peacefully on Sweeney's manly chest.[3] Sabukia decided quite finally to bring all her kittens into my side of the bed and though I spent all most [sic] the entire night gently but firmly putting her back in the wardrobe and tried all sorts of other places, nothing short of locking her in the cupboard did any good, and so I just had to get up and sleep on the sofa because I was frightened of rolling on them all when I slept. She still won't budge and when I put her in the sitting room, she was unhappy and so now John and I are just taking it in turns to sleep in Sweeney's bed! Goodness knows how it will all end.

A ring from Perceval this morning to say that Mary was ill and could she come to Heide and Matthew too. She hadn't eaten for three days

[1] Clare ('Doodie') Pitblado had been employed as a maid by Sunday's parents at 'Balholmen'. She acted as Sunday's companion and became a lifelong friend.
[2] Micetto was a male Siamese cat imported from England.
[3] Everard Baillieu (b.1912) is Sunday's younger brother.

and everyone was ill at Murru[m]beena so they are all turning up in the morning and I have no idea how we are all going to manage and I feel tired thinking about it and think I will run away. And now Goodnight to you both, I have to hurry to catch tonight's mail and you must forgive a scrambling silly letter but it has been a scrambling day and my thoughts are scattered everywhere. Love to you again, little one.

Ring up soon
S

Gar
Thursday (October 1951)

Dearest Sun
Your letter yesterday – I do hope little Mary is not seriously ill, you poor thing! What a pack of friends you have – we'll have to take it in turn to give you a holiday from us all and all the worry. We could arrange an evening off ... Perhaps John Perceval would look after Mary and Sweeney and Gray and I could stay the night with Mrs Smith as her boarder's room is vacant once again.

I have to go into town next Thursday, so think it over and see. Perhaps we could all meet up and see *Macbeth* that night – anyway I will ring you tomorrow – perhaps there is some way in which Gray and I can help you cope at Heide while Mary is there. If Weeno came up here for a couple of days the pressure might ease – or you may think of some way we could help. You could tell me tomorrow – I will ring about 1 pm. Will be in town in the afternoon. Have to see [Dr] Russell Howard to see if the 'pendix is OK. Is there anything I could [get] in town for you?

Would you like to stay a week at Gar and let us give you a rest? That does not sound a very good idea for you, but I feel sure you must be very tired, and then I think of all the involving things that go with your life, the kitties to be fed etc., perhaps after that. Anyway I feel well now and feel we ought to turn the tables and let me give you a help.

Gray has started to prepare the flat, John. It is costing a lot to say goodbye to the old quince tree – we have asked Johnno and Bill Sheridan if they would like the apple trees and they do not seem very interested in the idea of transplanting them which is rather sad.

Well we saw you bathing in Chanel and smoking Sobranies at Pitblado's. I'm glad you had a nice restful day. Perhaps your birthday will fall on a Sunday next year.

Did you see in the paper where Diana Barrymore said they were being very chic these days and doing all the things those Aussies do now and turned to her husband and said 'Honey, these are Australian Sobranies aren't they?'

Love to you and all the things at Heide. I hope the pussies are not scared of little Matthew. Tell Mary, I hope all goes well for her and she is soon better.

XX
Joy

PS   Got your birthday wire.

Heide
Friday night (1951)

Dear Joy

I started my nursery today and completed the first bed of irises in front of the old southernwood hedge in the veg garden and I should have hundreds of quite big clumps in twelve months and flowers too and plan to fill the whole of that rather dry area. I put in a lot of little things too from the spring garden. Sweeney and I enjoyed ourselves and while I crawled about in the wet and [the] leaves under the trees Weeno dug up (and beautifully) the finds and then we replanted them in a bed we had prepared along the boxthorn hedge, dividing the hens from the ducks. It is fairly sheltered and should be a good place for a start.

I decided the other morning just to go ahead quietly in my own way and asked John to fix the registration and he said he was happy about it and perhaps it will seem like a game but one day it may be useful to you all and in any case it will be good for Weeno to organise his energy and I think that nothing should be lost.[1] When I asked what you would ever

---

[1]   Sunday was interested in creating a separate title for the property and giving part of the land at Heide to Joy and Gray. There is no record of further discussions.

like best to do if you left Gar I suppose it was just because I have been thinking of you both so much. In the old days and even since we returned from France we have thought that finally Gar might evolve a way of living that in its turn would bring you both the kind of peace you need. But it is true I do not feel this now and the time that held these thoughts seems to have been worked through with the birth of Peregrine.

So my thoughts have been moving about till one day I imagined what if you were to take a little cottage somewhere near us and from there I thought of a nursery and if Heide could be a 'mother' garden and share herself with you. But then you see I don't know, not really, and if you would be happy to live away from the Aussie hills and in the middle of what one day will be a strange suburb and Heide a big secret garden behind the hollies. Would you ever find the cottage sufficient to build your own lives around, a place where Gray could plan his bird book and a door that will be home to Peregrine? Would you rather be in Sydney, the north, by the sea or anywhere in the world or even stay at Gar, and I wander here there and everywhere with you with love and when you come we will talk again. Thank you for the last poems. I loved 'There's one awake in the fern world'[2] and felt for the other one, too, though I could not tune myself to the last verse and will tell you more. But what could be happier for me than seven new poems on the mantelpiece!

Forgive me for not seeing you safely home the other day. Sometimes I am overtaken and the tears fall from my eyes so that I cannot see and stumble and know not what I say and it is best then that I am under the trees. Please try to put up with me, won't you?

I meant to tell you the health centre days but forgot to ring but I will and expect to hear from you Monday or Tuesday but Thursday or Friday would be a better day to set forth as we are going to Dorian's recital on Monday morning, and Tuesday [is] with Doodie.[3]

Goodnight to you both

S

---

[2]   'Awake' (1951), published in *Ern Malley's Journal*, vol.1, no.1, November 1952.

[3]   Dorian la Galliene (1915–63), composer and music critic for the *Argus*.

Awake

There's one awake in the fern world
in the forest of my heart
meeting word with word
linking countries to the eye
making bluebell of my hearing

groping the underworld
in frond places, you are taking
thoughts, separating eye-beams
reaching the pulse-magic
of my expression

so call for my heart
bud the daydream flower
turn the night, meet
the minutes' hour with stars
and leave no space for yearning

In autumn, 1952, Joy, Gray and Peregrine moved to Avonsleigh in the Dandenong Ranges. They had sold Gar with the intention of committing themselves more firmly to farming. Cherry's Lane, Avonsleigh, was a larger property of 15 acres with better soil than at Hurstbridge. They tried to make a living from the land by growing potatoes, keeping chickens, planting oats and selling wood but after a year they realised their crops would not give them sufficient income. Schemes to supply chickens to the local delicatessen at Belgrave, to evade the Egg Board and sell eggs on the black market or to pick blackberries did not work out.

Avonsleigh is an idyllically beautiful area, green, lush and hilly. Though it was further from the city, involving a trek by bus and train to town, they had an inside toilet and plenty of water. The house with its Spanish style arches was set on a rise. Concrete foundations, laid out for extensions, had not been completed by the previous owners. The middle room was a sitting room but the life of the house went on in the kitchen with its round table and open fireplace. Breakfasts were nourishing meals of fresh cream, wheatgerm, bran and fresh peaches. Scones were made from the bran and pollard of the chicken feed. Next door to the kitchen was an unfinished room where Joy sometimes worked. Joy was happy there although they missed Hurstbridge neighbours such as Florence Noonan.

Joy told visitors that the house had been an abortion clinic built by a city doctor.

Heide
Monday (Autumn 1952)

Dear Joy
Just when we were planning a day to come and see you your letter arrived and delayed us. No matter how tiny the sentence – in the middle of all the mountain air – your small thought around Barrie seemed to carry only the re-reassertion of an attitude that I think that does not bear the weight of our own relationship.

Essentially of course my feelings have nothing to do with Barrie. He told me not very much about the phone conversation he had with you. It is a long time ago now and we have not spoken of it since but if I remember he said you were very hard and I think 'Hollywood' and that you had announced that you did not trust anyone and advised him in effect not to worry. Obviously this is not the context in which these things were passed on and I only recall the words to explain what I mean by 'attitude' but my feeling is that [if] we were to contact each other now, in such a place, that sooner or later I would, or John would, or both of us would be certain to displease you and so recreate the unpleasant situation of being under fire again – a situation that has continued off and on since we returned from France for reasons unknown and known at Heide. It has now worn rather a hole.

It is true that Barrie was sad and true that he met something on the phone that he had not known was there but if as you say in your letter, it is also true that he met you for the first time, I know you will understand why all sorts of fears have been revived.

John told me that the night you rang him, when you were so upset, you had said that [you] had been thinking awful thoughts about us for months and I'm afraid that the stone has stuck somewhere and I tried to tell Gray when he rang (but he wouldn't listen) that mutually we thought it best to wait until these awful things, whatever they are, are resolved. To think awful thoughts about anyone for such a long time would I know make you very tired and I wish I could help yet in spite of this wishing I cannot believe it fruitful for any of us to repeat a cycle. This is neither critical nor defensive. My thoughts are just signposts to our own way home.

I miss you a lot. Perhaps as the days go on I will take heart and we will see you soon and perhaps in the meantime you will tell us just what plans you make and what you think to grow around your mountain house. There are so many little rooted trees at Heide, hawthorn, laurels, spindles, oaks, hollies and so on and of course hundreds of garden plants, herbs, roses, daisies and all the garden you know so well but we think it would be of little use to unearth them without really knowing just how much you want to do and just how much you want to look after.

The persimmon tree is mad with fruit and is so beautiful, reminding me of how we all loved them last winter and ate them together.

I do hope all is well with you both and the little one, Peregrine, and that you are warm.

With love
S

Heide
8 July 1952

Dear Joy
 I wonder if you and Gray would each give a poem.

John has dropped out of *Direction* and Barrie too, and Davison is continuing it alone but we who had been so personally involved find it difficult now to be uninvolved – for the moment anyway – and we are now harvesting and hope to go to press quite soon – with Barrie and perhaps Max.[1] We would like to come and tell you about it and talk

---

[1] *Direction: new literature in Australia* was L H Davison's idea. Its first issue in 1952 was edited by Davison and Barrett Reid. Subsequent issues until its demise in 1955 were edited by Davison. Sunday, feeling that she, John and Barrie had been involved in soliticing articles and poems, decided to go ahead with starting, 'harvesting', their own literary magazine. Max Harris was persuaded to participate, too. The result was *Ern Malley's Journal*, which ran from 1952 to 1955.

about poems and which one of yours and which one of Gray's you would like best – that is of course if you are pleased about it all.

But it won't be this week because we seem to be weathering a few mild storms and Sweeney was in bed last week with some frustrated bug and a hangover from a swig of whisky! Now I think I may have something too and as we have been in contact with German measles it would be wise on account of the little one [Peregrine] to wait and see. I will send you another message what day and if you [are] in town, do ring.

I felt your warm letter but somehow I have felt too quiet about us to write. You more than anyone know the world in which we all live and you know so much about us, and know so much about yourselves in relation to knowing about us. It did not seem true when you spoke of your inexperience, such things seemed so unreal that no thought of mine could meet it or rise again.

And so we have waited for the spring and the fresh green leaves.

Thank you for the little old painting which I welcomed home and the poem too which reminded me of one other. I did not feel it as closely as I usually do but it is always a happy moment when your poems flutter into the world and I so hope you are writing more and Gray too. It is nice to think I may be able to take them off the mantelpiece and put them somewhere for everyone to see.

Greetings to you both and it would be just a great help if you could really tell me just what you want from the garden. What little trees and plants and how many! I don't want to bring things unless you feel ready to have them and will be able to manage. I expect you have all sorts of more important plans on hand.

S

Please keep the *Journal* confidential for the moment.

Heide
Tuesday (July 1952)

Dear Joy
John didn't tell you the Peugeot has bust its bearings and will be out of action for 10 days or so – it has been

making funny noises for a long time and although we wanted to come up and talk with you both we thought we would never make it and now in fact are becalmed!

In the meantime I hope you have taken heart and are busy with plans for your first crop [of potatoes] and that you will let us know when to help and how you think it best to arrange it. Forgive me for involving you in my anguish about your trees. Gray was very gentle for which I thank him. Believe me that I do indeed understand the way the world is worked and the situation in which you are almost inevitably committed, but understanding does not stop me crying out against it and more and more as I grow older and the days seem shorter I suffer for my own part in all the muddle and you will find me in my garden, the tears falling while I turn under the earth all the growing things I love and name – the tiny blue speedwells and so many beloved little friends – just to exist the chosen way. God knows. Your poem said 'God knows' and thank you for two lovely ones and your letter[1] and the strange rose which I felt for so much – as you did.[2]

Your poems – I wanted to talk about them too and ask you both if you were happy not only to publish them but to subject them to open criticism. I told you, didn't I, that Max wanted to work in this way [in *Ern Malley's Journal*] to expose as it were the various sensibilities and positions. However, John and I do not really work this way at all and since Max is the only one with this kind of articulation it is obviously Max who will attack and Barrie who will answer! In your case you may feel to answer such things but goodness knows how it will all work out – one hopes for some further illumination that will bind us more closely but the early stages have been complex and I have been feeling rather strained somewhere.

As far as you are concerned I do not know if I want your poems to be involved in this way. Both of you. Anyway, I would like to have your thoughts about it. Incidentally, Max liked your last poem on the mantelpiece but I cannot tell you why this one and not another. Von [Yvonne Harris] went into hospital yesterday – I told you didn't I – and was operated on this morning and all is well. Max flew off to Adelaide to take Sammie[3] home and then flew back this afternoon all in the

[1 & 2]   Are referring to the poems reproduced on pp. 239–40.
[3]   Samela Harris.

space of a few hours. I'm sorry you haven't seen Sam. She is a lovely little girl, so irrepressibly gay and she laughed all day with Weeno, laughing and laughing at him. I took them to the ballet – it was like having two Weenos to hold onto and I thought it would be the end of me and between them when we came home they literally turned Heide upside down. Her quality is so like Max, as if you just picked her off the Max tree.

My love to all the spring mornings and all the growing things around you both. Heide is full of all sorts of plants for you to take away and we will come soon – as soon as the car works again – in between times let us know of course if you think to come to Melbourne. I hardly seem to have done anything in the garden, yet underneath I hope it is taking shape though perhaps it will seem to you all much less than more. The paths and the putting down [of] the gravel have taken away so many hours all through the winter, and the gradual planning of other paths and other ways and so spring does not come this year with as much blossoming and flowering and all the wild ways we love.

Seascape

Both are one, god knows –
the flower's secret heart
and heart's secret flower.
your forget me not eyes turn
a world – as moontides
our days along windswept shores
and dark places
to the quiet bay, and love
seagrass, seaflower, sandune
whispering your eye to me
every now and again
moonwashed liquid your voice
the whole of your eye is my heart
in your hand, on distant shore.

Freak rose

eternal tree, peculiar of love
fulfilling the moment twice
making days, years – history
perhaps a tear
at your eyes' corner.
so strange it is, a bud
within the heart of a rose –
remark the tree unique
that holds a flower
opening in agony, revealing
a bud, deep within
right at the heart's core!
a moment re-stated
such anguish! oh cover
my cry, freak flower
beholding such sadness
still unborn.

Joy Hester's birthday is 31 August.
Heide
Monday (August 1952)

Dear Joy
I have been thinking of your birth-
day-day on the 31st and wondering if we will be able to share it with you
or have you made plans? I expect Mrs Smith will be thinking of you too
and hoping to see you. We would like to do just whatever you like best
and Gray I think suggested that we celebrate at Avonsleigh or just as an
alternative idea you might like to come to town for the night and then we
could have dinner and go to a beautiful film! If you felt like this then, in
any case, we will come to see you or if you are in town we could perhaps
drive you home again? What do you think? What is happiest for you this
year? I imagine bus fares and all else are a worry these days but if you journey forth for your birthday, I would like to take care of all the expenses.

I had really thought to entice you to spend a long birthday weekend at Heide so that I could have you in the garden for a few days and that would be nice for me now that spring is coming but now Max has decided to come to Melbourne for a few weeks and bring Von and Sam who don't seem to have any idea where they will stay and I think they will arrive around about your birthday time and perhaps want to come to Heide. I am sure Sammy will anyway – and so we will have to postpone our time together till a peaceful moment. I so hope there will be one some day. I am tired and feeling very old now.

Max flew over on Saturday and surprised us and flys away again today. He looked like Max this time, his eyes were all over his face, smoking and soft, and he had not had a shave.

Goodnight and love to you all in Cherry's Lane and if we are coming first then when you send me a note include all the little things I have missed for your garden so that I can bring them. How did the broccoli go[?] Your heath is by the dam. Gray did not say he saw the red paths or if he saw them he still did not show any surprise and we thought he must have felt strange with them or is [it] that nobody says anything anymore[?][1] When we came home from France John and I said we will never again say 'Look' in our garden and then we will know. And ever since it has been quite quiet and secret and nobody ever looks now or speaks.

I look forward to publishing *all* your poems before it is too late for me. It hasn't anything to do with the *Journal* but is only to do with me and with you and John and I hope you will help me to start putting them together.[2] It may take a long time. Please keep writing won't you? It seems a long time since a poem came from you and you did not send me Gray's. I wondered if you had changed your mind and felt they were too close to you up there. Max says you cannot write associative poetry anymore, not in the atomic age. Does he mean it do you think? For instance in the 'There is one awake in the fern world' it must not just go on having more ferns and fronds and underworlds and gropes. Words should not spring out of each other to the next line but how can they help [it]? In his [Max's] own it is Jesus meekness and Kingdom come but

[1] Red gravel paths were put in at Heide.
[2] Joy did make a typewritten selection of her poetry, presumably for the proposed volume Sunday mentions. The manuscript is titled *Joy Hester Poems*. Original now lost. Photocopy, collection the editor.

I know I suppose what he means for himself, but how can he mean [it] for another[?]

S

Send a note soon.

Cherry's Lane, Avonsleigh
Wednesday (August 1952)

Dear Sun
Just a note to thank you for your thoughts about my birthday, and coming to town, which would be lovely but trains, buses, Peregrine and Celtic seem to madly complicate these things and somehow halve the pleasures for all concerned. But if it is a nice day I would love for you all to come and have a cabbage leaf with us. Perhaps you could milk about 3.30 pm or some time that could make it easier for you to have dinner with us without having to tear away right after. Anyway, see what you feel like and drop a line.

The other night Perceval called for us and took us to 'The Grange' and we had a happy night ... We saw Arthur's mural which moved us very much for neither of us had imagined it quite like that at all.¹ But what is disturbing is that the place is up for auction soon and some person will paper flowers over it or paint it white – so I wrote to Daryl Lindsay about it.² Told him to go and photograph it – I don't suppose he'll even read the letter but I *do* think some record ought to be made of it, don't you? Perhaps if Johnnie Yule has not yet sold his camera you could entice him to photograph it.³ Perhaps ... Clive Turnbull or an

¹ In 1948–9, Arthur Boyd completed a mural at 'The Grange', Harkaway, near Berwick. Built by William Callender à Beckett in 1866, the Boyd family home was bought back by Martin Boyd on his return to Australia in 1948. Martin invited Arthur, Yvonne and their young family to live there. The frescoes, depicting Biblical stories, were destroyed but not until the early 1960s. See Patricia Dobrez and Peter Herbst, *The Art of the Boyds*, Bay Books, Sydney, 1986.

² Daryl Lindsay, Director, National Gallery of Victoria, 1945–56. In Lindsay's reply, 20 August 1952, he said that while it would be an 'excellent thing to keep a record of these murals' there was no Gallery photographer and no funds for the purpose (Smith Collection). In her letter to Lindsay, Hester signed herself Mrs Joy Smith though her divorce from Tucker was not finalised until March 1959. She and Gray married in November 1959.

³ John Yule photographed Hester's exhibition at the Melbourne Bookclub Gallery.

Argus boy [could] do a color page in the *Post* or the *Argus* supplement or perhaps if it can't be made public Simmer [John Sinclair] would go down and do it justice. But the thought of all that lovely Hark world of Arthur just being painted over with kalsomine does something to me and I feel if perhaps all else fails a Box Brownie would be better than nothing.

Thank you Sun for the darling violets which were so lovely. I gave them to Rosemary who was in bed with her new baby, in the balance so to speak of two worlds and the violets looked so secret and smiling and the hour lived spring again.

I suppose you are all madly copy or proof reading. I hope all is going well. Gray said you had a good article of Johnnie[Yule]'s this time. What a business that proof thing is! Has a name been finalised yet? And so much more we'll know when we see you. Perhaps by now it is printed and selling?

The broc[c]oli's coming [along] fine but does look suspisiously [sic] as though it may flower any minute ... The holly doesn't look as though it's quite adjusted itself yet to the new soil. Perhaps I should put a windbreak around it for a while. The bellis perrenis has not stopped blooming since you put it here ...

Gray saw a wedge-tail eagle flying low here the other day. He was huge and I missed him.

Love to you all for now
Joy

(in haste as usual, the bread man takes the letters down)

PS Yours today just before posting – with all your lovely thoughts for my birthday. If Max and V don't arrive on 21st it would be lovely for you to come up if you felt like it – will have to leave you to let us know as you don't I suppose know what date they'll arrive yet. If they come earlier than 21st and get settled at Heide and you'd all like to come – do – it's no more trouble to cook a cabbage for 2 more – so don't worry about inconveniencing me. I had not felt to come to town next week as I've been a bit off color this week and find a journey to the bright lights tiring if I do not feel fit – although it is a lovely suggestion.

Anyway if you drop a line the day before to let us know if you are not coming so we won't be too disappointed – telegrams have to reach Avonsleigh PO before 11.30 am. if we are to get them at all.

The thoughts about my poems make me feel happy and I don't agree with Max but as you say if it works for him then it works. I'm old fashioned or perhaps not that. I just couldn't work that way, though I love people who can. This is just a PS as the bread man is tooting. As to plants – porges [sic] laurel, ordinary cooking laurel, spindles, flowering raspberry, southerwood, mullen to name at random. Love to you dear one for your constant thoughts and all you are under the judas tree in the fern world and the spring bulbs by the drive.

PSS [sic]   G did see the drive and veg garden paths and how! also the cattery – and told me all sorts of details – in haste.

Heide
(August 1952)

Dear Joy and Gray

Just to say that unless we are overtaken by some unforeseen event we will be with you on Thursday. Our present plan is to arrive for arvo tea and stay for the cabbage leaf if you will have us, but we also thought that if it is a beautiful spring day you might like a drive in the hills or a trip to somewhere, in which case instead of arriving at four we will try and arrive at two. However, if the weather is against us it may not be worth all the complications of an early start and all the problems to do with milking moos and feeding pussies have yet to be resolved. Will it worry you then, if we leave things in just that way? Roughly speaking expect us at two but you never know!

One other thing – would you like me to ask Mrs Smith to join in the day? I felt she might be disappointed but I think too that you and Gray know best and I suppose there might be difficulties about the shopkeeping but should you think it a good idea then will you let me know in plenty of time so that I can ring her? Unless I hear then we will set forth just our three selves.

Max and Von are not coming till possibly the 29th and have made plans in any case to stay with their doctor friends the Lewis family. It would have been fun to have brought them with us but it will have to be another day.

I better warn you – I'll bring a cooked chicken – poor little thing when I write it I feel I can't – but I will and a glass of wine and a little cake and I'll leave the rest of the celebrations to you!

Love to you, get well
S

Avonsleigh
Monday (August 1952)

Dear Sun
Yes it would be lovely for you to bring Mrs Smith, I'm sure she'd like to come with you – I told her you'd ring her. It is pouring with rain tonight, but Thursday is a while off. We will pray the sun shines for you to come – it makes it such a journey and if you come – be it evening or afternoon it will be so much nicer should old man Sun shine for us all – the chicken and the wine sound so festive. I will do my best to make a nice salad for you and some mayonaze [sic] and we have some coffee. It makes me feel [as I did] when I was little and my mother used to prepare bread and hundreds and thousands – and lemonade.

Love to you all and spring in the wild garden
Joy X

Heide
Saturday (September 1952)

Dear Joy
Sending an extra birthday pressy. Are you better? This is in great haste but John said Gray rang while I was out and that you were still having headaches. I wish I could get up and see you but without car the day just wouldn't fit. Max wants to see you too, and Von, before they return. At first Max thought to drive us up in his car this coming week but then he felt that Von would be disappointed and suggested that we wait until she comes out of hospital, probably at the end of the week and so far I have not been able to get arrangements past that point.

I'm afraid our own car won't be ready until goodness knows quite when because the garage wouldn't take it this week and it is just hanging by a thread! Would you perhaps like to come down for a night and have dinner at Heide through the week (if I pay fares)[?] Max sometimes has late dinner with us after he has been in to see Von.

Do you think you ought to see Sewell? What can I do to help, darling? Please if you send a note let it come from *inside* your world. So much lately has been outside and from there it is not easy to know how to help. Perhaps I do not deserve more than that now. I am so tired.

Max fell in love with your 'Micetto' poem[1] and also 'Try me again, repeat the hour'[2] and wants to publish 'Micetto' and perhaps the other too and so now there is nothing to argue about and gradually we all seem to be finding out things – send me a note, won't you?

S

Micetto, Father of Kisses (1951)

he smiled some flowers
and laid a wish
across the spring
turning the seasons,
without a rosebud blowing

a moonlit butterfly
set passion
as a jewel
within her eyes – and
love made deep her speaking

quiet as a fog
birth music
its endless word
six times enfolded
smile with tear, and kisses

[1,2]   References to the poems reproduced on pp. 246–7. 'Micetto' was published in *Ern Malley's Journal*, vol. 1, no. 1, 1952.

Try Me Again (c.1952)

try me again, repeat the hour
make the wattle bough come heavy
so I may hear the forest dream
and join the birds in chatter

take all the things a river knows
place them beyond the reaches
then I will see the summer dawn
and love arrange the seasons
tell me the words you used to say
that make the spring's eye widen
so I'll recall a wayward love
and place my heart's-ear nearer

Heide
Thursday (October 1952)

Dear Joy

Thank you for thinking of me. My
birthday is the 15th, I think next Wednesday week but don't worry a bit
about dates, just come when it fits in with your plans. I expect you are
busy with potatoes and John said to ask Gray if he would like him to
help with his labours for a day. When are you putting in the seed I
wonder?

Our little jet [car] has now been returned to us and so we will be able
to climb up to your mountain tops again. Our own ties are as ever but
perhaps it [is] difficult for you to plan a visit to Heide. I don't really
know how it would work out for you, whether Gray could be spared or
whether either of you feel sufficiently relaxed to gather together Celtic
and all else for a journey to Heide. I would rather you sorted it all out
yourselves and just tell me. It would be fun to have a night at the
movies if we can find a good one to look at but it would mean that Mrs
Smith would look after Peregrine or would it[?] I don't think we could
leave Sweeney in charge. Perhaps a night in town would be more peaceful for you both than several nights and so let me know as the days go
on what you think. We would like to come up anyway.

Are you greeting a beautiful Scotch mist, all warm and soft over the hills and are you both better? I feel relieved to know the X ray was negative and hope all the Vitimin [sic] Bs will do the trick. Have the headaches gone? You do not say a word about them in your letter. I think I have millions of Bs in the bathroom cupboard which you can have if they are [of] any use at all.

Yes, I love reading Hardy too. He seems to come sometimes when I am not really looking for him and like you I feel he is close. We must read the Mann books and share your thoughts. I don't think I have ever known about them and only followed John's somewhat vague thoughts years ago. Love to you both. Forgive this hurried note to catch the mail. I have been feeling frustrated in the garden. Everything is so much behind and we will be living off the greengrocer for months. If I had four hands and four legs I might catch up with the seasons and travel round the garden in time. We have not felt the same joys of spring this year and we are fluttering round the house thinking of snakes all over again and the pussies and I know I could not take it again. We have made grass on the old rose garden so there will be no more snakes there and if we go on making safe little places everywhere for years then one day we will get back to the beginning when old Mrs Lang knew best and had Heide with nothing but a pepper tree.[1] And that is the way the world goes round I suppose, everybody knowing best for a little while and it is all over, quite quite over for them forever.

See you soon one day and how is the little boy Peregrine and greet the peony rose for me and all else and wave to the mountains. I'm an awful flop these days.

Forgive me
S X

I am so sorry writing on both sides – I can't read it myself.

---

[1] Mrs Lang was the previous owner of Heide.

Fragment which starts on the second
page; Sunday is at Sorrento.
Avonsleigh
(Summer 1952)

... Yes, this is our land and the place
of peace for us (although we did not know it so clearly before we found this
mountain entrance) built with thick walls between us and the Lord's world
– *in it*, yet above it, and surrounding us with our dreams – here is the place
we can start to find (have started) ourselves and our deepest Aussie heart.
There is air to breathe and peace to survey the world about us that is *in* us
from the beginning but one has to *rise* to see clearly.

Here is where we can work and want to, we are determined to stay on
by hook or by crook! And so it is four years of hard work, building bit by
bit the heart we belong in – it is well to be forced to work for 4 years
hard with the red soil, and not have too much time for we shall be
assimilating the great space and out of it will come the true expression
of ourselves – and our thoughts will collect and sift themselves over this
time and poems and drawings will come from the pure Aussie heart and
we will fulfil truly the things we are – but it is hard.

I look around and I love and embrace and breathe and live the beating heart here and *my* heart races with what the old hills whisper, but it
is too soon yet to speak with it or of it. I just listen, overwhelmed by the
'familiarness' of the words and voice – so soft it is and so dear to us all!
But there seems so little time from without and cities are spilling over
our land so quickly now and our sons marry another world and it seems
another world will speak before we can state what *is* for it must be said,
the land demands it.

So meantime Gray and I work all day to retain the spot that we have
chosen to see – it is a struggle against a lot of odds but it will come. This
sounds all rather selfish and self-centred. It is to a degree, but ultimately
not, for it has to be. It is so necessary to the life within us – and we all
have to struggle to retain these things that we are.

To continue this we have acquired 4 chooks. Ludicrous as it sounds
we hope to put settings beneath them in spring and have 40 chooks and
so gradually build what we hope one day will provide some of the means
to ultimate expression. We plan to turn part of the shed into a chook
house. Still those 4 chooks are a beginning. Doesn't it sound silly?

We have both been picking blackberries for Camms Monbulk jam factory, about 280 pounds of them so far, between us, at 9d a pound. You can work that out, too much for me! It is nice work and you should see my hands. I look a bit scratched here and there as though I may have had a fight with a woman . . .

And your world dear ones – I hope the new cats are feeling more security than they have lately and will unfold themselves to your cat ways, as we have seen so many of them do – revealing their world with its controlled barbarity, so sure, so gracefully – and the thing creeping, creeping, into our hearts and lives of their actuality and all the actualities they have come to symbolize and be for us all in our, and their different ways. It is lovely to have had the pussies, all of us.

Will we be coming to town? We both feel that we want a stretch up here without setting eyes on the city for a while – we seem never to have done this before – at Gar or here, to *have had it with cities in a solid block* for months on end, this is what we desire at the moment. The feeling seems an essential part of our building the necessary strength and for the world about us to speak with more clarity, of course this too is difficult with dentists and things cropping up every now and then.

How is the building going? Is it still going? I wish I had a wand and could do it all for you without the necessary but niggardly details of builders etc. tramping you down everywhere.[1]

. . . I hope the *Journal* is not discouraging you, have faith – it will come. We must have faith, darlings, *one can never let it go* or one is lost, gone and sunk. I feel perhaps your faith is wavering somewhere lately. Don't let it. It is hard to hold, I know, one must though – the same as a tiger must hunt or he dies. Humans must hold faith . . . That is instinctive and necessary for survival and we are animals too with other necessities for survival. *They are a must* or we *sink* and you say perhaps why not[?] What the hell does it do holding on when all is fading before the sight and senses[?] But it is the Lord's way – it's out of our hands. We must, we are here for that very purpose.

---

[1] Extensive renovations to Heide were being carried out. A new sunroom and bathroom were created, and two bedrooms knocked into one. The library, whose walls had been painted a brilliant ochre by Nolan, was repainted and new shelves were designed and fitted.

My love goes to you with strength for you must both take it from me – where I have it for you, same as take from you – your strengths and we survive.

Joy XX

Untitled

I see no reason
to doubt a good man's word
and things shall Be
God has said –
take strength, dear heart –
take all dear one,
and as love does echo
I am there with you.

Heide
Sunday (Summer 1952)

Dear loving river

Did I tell you that Gethsemane had been very ill this summer? One very bright morning I decided with a beating heart to bathe her in the laundry trough and to my amazement she floated lying gently on the surface with her arms outstretched as you or I might. She looked so happy, really happy, and I called the boys to see her and to watch her swimming while I washed her flaxen hair.

Perhaps she stayed there too long and felt the cold, I don't know but suddenly I felt she wanted to come out and I carried her to a sunny spot by the violets and left her sunbaking – I can see her now, her hands over her face. Later when I returned I found her, poor little soul, unconscious and her body was scorched and covered in darkness. For days she was so terribly ill and I thought I would lose her but I kept her in bed and when she was stronger she had several serious operations and gradually recovered till one day she looked quite herself again and as radiant and beautiful as ever. I took her to Sorrento for a holiday and because it was a special occasion in her life. I am sending you two not very good little pictures which I took one day while she sat on the sofa with the sunlight on her sweet face.

We are having a terrible time organising a kind of packing up drive[1] – already the paintings have gone from the ugly shelves to the dolls' house and perhaps you and Gray will not see the room again just as you have known it for so many years.[2] It is a strange thought and sometimes I am frightened to change anything – nothing very much has happened yet but next week I hope Freeman [the architect] will come and then I think it may all begin. We go on every day, clearing one muddle and making another and from the fire to the frying pan all day and I am becoming more and more unbearable every moment . . .

Our Peugeot has been and still is in the garage, and so I have not been able to carry out my plan to see the morning with you but it will *be*, I know. I loved your last letter coming as it did like kisses – *your* kisses, travelling from the heart to the face like a river. I can't tell you how glad we feel that so much has unfolded for you in the mountains and that so restoration takes place in you both. Glory be little Joy and the harvest gold.

It is true we have been sad but not, I think, because of Ern Malley who in his own way trots along behind the boys peacefully enough but just sad in ourselves and to each other and around us because perhaps the years have been heavily laden and lately I do not seem to have met them in the same way, and I have failed more than is good for one's face so that I wonder if my mother or my father would know me if I passed by. My little lily of the valley, my mother would write, I kiss your soft face. Oh darling I kiss yours back *now* so many years and years after. Our love to you both waiting each day for the blessed rain while the seasons change and we feel the cold coming thro [sic] the windows.

Come soon

S

---

[1] Sunday is referring to her preparation for the renovations at Heide.
[2] The dolls' house was an outbuilding in the garden near the milking shed. After it was waterproofed in the early 1950s, paintings were stored there.

Heide
(26 December 1952)

Dear Joy and Gray and Peregrine

This is just a note to say goodnight before I go to a much needed tuckbyes and to thank you all once more for your loving Christmas greetings which still continue to greet us while we wend our way through the bright Christmasy days and I have been wearing your little blue Joy-stitched chemise over my heart and Weeno has been playing under the hose in his gay French swimmers (they fit perfectly) and John's diary rests on his dressing table awaiting his New Year pocket.

We hope to see you soon and wonder when and how and what is happening to you and to us between now and then and if the potatoes are up? Will you come to town to kiss at midnight or will we have to blow ours to you? I hope everyone ate your Christmas up because nobody ate mine and my plans to have a cold dinner party made no impression and left me just as tired. After cooking all day I seemed to cook all night as well and the poor little ice chest just wouldn't make anything cold in time but Sweeney and Matthew pulled crackers and scattered crackers all over Heide and we all sat in panting little heaps drinking iced wine and smoking Sobranies and now may the New Year bring you all sorts of lovely things, that is our wish, and forgive this note, so different to your own, so beautifully full letter, and your description of the children's Christmas-tree party and little boy Smith cheered us up and I wish I had been with you.

I had been saving a long line of peaceful thoughts for you but last night we went to hear the jazz boys at St Kilda and they have blasted them all away and I must go to bed. We are off to town quite early in the morning to see Simmer married in the registry office.[1] Joyce [Good] is coming, too and tonight Simmer said he would like to come to dinner at Heide and bring Joyce and so I will ring through just to see where you will be and perhaps should you by chance be in town you will have a drink with us to wish them well. I am thankful they have forgotten about parties.[2]

---

[1] Simmer was John Sinclair's nickname. He and Jean Langley married on 27 December.

[2] Joyce Good, Rosemary Smith's sister and a friend of Joy's. Sunday and Joyce were the witnesses at the wedding.

Outside the windows the stars twinkle. Come soon again, the lavender hour and a thousand bees move through the flowers like a breeze, plums fall and butterflys [sic] and everywhere in the garden there is summertime – sometimes I feel I can hear something as if I can *hear* the sun shining and the shadows moving their places under the trees, a very faint sound that seems high up in the air like an aeroplane but everywhere a tiny summer engine, sweet sweet oh so precious world how greatly I love you … and kisses to you and Gray and the Peregrine to the snow hills and the gums beneath and around you and the little rusty dampiers and now in you go letter, into Gray['s] rusty letterbox on the road with the bread, in with all that comes and goes with the days every day and the hand that takes and so closes the door gently to wait for tomorrow.

Haste XXX
S

Heide
May 1953

Dear Joy
     I'm glad you wrote to me. We must have letters sometimes although I don't know that I agree about the telephone – only yours – and lately it has been difficult to hear either of you. Why, I wonder?

You know I never suggested to Mrs Smith that she should 'go on Hay'. It just happened that towards the end of our evening together when we were pouring out the third gin, the word for no reason cropped up and Mrs Smith said 'Oh, by the way will you lend me your books[?]' Really, I must be absolved from all blame and bones to pick. Actually, I felt sad. Your long list of weekly rations impressed me yet I hardly know what to think. Are you cross with me about something? I don't try to get away with the salmon and rice do I? Do I try to get away with your beautiful potatoes, too?

But surely it must be a hundred years since I talked about 'starch and protein'. I've forgotten what to say. I suppose we have been left with certain prejudices. Mr Hay gave me such a talking to, in the early days, I have never recovered. Perhaps out of all that, and the years, we have learnt a way of eating and thinking about food that seems to fit in some-where with all our other funny ways but whether finally it [has] much to do with salmon and rice or even Mr Hay, I don't know. I only know that nowadays if I ate too much salmon and rice, I should not feel well and so I don't, on the other hand I know some people who would die on orange juice. So there you are. It's a sort of voyage of discovery isn't it? Every man for himself. But why all this?

I'm sorry you didn't like the second *Journal* so much. I hope the third will be better. I think I'm too much underneath or round about, to know the answers offhand. We hear that it is 'a flop' and that Neil Douglas threw his copy out of the train and that Martin says 'someone should tell us'. So you and Gray are not the only ones. No, I thought it was good Peter although it is true that I did not enjoy the story as much as I have enjoyed others. It was just not so much my story but I did not blame Peter as much as you did.[1] Greville's translation I read as a poem and in that sense I felt for it and forgot it was a play.[2] But I agree it *is* and might lose some total implication. I don't know. Since we could not publish the whole work we thought it would be nice to put down that much and were so thankful and, as far as the *Journal* is concerned, there is a strong emphasis on greeting a rare translation. Your word 'pretty' shocked me – it moved through death like 'Child of the High Seas'.[3] I think Barrie has the play and so I will keep it for you . . .

I am close to Barrie's work, as you know, though I do not feel happy about a number of his poems [being published] together (or anyone's for that matter) and feel in publishing them that just one should be left to lie in the air till next time. John's small *Festival* I thought adequate enough[4]

[1] Peter Cowan, 'Escape', *Ern Malley's Journal*, vol. 1, no. 2, March 1953, p. 21.
[2] 'Asi Pasan Cinco Anos' by Federico Garcia Lorca, translated by Greville Texidor, ibid., p. 39. Texidor (1902–64) heard Lorca read in Barcelona in 1935. Impressed, she began translating his poems and plays. Twelve of his translated poems appeared in *Angry Penguins*, 1944, along with Texidor's short story 'At Home and Alone'. Joy liked Lorca's work and did several drawing inspired by Texidor's translations. In the same issue, Reed & Harris advertised Texidor's forthcoming novel, *These Dark Glasses*. Reed & Harris folded before the novel could be published.
[3] Jules Superveille's melancholy and touching short story 'A Child of the High Seas' (1948) made a deep impression on both Sunday and Joy, inspiring Hester's *Child of the High Seas* (c.1948, National Gallery of Australia). A sailor, whose daughter had died, conjures up her presence – and her village – on the high seas where the child is doomed to wait for, but not gain, death. See Janine Burke, *Joy Hester*, pp.153–4.
[4] John Reed, *Melbourne Film Festival*, op. cit., p. 45.

and Yule's article rather a muddle of sorts but probably the muddle is on the good side.[5] He always seems happy to work and that's about all isn't it, or at least it is nearly enough to make a sort of reality, even if at a distance we are not bowled over. I'm sorry all the young ones are turning up their noses. It would be nice to have their warmth and sympathy.

Yes, I understand about you staying put in your mountain top and it is not easy I know to bundle yourselves up and off to town but even so I think it was a pity you did not come to see the paintings and seeing them at home seemed not the point. Do you think you would have said that just when your own lovely little drawings were hanging around the walls? Something is stated then and something goes out and is received that otherwise doesn't take place and more particularly in Charles [Blackman]'s case because his schoolgirls seem to need just such a moment in a big room.[6] Never mind.

I write or try to write with pussies everywhere waiting for supper and bed time and the phone going and some kind of tiredness in my head that won't budge nor will it write. I may dash off to Sydney for a day on Friday to see more pussies so you better ring John on the weekend to see if he is lonely.

Love to you both and Peregrine and Hannibal. No don't for goodness sake worm the little thing. Cats *can* be wormed if they have to be but it is a touchy business and very unwise unless it is really necessary. If you do not come to town then we must come up soon and here's hoping the potatoes are all dug *and* sold. And no news of the bath heater? I told Gray to get the plumber. What happened?

S

Heide
Wednesday night (June 1953)

Dear Joy and Gray
For so many years, ever since I came to live at Heide and perhaps before, I have wanted to share whatever I

---

5   John Yule, *Cloaca Maxima*, op. cit., p. 48.
6   Charles Blackman's *Schoolgirls* series was exhibited at the Peter Bray Gallery, May 1953.

have that others are without. But for all sorts of reasons this is not easy to do – living is just not simple in that way – nevertheless, it is true of myself. As the years have gone on these feelings have become more and more pressing, not less and less, and correspondingly those around me have needed more and more. So the demand for what it is that I have and others haven't has gradually become far, far in excess of what either my income or my more mature consciousness can survive in peace.

Counihan once said when the money box was stolen, 'Well, you deserve it, you shouldn't have so much money anyhow' – or some such thing – but I have never forgotten, nor have I forgotten for that matter so much that has been said and done in and out of Heide and now I have come to believe that it is true, and I should not have what others haven't and over and over I try to think how I can pass it on to you all and run for my life.

It is very lonely and very strange to be different to those you love and to be told so many times [that] my cheeks are always hot. But here again, life isn't simple. How can I run? You more than anyone know how it is that I have never yet run to anywhere.

I tell you these things because Gray's letter the other day was a part of what has now become a very deep conflict in my living and out of it all there appears yet to be no solution, only to try and live *with* my life and to do with it as much as I know – yet unfortunately it doesn't end there and particularly because my nervous structure is no longer steady and where in the past I have lived with these things privately, now, more often than not I expose distress. It was just this that prompted me to tell John to tell you that your letter had upset me, since it came to me, I confess, without the slightest feeling in it that such things might be possible. I told him to tell you that it was, I thought, the sixth request in the last month or so. Not that it is wrong to be asked but wrong for me to live like this. Thank you, Gray, for writing again so quickly, yet I did not think your letter very real for myself and perhaps even less real for John whose letter did not carry an unstated reprimand but the reflection of my own extreme fuss that was and still is.

I'm afraid all this does not really tell the full story but perhaps it is enough to ask you to forgive me. I have disappointed and upset you, too. I'm so very sorry. I so hope – you know that I am always hoping that all will be well in your world one day and why I wonder do you not tell me more about it in the moments that come and go between us. I do not like being one of the many avenues of investigation – that is rather lonely, too, isn't it? Never mind.

S

[handwritten along side] I have no capital at all and when I go my income returns to my brother.[1]

Heide
Thursday night (Spring 1953)

Dear Joy
I don't think I deserved another long letter but I do thank you all the same – please forgive me for not writing sooner.

I am sorry that you misunderstood me – I said a long time ago that your letter came from another world. No! I did not mean that you had changed or were changing or that we were losing contacts. My thoughts were quite specific and referred to my previous letter and your response to it. I had written from a deep place and at the time I felt you had set aside deep answers. There did not seem to be any reality in telling me not to probe too deeply that which I know I can never probe deeply enough – nor can anyone so far – and like the neighbour over the fence there must be 'no recrimination on either side'.

Yes, I did wonder what mountain you were living on. I suppose I do not feel human relationship as you and Gray do – that we do what we can when we can and so on – it is, I'm afraid, rather like the world where everything eats everything else but man comes out on top and God said so. I always feel God said a lot of other things too (if we must

[1] John wrote to Gray, 'If Sunday and I were in a position to let you have this money you can be quite sure Heide would have been altered, reconstructed, renovated and rebuilt ages ago. As a matter of fact your letter upset Sun a great deal ... I have very little income and no capital on which I can draw, and as Sun has already told Joy she has no capital either. We live and try to help as far as possible on Sun's income which as often as not is grossly overdrawn. This is about the sixth request from our friends in the last month and I think Sun feels her position with her friends has now become quite out of hand.' John Reed to Gray Smith, 17 June 1953, Smith Collection.

talk about God) and more often we try to do what we can when we can't, and roughly that is what responsibility is about. But I'm sad about all the muddle. It was a silly comment of mine yet it is strange – strange because I always feel you understand somewhere in yourself. I should have said more but out of tiredness I just didn't and out of tiredness I won't go on but it is quite time we were all together again and at any moment we will be on our way. I am so happy of course that you say all is so well with you both and that you are feeling quiet and at peace and rich, too. I so envy you. And now much love to your springtime chickens and all else and your two selves. Rose is having kittens again and so the clock goes round once more and we must come before the hour strikes.

S

Avonsleigh
Friday 26th (Spring 1954)

Dear Friends
                    The days pass and we don't see each other but how very often you are in our thoughts, our living! . . . I see a pattern in our givings and takings of each other, but I do not understand the pattern – but over the months we have not seen each other I feel I know the design a little better and the illuminations grow brighter and I treasure them more – I don't think I know all about why they shine so brightly for me but I am happy and so glad they do . . .

Fern is tiny – a tiny weeny one – but very different to Peregrine and she smiles a lot and doesn't cry much at all and has one hand bigger than the other – not much but definitely bigger . . .

All the wild flowers are about us again in the bush, fringed lilies everywhere, and orchids and we have now a phantom footstep which goes padding by and makes the dog bark. We were given a dog called Bluey by a neighbour who is [sic] a heeler . . . but [he] is only 4 months old and quite large already, [although] very thin. We are giving him garlic as we suspect a tapeworm – though except for being thin he looks well and shiny . . .

John sounds thick with hay fever again on the phone. I hope it won't last too long and that except for the inevitable hay fever everyone is well, cats and all the cows. For now love

Joy

Heide
(1954)

Dear Joy

I know you will be worrying about the silly bumps that have popped up on your poor little head and I do wish you had told me when you were here. I noticed that your eyes did not look very well and felt that somewhere in yourself you were strained. It was selfish of me not to ask you – not to take more care of you – but these days our times together are quick – almost rough – and the moment of quiet companionship is always just out of reach.

But do not worry unduly darling, will you, [as] so many strange things overtake us and I suppose that it is not really surprising – they stay and worry us and then pass as if they had never been. I do feel that all will be well soon. Don't come to town without phoning – perhaps you will think me too close to measles to see you when you come on Tuesday but I will ring in the meantime. Do they keep you for hours in the hospital? Could I sit and wait with you?

Sweeney has ploughed his way through all the usual symptoms. First eyes then cough then swollen face, temperature etc., and finally rash. I had forgotten all about such things as measles and just couldn't think whatever was happening to him and he kept telling us to turn out all the lights because he felt like 'here we go round the mulberry bush'. I never knew a more adjusted patient. He is a perfect example of an angel in bed and so made a rapid and lovely recovery and is now singing his heart out with a brand new Meccano set. But it is really a horrible illness and I'm sure he suffered a lot for two or three days. Do watch your little bird [Peregrine] this weekend. The 10th to 14th is [the] time of incubation. I feel sure Sweeney had taken it on board when you were with us but [I] don't think at that stage he passed it on – [it's] not till [the] cough starts, apparently. Love to you all three in the mountain tops

S XXXX

The Mirka Cafe was run by Joy's friends, Georges and Mirka Mora. Joy was surprised and delighted when Georges offered her an exhibition there in 1955.

Arriving from Paris in 1951, the Moras did much to civilise their new home. The Mirka Cafe was one attempt. In a narrow restaurant at 183 Exhibition Street near Her Majesty's Theatre, Mirka cooked French-style food and fresh coffee was served. Artists were drawn to it. Sculptor Julius Kane constructed the bar while abstract painter Ian Sime decorated the staircase; Clifford Last made a special sculpture for the ceiling. John Perceval's ceramic mugs were available at 1/- each. The Cafe grew out of the Mirka Studio at 9 Collins Street where, in 1953, the first meeting of the revived CAS took place.

The large, monochromatic drawings shown at the Mirka Cafe in July won the first (and only) faint praise Joy received from the critics. Alan McCulloch, an early supporter of Charles Blackman, described the show as 'striking in its originality, somewhat bizarre in general feeling and . . . resembling the negative print in photography'.[1] Arnold Shore admitted Joy's drawings were 'individual'.[2] For the first time, Joy signed and dated her work.

The same year, unable to meet the mortgage repayments on Avonsleigh, Joy and Gray lost it. They moved to the small township of Upwey, also in the Dandenong Ranges, where they rented 'Wildwood', built as a weekend cottage. It was a comfortable house on a big block, facing south.

After a scare in 1954, the symptoms of Hodgkin's disease resumed in 1956. In a letter post-marked 3 May 1956, Sunday wrote to Jean Langley, '. . . Joy and Gray and the children have been with us . . . Joy's so serious illness has returned and we are disturbed and I have had no time to myself.'

Sunday wanted Joy to leave Upwey and move closer to town. After a few months, Sunday bought Joy a large weatherboard house at 18 Clydesdale Street, Box Hill. There Joy had her first properly set-up studio where she worked at night, completing the *Lovers* and *Child* drawings.

[1]   Alan McCulloch, *Herald*, 27 July 1955, p. 20.
[2]   Arnold Shore, *Argus*, 27 July 1955, p. 8.

Heide
(1956)

Darling Joy
Your brave and lovely letter felt like
the soft kisses of long ago and though I cried when I read it I felt so
warmed and so happy [and] close to you. Your courage filled the sky with
bright stars. You know that I have always believed that *you* precede the
Hodgies, even though it now seems to be the reverse – these things are
mysterious and the line between us so fine sometimes that it barely sepa-
rates us from the devil. Yet I continue to believe it does and that finally
the real battle is the fight for survival of our own identity.

Often I question myself would my father still hug me to his breast and
tremble lest my mother, who called me lily of the valley, fail to know me
now[?] Forgive me [for] being so inadequate tonight and tired but I do
want you to know how deeply I hold to your strength and heart. When
you were first so ill I know the deep ray helped you to get better but it did
not keep you well for eight years. YOU kept YOU well and I know that
you will find a way to keep you well again. It may not be the same way
but some change will bring the change you need to greet the sunrise
again and I expect that it is this we must somehow discover and seek till
we find.

Ages ago I felt you should leave Upwey for just this reason – it did
not seem the right place to meet this search, which is so terribly important, and I have continued to think in this way although I feel so affec-
tionately for the place you have made so much yours and the place
where you and Gray and your two little birds live and love in and out of
the trees. But don't resist comfort and help, darling, because you need it
so much, more than anyone, and I so hope you will be able to look
deeply inside your world and know deeply now and urgently where it is
best and how it is best to make changes that will help and that you will
move towards them gently and without fear and distress, which I think
feeds Hodgies more than anything.

This is a muddling kind of note to send to a sick girl but my thoughts
are scattered in all directions. I had intended to write at once then
thought you would be in town on Friday and waited for a ring from
somewhere and now perhaps it is too late to ask how to help or if we can
during your treatment time. Could Gray ring John at the Gallery [of

Contemporary Art] soon – this is more certain as I do not always hear the phone – I would love to know how you are and cannot bear to think you are feeling so miserable and [of] the journeys to and fro – how often? How much I wonder.

And I wonder would it be a good idea if we come up? Would it help you to try and make plans together or would you like to first work things out on your own[?] Would you like me to come up and drive you to hospital? Please let me know. In the meantime we have just seen such a lovely French film called *The Red Balloon*.

I do wish you had been with me. It was like a poem – almost quite silent – about a little boy in Montmartre who had a red balloon that followed him everywhere. When he went to school it went with him and waited and when he got on the bus, it followed the bus and when he called it, it would come down and when he went home it would drift up the side of his house and wait till he opened the French windows and let it inside. There is no story except this and all the other boys who try to catch it but can't and then finally go and bust it with a shanghai and it dies beside the little boy and then every balloon all over Montmartre moves out. They leave the windows, fly out of the hands of the balloon sellers and every child loses their balloon and everywhere there are balloons and all over the sky and up and down the lovely old streets and they all move towards the little boy and float down on top of him and around him and you see his face in them and behind them, till he takes all the strings in both hands and is very slowly lifted up and drifts across the sky and out of the film. It is colour, of course but very gentle and transparent. Perhaps if you feel well enough we could see it one day. It is only about half an hour. My heart is with you. You give me so much more than you will ever know.

XXXXX

Heide
Saturday (1956)

Dear Joy
I've been reflecting on all things since we talked by the fire and feel now that your own thought that I

should find a house by the beach is perhaps best to fill this moment – somewhere not too far away, somewhere to brown your faces and paddle about with the children. Later when you feel stronger and the sea has blown away the cobwebs then you may like to do something else, and anyway these few words just in haste to say I will go ahead and look towards the sand dunes and the blue sea and hope we will have good luck. I will try to get up to see you and report progress early next week. In the meantime love to you Joybells and don't worry about anything, will you.

See you soon
S

Joy is staying at Mt Martha on the Mornington Peninsula.
Heide
(December 1956)

Dearest Joy

I felt impatient for your letter and so thrilled to hear that [Dr] Parsons had seemed 'quite cheerful' about you. In spite of the appearance of other glands we must rejoice that the ray has done its job and have faith, little one, that next time will surely be the end of it all. I know how frightened you must be when you think of going through it all again but if the sea and sun warm you first then I feel you may not be ill this time and I do want you to do everything you can in the world to renew your strength.

For a start you must be completely nourished and I would like you to buy all you need at my expense – a case of oranges, fresh fruit in ample quantities, and cream as well as milk, and lots of wheat hearts and everything else that is good for you. I don't suppose it matters if it's Hauser[1] or Hay but you know I still have enormous faith in diet, and though perhaps I make you cross and in spite of your appendix I still feel quite strongly that your best years were the years you leaned a lot on Mr

---

[1] Gayelord Hauser (1895–1984) a popular American nutritionist and author. A health-food advocate, Hauser emphasised the nutritional values of yoghurt, wheat germ and brewer's yeast.

Hay. I know when we were in Europe how the change in eating affected my own glands and I came home, you remember, with a swollen face and cramp in my legs and all sorts of curious things.

We sometimes bring you all sorts of mad things to eat but this is [only] sometimes and over a long period. If you will be a good girl I am sure you can do an enormous lot to release your body and restore resistance to colds etc., which is so terribly important and vital in your case. Bear with me, please, darling and promise to take every possible care of yourself. Somehow we must, together, bring in a new era and I do not mind paying bills you cannot meet.

The next on the agenda is where you will live when you commence treatment and when it will be necessary to begin. This I imagine you will know more about after your visit to [Dr] Pearce – (is that his right name?). John and I want you to take a small flat or a little house that you can move into as soon as you leave the beach. I thought if we can find a nice girl to come in the mornings you go to hospital then Gray could always be with you and the children would be safe and organised. You cannot possibly anticipate journeys from country places and both John and I think it very unwise for you to return to Upwey – in any case you could not do so while you are having treatment. I would like to talk this over at once because if you confirm our thoughts then it will be necessary to commence our house hunting immediately and if you are in agreement with the idea then I would like you to tell me roughly where you would prefer to live.

Would you for instance prefer to be somewhere near a beach? Elwood, St Kilda or Brighton or one of those suburbs. Or do you think some more convenient area where the children could visit Rosemary's children without a great panic or would you prefer to be rather more isolated? These things you must tell me and we can have a word I hope when you are in town on Wednesday. And that is another point. I rang Mrs Smith to find out if you had a good weekend and said I would order a taxi to meet you at the station if you were all coming up so that the children could be organised without a fuss and I am sure Rosemary will be happy to have them for the day. Should you decide to come alone you had better give me a ring before 11 o'clock.

There have been all sorts of goings on since we last talked – opening days, jazz nights (till four in the morning) but I expect you will get a full report from Barbara [Blackman] so I won't begin telling you tonight. It is late and John is weary with hay fever and there are many kittens to wean and a suitcase to be found and goodness knows what else, so goodnight and sweet dreams and love to you all and kisses to the seagulls. I do pray the sun shines on you. Put on your little swim suit and dream while the waves lap around your feet and don't be depressed – all will be well soon.

Forgive this mad scramble of a letter. I've broken John's glasses and am now using your grandmother's again. I can't see very well with them.

In haste
S

Dear Gray, I hope you are better, too.

Heide
Monday (December 1956)

Dear Joy

I hurry to catch the evening mail from our part of the world and write somewhat frantically between shelling peas and feeding cats just to thank you for your last letter of love and to tell Gray how lovely it was to hear from John that he had given his painting to Heide and it was in my thoughts when we were together at the Florentino then for some reason the moment was lost. [Seeing the painting in] the Gallery only reassured me how much I feel towards it though not more or less than my first vision in the cottage and we are very happy and rejoice that it is to stay.

Please forgive me for what must seem a long gap between the time of giving and acceptance – it is not so in my heart but only the hurly burly of busy days and frustrated plans as we hoped very much to join you at the beach yesterday. Then Danila arrived for the weekend and although he and John hung the watercolours on Saturday I did not like the hanging and we decided to completely rehang it last night and were in the Gallery until nearly midnight.[1] Watercolours are very difficult. What with all the glass and frame there seemed at first sight nothing there but

---

[1] Danila Vassilieff's exhibition of watercolours opened at the Gallery of Contemporary Art, Tavistock Place, Melbourne, 11 December 1956.

a long line. However in the end I put two or three meshes out from the wall and broke it into groups which I think is much better. I wonder if you can make it to town to see them again as Danila has brought down a lot of new ones which are so exciting. A wonderful red moon with a face that Peregrine would love and [which] made me think of the sun going down that night we were all together on the beach.

Our house hunting is proceeding but I realised that flats are out because of Bluey [JH's dog] – nothing to report as yet but more later – in the meantime what do you think about Christmas? Will you let me know your thoughts soon[?] Do you anticipate being in town with the family? Are you expecting your Uncle to join you at Mt Martha? My own thoughts turn towards a picnic dinner on your beach which I would bring in a big hamper and [a] tentative suggestion that we bring Charles and Barbara and Mrs Smith.[2] If I make the feast do you think you would survive such numbers? Would you prefer to be on your own, would you prefer no party this year or if the family are coming from Sydney then I rather feel your hands may be full.

Anyway time is marching on and I will feel less fussed to work it out in advance and it will be best for you too. Talk it over and let me know. We must get down for a swim soon. The weather was so summery today I could smell the sea and raced to you all in spirit. Will you let me know too what about Gray's paints and things at Upwey. He must work and could we make a journey perhaps and collect something for him[?]

It was lovely to see you looking so much stronger and so pretty the other night. I only hope that the feeling of being better is becoming more and more real as the days go on, and more permanent. It is easy to be better for one day but I will not rest till you are better for days on end and now off to the post and away goes our love to you all. Wave to the seagulls and pat your gay umbrella for me.

Kisses
S XXX

Between 1956 and 1958, Joy exhibited in four CAS group shows, as well as having a solo exhibition at the Gallery of Contemporary Art, Tavistock Place, in April 1957.

2 For a tipsy account of the lunch that followed see Barbara Blackman Velhoven, 'Portrait of a Friendship', *Island*, Autumn 1994, p.12.

Many of the *Child* drawings were shown, together with several of the 1956 *Lovers*. It was an impressive exhibition, yet it was met with the same reticence that greeted her other shows. To Alan McCulloch the drawings had the 'psychological drama' that seemed to 'emanate naturally from the atmosphere of the CAS'.[1] 'Curious' and 'highly emotional' was how he summed them up. The *Age* art critic pronounced 'Miss Hester can obviously draw' but satirised the faces which have 'exaggerated eyes like head lamps . . . in [G K] Chesterton's words: "They haven't got no noses". '[2]

By early 1960 Joy was spending longer periods of time at the Alfred Hospital, Prahran. An operation to remove an enlarged spleen was performed. As the year wore on her resistance to the disease lowered significantly, although she remained generally in good spirits.

Joy wrote to John, 'I loathe this place so much – that when one of the doctors asked me why I didn't sit up in bed and draw the people around me I nearly spat at him. Somewhere I will never draw the people around me again, I will only draw what is around people – which is always there as the people fade away . . . After being in this place a second time, I'm convinced very few people "fade away", the[y] go with a terrible groan which goes right through me. I can never remain detached from [it] no matter how much I try – they groan and they rattle and the agony remains forever in my heart and ears, it is almost more than I can take, but I have only two weeks more and I stay gladly until I know how these chemicals react on me – for I feel perhaps their poisons will change to healthy blood within me and revive me. I was sorry I had to put Weeno off the other day but some other time when it's all sunny again.'

Joy Hester to John Reed, (1960), Reed Collection.

18 Clydesdale St, Box Hill
Wednesday (1960)

Dear Sun
The days come and go and I think of you – and want to write but can't express my thoughts well enough – and so I don't write. But clumsily, your flowing thoughts constantly to

[1] Alan McCulloch, *Herald,* 10 April 1957, p. 29.
[2] The *Age* art critic, A Cook, *Age,* 9 April 1957, p. 2.

me over the years make my self shake with my own inadequacy. The spear of your warmth and guidance reaches perpetually to my heart. I rejoice. [I] am happy – but how can I do this for you? I fail hopelessly. Forgive me. No, I can't put it into words. Spring is coming and the borage blooms and I have been to [Dr] McLean yesterday and he is very pleased with me. I feel such an oaf always being sick but perhaps this is the beginning of a new era.

I have been doing a bit of painting since I have been home, [and] this disappoints me a bit. I feel I can't go as far as I would like to and each drawing seems bound so much in a piece of paper with four edges but I have bought calico for my screens and perhaps it won't turn out as I imagine but here's hoping.

I am so conscious of my own limitations that I'm afraid I'll never do the things I dream of – but always I think of you and wonder what you'd think of it – and once again feel I have never done what I would have liked to do for you. And how you have always given me so much pleasure because you bothered to follow what my silly dreams were – I see I have written on one of the children's bits of paper with spots on it.

Love to both of you – come and have coffee with us again soon

Joy

Joy died of acute peripheral circulatory failure on 4 December 1960 at the Alfred Hospital. Gray was with her.

Sunday wrote to Jean Langley, 'For Joy I can't think of anything more terrible than her last week in hospital. It is easy to say her suffering has ended but as her life has ended too this does not comfort her. I saw her the night before sweating and dying and she said goodbye darl. In the last few years her struggle just to survive and to be with her children and Gray almost completely isolated her from the world, a world in which I found she could no longer cope with other relationships or loving. But I did see her in an ordinary way, not I suppose often, but fairly regularly, particularly this last bad year when she was in and out of hospital . . . We would look at each other and our eyes would reveal some kind of certain knowledge – as if together we had made something and that it had been completed . . . The deep river flows on locked in my life with Sweeney.'

(December 1960), Langley Collection.

270 | Dear Sun

Picture Credits

Plates 1, 20, 25–26, 31 courtesy Fern Smith

Plates 2, 4, 24 courtesy Jean Langley

Plate 3 courtesy Wendy Bradley

Plates 5, 16, 36 courtesy Peregrine Smith

Plates 6, 7, 10–14, 18 courtesy Albert Tucker
(all except plate 6 taken by Albert Tucker)

Plates 8–9, 33 courtesy Museum of Modern Art
at Heide (plate 8 taken by John Reed)

Plate 15 courtesy State Library of Victoria

Plates 17, 19, 21–23, 27–30, 32 courtesy
Barrett Reid (plate 32 taken by John Yule)

Plates 34–35 courtesy the editor

Index